Return to the Center

# Return to the Center

ROGER FULLINGTON SERIES IN ARCHITECTURE

*This book is published in association with the Center for American Places, Santa Fe, New Mexico, and Staunton, Virginia George F. Thompson, Founder and President (www.americanplaces.org).*

# Culture,

# Public Space, and

# City Building in a

# Global Era

TEXT AND PHOTOGRAPHS BY

LAWRENCE A. HERZOG

University of Texas Press ⟵⟶ Austin

The maps on pages 39, 105, 128, 130, and 186 are by
Ed Woch, Department of Geography, San Diego State University.

Requests for permission to reproduce material from this work
should be sent to:
Permissions
University of Texas Press
P.O. Box 7819
Austin, TX 78713-7819
www.utexas.edu/utpress/about/bpermission.html

∞ The paper used in this book meets the minimum requirements
of ANSI/NISO Z39.48-1992 (R1997) (Permanence of Paper).

Library of Congress Cataloging-in-Publication Data

Herzog, Lawrence A. (Lawrence Arthur)
  Return to the center : culture, public space, and city building in a
global era / Lawrence A. Herzog.— 1st ed.
    p. cm.—(Roger Fullington series in architecture)
  Includes bibliographical references and index.
  ISBN 0-292-71261-8 (cloth : alk. paper)—ISBN 0-292-71262-6
(pbk. : alk. paper)
  1. Public spaces—Social aspects—Spain—Case studies. 2. Public spaces—Social aspects—Mexico—Case studies. 3. City planning—Social aspects. 4. Architecture and society. I. Title: Culture,
public space, and city building in a global era. II. Title. III. Series.
  NA9053.S6H47 2006
  711'.40946—dc22                                          2005028163

To my grandfather,

**ALBERT HERZOG,**

a New Yorker who personified city life

in the twentieth century . . .

and

to my son,

**ADIN HERZOG,**

who surely will reinvent it

in the twenty-first.

# Contents

**CHAPTER EIGHT**
Return to the Center? Politics, Latino Culture, and Public Space   223

# Preface

Scholars and practitioners of urban design, planning, or urban studies are united today in their attempt to grapple with a dramatic revolution in the relationship between people and urban space. The buzzwords in urban theory—globalization, postmodernity, cyberspace, deconstruction, simulation[1]—evoke a spirit of change in the air. Healthy debates are raging as to which paradigms will define urban space in the new millennium. There is a consensus that global, technological, and social forces have broken the bonds that traditionally shaped city structure. A new urban order is forming in a world of virtual space, changing territorial behavior, and reinvented communities.

One set of writers argues that the traditional city—the metropolis of tangible physical space, from pedestrians and streets to buildings and town squares—is on the decline.[2] It will be replaced, they tell us, by a new prototype—whose spatial form will mimic Los Angeles, the postmodern metropolis that has given birth to its own school of contemporary urban theory. L.A. theorists are convinced that Southern California is the best laboratory for understanding twenty-first-century urbanization.[3] A spin-off group believes cities will morph into cybernetic spaces that will increasingly eclipse visceral, material places.[4]

Unquestionably, these are innovative and critical discourses for the urban studies field. However, in our zest to embrace new paradigms of urbanism, we must not be too quick to dismiss the significance of physical, material space, which I would argue is still the essential element that distinguishes the science (and art!) of the study of built environments—principally urban design, planning, geography, and architecture. Further, we should exercise caution in undervaluing the importance of traditional urban places, especially the historic centers of our cities.

The late twentieth century witnessed a fashionable trend in urban studies: to write about the death of physical space, the fragmentation of territory, or about life on the new periphery. But, as the saying goes in Spanish, "Vence pero no me convence" (It may win the day, but I am not convinced). An underlying motive in writing this book is my belief that scholars and urbanists should literally and metaphorically "return" to our historic centers and urban core areas to examine and rethink these critical fragments of our metropolitan regions. These are, ultimately, the places that retain the most consistently important examples of historic preservation, pedestrian-scale urban design, socially cohesive community identity, and sense of place.

Over the last decade, the redevelopment of central cities, once considered a dull pastime best left to bureaucrats and planners, has captured the attention of mass audiences. The revitalization of old downtowns in Barcelona, Berlin, or Bilbao have been celebrated in the mass media. For the first time architects and urban planners are attracting the spotlight usually reserved for media superstars. This scenario reached its zenith at Ground Zero—in post-9/11 New York City. The debates about the redevelopment of Lower Manhattan, including questions of the design of a memorial public space, were followed in the global media by millions of observers. The planning for the redevelopment of Ground Zero has surely been the most spectacular urban design media event in history.[5] The urban design, planning, and architecture professions are now "on the radar" of everyday citizens. So, too, is downtown. The inner city, after years of neglect, has reentered the public consciousness.

Meanwhile, the postmodern celebration of "edge cities" and suburban life can at times lead to distorted generalizations about the future of cities. This fact was highlighted for me at a public art conference in Southern California in the spring of 2004. In a keynote session entitled "Urbanisms," one of three invited panelists, a professor of architecture, told the audience that traditional urban downtowns, from New York City to Los Angeles, were dying as centers of business and innovation. In their place, the professor argued, were the new spaces of dynamism—the suburban realms epitomized by the region of Southern California called the "Inland Empire," the eastern edge of the greater Los Angeles region mainly comprising Riverside and San Bernardino counties. The presenter went on to point out that these regions were seeing growth in jobs, housing, and commerce, while spawning new infrastructure—freeways, high-tech office complexes, and telecommunications facilities. These regions are blanketed with the worst form of sprawling, low-density suburban developments, but the speaker confidently announced that this kind of urbanism was the undeniable trend of the future, and should be embraced by architects, planners, and urbanists. To not do so, the speaker told the audience during a question-and-answer session, was to engage in an "elitist" celebration of historic inner cities.[6]

Sadly, this kind of pop-intellectual commentary on suburban growth exists in a kind of nether world of trendy discourses, many of which end up being labeled "postmodern." But it fails to answer a fundamental "reality check" for urban planners, designers, and architects: If developers and investors are marketing new regions for low-cost housing, resulting in inefficient, car-oriented, low-density, sprawling morphologies, such as those in the aforementioned "Inland Empire," is this kind of unsustainable urban ecology something that should be celebrated? When population and investment shift to a new part of the metropolitan region, do we not need to evaluate critically the kinds of spaces the private market is creating, before we endorse them? Should we not question whether such places, however fast they are growing, are sustainable and desirable as urban design models for the future of cities? For example, urban citizens want and deserve a healthy public life; but do such placeless suburbs offer residents adequate "third places" to mingle between home and work? Where will people find the "city comforts" of public life knitted into the fabric of this urban form?[7]

Further, the cheerleaders of edge-city growth, who would have us believe that all traditional cities are in decline, have not been following recent trends. The fact is that the core areas of many large cities in North America have been booming in the last decade—in Portland, Seattle, Las Vegas, Boulder, Denver, Pittsburgh, Austin, Vancouver, and countless other cities. Indeed the irony of the lecture at the public art conference was that it took place on the edge of downtown Tijuana, which already has high-density development in its urban core, while eight miles north across the border, a similar boom was unfolding in downtown San Diego, California.

People are moving back to the urban core, in part because they want the stimulation, the complexity and serendipity of street life, the conviviality, and the energy savings associated with living closer to the urban center. Businesses move there when they recognize that these amenities can enhance profits. One study recently documented evidence of increasingly robust economies in the urban core. It reported that in the New York metropolitan area, while the suburbs continued to add jobs and residents in the 1990s, the core areas of New York City also gained in those same categories, and at nearly identical rates of growth, thus reversing a pattern that had begun in 1945.[8]

Notwithstanding the outpouring of legitimate interest in the transformative effects of cyberspace, the obvious fact is that physical space continues to exert a powerful influence on urban dwellers. One need only fly in a helicopter over the average large metropolitan region during rush hour to see hundreds of thousands of automobiles trying to overcome physical space while trapped on freeways. Los Angeles, the quintessential gridlocked metropolis, is certainly a tangible example of a new pattern of postmodern urbanism that is becoming dominant. But is it the only form of urbanism to which writers and scholars should be paying attention? My simple answer is no. As one travels the great cities of the world, it is obvious that the greatest streets and public spaces remain in or near high-density historic centers, rather than in the diffuse suburban rings.[9]

The importance of historic city centers is particularly evident in the Spanish-speaking nations of the world where I have spent a good part of my career as visitor, urban explorer, part-time resident, and field researcher. In Spain the central cities of Sevilla, Toledo, Barcelona, and Madrid are not only filled with phenomenal works of architecture, they harbor numerous examples of good urban planning and design, from the smallest neighborhood plaza to pedestrian-friendly streets and grand promenades. The historic downtowns illuminate the importance of harmony in scale and proportion among buildings, public spaces, and city dwellers. They embrace an important model for humanly scaled communities.

Meanwhile, some of the worst examples of planning are found on the peripheries of those same cities, where belts of tower block apartments sprawl along highways and around industrial complexes. In these "modernist" suburbs, community, sense of place, and pedestrian life have virtually disappeared. People tolerate living in Corbusian-inspired, failed satellite towns, but they religiously return to the city center each week to find the urban quality of life that is lacking on its edge. Indeed, many of these cities are experiencing a powerful surge of return residential migration to the inner city.

In Mexico the distinction between center and periphery may be even more striking. Mexico boasts a number of cities where the downtown colonial districts have been declared World Heritage Sites by the United Nations Educational, Scientific, and Cultural Organization

(UNESCO). Many of these colonial centers have been restored and reorganized into thriving living and working spaces. Historic Querétaro is a case in point. This emerging high-tech metropolis along the central Mexico "NAFTA corridor" has been extremely successful in preserving its valuable colonial historic district, as well as in creating a lively system of walkable spaces, pedestrian promenades, and streets that allow citizens to stroll and live in downtown. This in turn has galvanized business in and around the city center, contributing both to its popularity and economic viability. Querétaro's historic center offers a model of urban design that could serve as a guidepost for growth in other sections of the city. In the words of one foreign observer:

Every time I visit Querétaro I walk along the old Spanish colonial streets and feel the quality of the cut stone under my feet; and with every step I appreciate the skill of the anonymous stone-cutters who, generations ago, knew exactly how to make pavers and gutters and curbs. Then, I hear the bells of your churches ring out across the roofs like spoons beating in tin cans; and I enter the doors of your churches and I smell the fragrance of incense and I see the iconographies of your worship that relate to the spirituality of our everyday lives to similar truths of nature, fertility, birth, and death; and I tune into the "collective memory" of your beautiful town and of the people who inhabit your streets and courtyards and squares.[10]

On the outskirts of Querétaro, planning and urban design mistakes abound. With its population growing from only 50,000 in 1950 to nearly 1 million in 2000, Querétaro has experienced the kind of suburban boom typical of a North American city. Sadly, like its counterparts in the United States, Querétaro's suburbs have largely failed to re-create anything resembling the sense of place and community that is so prevalent in its rich historic center. The suburbs are essentially laid out for automobile travel. The lack of alternate transit forms has rendered the metropolitan region increasingly congested, polluted, and socially fragmented.

No attempt has been made to introduce elements of the historic center's rich pedestrian life. For example, to the north of the city, two of the wealthiest suburban towns—Jurica and Juriquilla—would seem ideal places to create well-planned, pedestrian-scaled communities. Jurica, built first in the 1960s on a former hacienda, is a pleasant, quiet residential suburb, with cobblestone streets that keep automobile speeds down. Yet, there is almost no destination to which one may walk in Jurica, and all of its residents must use the single one-lane auto entrance/exit into the community. At least four times a day (morning and evening rush hour, and the midday ingress and egress for "comida"), traffic is paralyzed entering and exiting town at the freeway. Many services are lacking, adding even more automobile trips to the daily life of residents, and most locals commute to work elsewhere by car. Jurica also lies adjacent to one of the major industrial zones of the city, seemingly a grave error in land-use planning that everyone acknowledges, but that no one seems prepared to change. Most of Jurica's residences are surrounded by 10-foot-high walls, further adding to the lack of pedestrian quality, and converting this community into the "fortress city" many American writers have lamented.[11]

Beyond Jurica lies Juriquilla, a newer suburban town begun in the 1990s, surrounding another hacienda and a small village-scale pueblo. The pueblo would seem to offer an excellent opportunity to create a planned community with a discrete center. No such plan exists; indeed, most of the new growth is dominated by private developers who, once they receive permits from the city, plan the streets and housing to ensure privacy and ease of automobile travel. In essence, the old village of Juriquilla houses the indigenous poor, along with the stores and services used by the wealthy residents, who live mainly in gated communities and suburban subdivisions arrayed outside the original pueblo. As in other parts of suburban Mexico, local and state government allows the new subdivisions in Juriquilla to be laid out by private developers, only later followed by supporting infrastructure. Once all of this is in place, a town plan is created.

These observations from Querétaro, where I have lived and returned to visit many times, are repeated in most cities in Mexico. As in Spain, they contribute heavily to my conviction that only by returning to the center, can we better understand the future of our metropolitan areas. In this book I have chosen to focus on two nations of Latino heritage, Spain and Mexico—whose strong urban design and planning traditions offer valuable lessons for historic city centers.

Few people who have traveled to the historic cities of the Iberian Peninsula or Latin America would disagree that these are some of the most people-oriented urban centers in the world. The downtown quarters feature mosaics of streets, parks, and plazas enlivened day and night with diverse sounds, bright colors, exciting architecture, and spicy flavors and smells.[12] Vendors, shoppers, shoeshine boys, and workers flow across street and square with the expertise of skilled navigators. While other cultural regions of the world share the distinction of great public spaces, the lessons of Iberia and Mexico seem particularly relevant to U.S. scholars. The United States and Mexico are locked in a global economic partnership driven by the North American Free Trade Agreement (NAFTA) of the early 1990s. The United States has much to learn from Mexico's urbanism, if it wants seriously to embrace a cultural, economic, and environmental partnership in a region where borders overlap. In turn, American understanding of Mexican urbanism is partially dictated by Spain, which colonized and built all of Mexico's major urban areas during the 300-year-long colonial period, and whose influence on Mexican city building continues to manifest itself in the modern era, as the nostalgia for colonial landscapes grows.

The art of Spanish and Mexican city building is distinguished by the rich tradition accorded to civic life and ritual; in the urban design realm, this is manifest in a strong priority given to public spaces. The future of public space in a rapidly globalizing and privatizing society is indeed one of the great debates facing urbanist thinkers in the twenty-first century. Early in the new millennium in the Americas, it seems appropriate to look south and trace the path of our immediate neighbors in Latin America, and to their colonial relationship with Spain as a way of exploring how these cultures created, struggled with, and reinvented public life in their urban centers.

My concern in this book is to focus on different forms of public space as they evolved in Spain and Mexico in several large metropolitan areas, principally Madrid and Barcelona in Spain, and Mexico City, Querétaro, and the northern Mexican border in Mexico. I am interested in the visual landscapes of these spaces, the forces that cause them to change, and the policies that help them survive in two cultures that contrast sharply with that of the United States. The evolution of public space is a historical as well as a political process; thus I focus on both the origins of public space and their transformation through the processes of urban politics and planning in the twentieth century. In a recent study of plazas in Costa Rica, an anthropologist offers a comprehensive and well-documented argument for preserving the public square—as a material form that allows people to engage in meaningful social interaction and as a way to preserve a humane city.[13] This inspiring volume makes clear the need for more writing on the subject of public space in a Latino or Latin American context.[14]

Chapter 1 in this volume offers an introduction to some of the key debates surrounding both the general subject of urban public space and the specific public spaces of Latin America and Spain—in particular, the public plaza. Chapter 2 takes us to the origins of urbanism in Spain, where I review the emergence of town squares during the Renaissance and Baroque periods and the different forms these public places took historically, particularly in the nation's capital and largest city—Madrid. Chapter 3 looks at the evolution of contemporary Madrid, following the political processes that transformed squares in the historic center, and the larger politics of urban planning that have led to the public space crisis that the capital faces today. Chapter 4 reviews the amazingly different story of Barcelona, which has been influenced by global political and cultural forces, as well as those internal to Spain. The results are striking—Barcelona's public space story is embedded in a larger regional political movement to reinvent the city after the death of Francisco Franco in 1975. Barcelona found a way to modernize while at the same time recycling run-down spaces into vital public arenas that have become showcases for urban design, community identity, and social interaction. Through an alliance of business, global investors, local political leaders, architects, urbanists, and members of the community, Barcelona revitalized its city center and reintroduced successful public parks, plazas, promenades, paseos, and commercial streets for pedestrians. All of this was done while the city boomed economically and while inner-city neighborhoods flourished. Chapter 4 seeks to flesh out the forces that shaped this monumental transformation.

In Chapter 5 I move across oceans and sea to the Americas, taking on the general case of Mexico and the evolution of its urban public spaces, principally in the historic center of the national capital, Mexico City. This chapter offers some important contrasts with the case of Spain. I outline details of the history and politics of specific public places in the historic center of Mexico City as they have evolved over the centuries. Chapter 6 explores the contemporary urban landscape of Mexico City, the largest metropolis in the Western Hemisphere. It also looks at the city of Querétaro, a medium-sized, but rapidly growing urban center to the north. Mexico City has been a much-debated urban case, especially since the signing of NAFTA, when its air pollution problems were extensively written about in the U.S. media.[15] Mexico City's historic district has the largest collection of colonial-era buildings and public spaces in all of Latin America, and has been designated a World Heritage Site by UNESCO. Yet, it is also a highly contested arena for urban politics and planning due to a variety of conflicting views on how to transform it. Chapter 6 analyzes interest group politics as it impacts the future of public space in the historic downtown, focusing in particular on the example of the zone adjacent to the Alameda, one of the most sacred colonial squares in all of Mexico.

One of my goals in writing this book is to bring the discussion of public space and urban planning to the context of the United States. Chapter 7 looks at urban design, politics, and public space in the northern Mexican border region, including its transnational sphere of influence across the border in the United States. I focus, in particular, on the Southern California–northern Baja California subregion, especially Tijuana–San Diego–Los Angeles, the most dynamic cross-border urban region in the world. Chapter 7 explores the idea of a "trans-national metropolis,"[16] where a Mexican urban area (Tijuana) overlaps with a U.S. city-region (San Diego/Southern California). It ponders the future of public space in such a region. The discussion seeks to disaggregate the region, exploring the politics of public space on either side of the border. It contrasts urban spaces and the influence of U.S. and Mexican cultures upon them. In the end, we find, along this border, an example of the globalization of urban space. Public spaces are shaped by cultures on both sides of the boundary; public space traditions struggle to survive in the frenzy of trade, global manufacturing, cross-border flows of labor and illegal narcotics, amidst an urban boom around and across the border.

In the final chapter I seek to recap the different stories of Spain, Mexico, and the transnational Mexico-U.S. border, bringing them together through recognition of common themes. As distinct cultural forces, histories, and design traditions are tested by the forces of politics and planning, the survival of public space in historic city centers is ultimately linked to the larger politics of downtown redevelopment, and that, I conclude, is a crucial policy arena for understanding the future of public spaces in the Americas. The ability of countries to reinvent their downtowns in a global era will demand a more critical role for public places. Streets, squares, promenades, parks and other spaces have inherent virtues, even in the high-tech, global future.

The task of crafting sustainable and livable urban settings will not fall merely to the urban design profession. Political processes will continue to create crucial roles for the media, educational institutions, as well as design and planning interest groups, all of which must do a better job of understanding and promoting the virtues of a city of dynamic pedestrian-oriented, public places. The alternative is already on display: the contrived city of private shopping malls, artificial streets, increasingly undesirable simulated places, and gated communities.

Global investors tend to assume that modern Western models of development are superior, but in the world of urban design I argue here that history and culture matter too. Perhaps more study and reflection on the virtues of Hispanic urbanism will help develop better public space plans for our cities. Successes in places ranging from Barcelona to old Querétaro suggest that it is possible to build a global city of the future while preserving the public city of the past.

If public spaces are the vehicles for telling my story, I have also emphasized the tools of the historian, the interviewer, the urban design observer, the political journalist, and the photographer. In particular, I value the triangulation of these different prisms as they are layered across the urban landscape. In preparing this manuscript I became increasingly appreciative for my growing portfolio of photographs (slides, black-and-white prints, digital images), which I hope will serve as a source of information and even inspiration to the reader. I have certainly found that these images remind me of both the visual details and the emotions that the return to the center inspires in me, each time I make the journey.

Querétaro, Mexico, and San Diego, California

2005

# Acknowledgments

This book has been a labor of love across nearly a decade. It weathered the usual interruptions that life, family, and other work throw across one's path. I am grateful to many friends and professional colleagues who offered an extraordinary degree of assistance and support during the different stages of the book's evolution.

At home in California my colleagues (and our excellent staff) in the School of Public Administration and Urban Studies at San Diego State University provided an atmosphere of friendship and encouragement; I am especially grateful to Louis Rea, the Director of the School, for his support and good humor, and to Nico Calavita and Glenn Sparrow for their friendship and intellectual stimulation. I am also thankful to the Dean's office in my college (Professional Studies and Fine Arts) for support, and to the university for two sabbatical grants in 1993–1994 and in 2001.

In Spain Professor Javier Espiago González opened the door for a fruitful affiliation with the Autonomous University of Madrid in 1993. The Department of Geography received me as a Visiting Professor and provided logistical help in gaining access to research materials at the university and its affiliated institutions. The late Professor Rafael Más Hernández, an expert on Madrid, provided numerous insights during field visits and tours. I was fortunate to meet architects, city planners, journalists, and writers in Madrid. They were generous in speaking with me about the city and the political discourses embedded in its design and planning challenges. Luís Fernández Galiano, architecture critic for the newspaper *El País,* was particularly helpful.

In Barcelona, in 1998, my colleague Nico Calavita opened his temporary home to me and assisted in identifying architects and planners interested in meeting with me to chat about design and public space in Barcelona; for his hospitality I am extremely grateful. I am especially pleased to have met Amador Ferrer, a Barcelona planning official, who offered intriguing conversations about the city, as well as introductions to a number of experts with whom I subsequently spent time.

In Mexico City many colleagues and new friends shared their insights and knowledge about urban design with me; they included Boris Graizbord from the Colegio de Mexico, Daniel Hiernaux from the Autonomous University of Mexico (UAM), Xochimilco, and Oscar Terrazas and Sergio Tamayo from the UAM, Azcapotzalco. In Querétaro Jorge Ozorno, Ramón Abonce, and Ernesto Philibert from the Tec de Monterrey offered logistical support for my research—by providing an invitation to serve as Visiting Professor during my sabbatical visit in 2001. I am also grateful to the U.S. Embassy, Office of Cultural Affairs, for support for my Querétaro work via a research grant. I continue to value my many friendships with scholars, architects, and artists along the Mexican border, who help me think and write about the region.

In New York City I was fortunate to spend a semester of sabbatical leave in 1994 at Columbia University, where I was invited as a Visiting Scholar in the Graduate School of Architecture, Planning, and Preservation. I am grateful to Saskia Sassen, who at the time was a member of the faculty there and facilitated my visit, and to several members of the faculty who offered friendly advice and feedback, including former department chair, Elliot Sclar. The Library at Avery Hall was an important source of background research materials.

I wish to acknowledge the support of the Graham Foundation for Advanced Studies in the Fine Arts for a research grant that made possible my work on public space in Mexico.

I am grateful to William Bishel, my editor at the University of Texas Press, for his always helpful feedback; I also thank other staff at the Press for responding to my needs at various points in time. Thanks are also in order for George Thompson and the staff at the Center for American Places for their continued support of this project.

Other colleagues who contributed directly and indirectly to my thinking about this project include: Mike Davis (University of California, Irvine), Michael Dear (University of Southern California), Gareth Jones (London School of Economics), Ralph Sanders (State University of New York, College of Environmental Science and Forestry), Leslie Sklair (London School of Economics), and Peter Ward (University of Texas).

Finally, I must thank new friends—artists and photographers who have helped me take small steps in the long journey toward crafting compelling images. They include Marion de Koning, Suda House, Mario Lara, William Mosley, and Judith Preston. I am especially grateful to Eunice Miranda, who opened my eyes to the "decisive moment."

**Return to the Center**

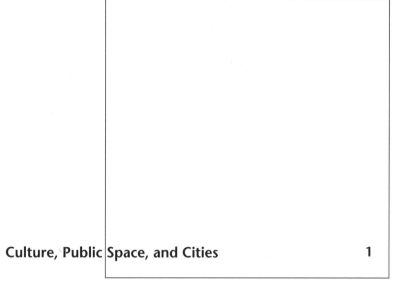

# Culture, Public Space, and Cities 1

*Had I but plenty of money,*
*money enough to spare*
*the house for me, no doubt,*
*were a house in the city square.*
*Ah, such a life, such a life,*
*as one leads at the window there.*
ROBERT BROWNING, "UP AT A VILLA DOWN IN THE CITY," MEN AND WOMEN

Every new century begins with a kind of soul-searching. As North Americans, the entrée into the twenty-first century compels us to confront the critical place where most of us live—the metropolis. Several broad trends that ushered the close of the last century—globalization, privatization, and simulation—will continue to define the debates about urban form and function in the new millennium. The increasing globalization of urban development decisions raises concerns about the loss of local control over urban design. The continuing shift toward the privatization of urban space suggests that the already diminished importance of "public interest" in city planning may be further weakened. Meanwhile, the digital revolution has had a huge impact on the daily life of urban citizens, implying even greater distancing from the physical space of the city, from its design, and from previous historic eras that emphasized the creation of livable spaces for pedestrians. The postindustrial age has brought a new practice to the making of urban landscapes: the creation of artificial or simulated spaces—shopping malls, festival pavilions, video arcades—as the primary places where urban dwellers meet. The computer and its spin-off technologies, such as the Internet, pose radically different forms of urban interaction—cybercommunities and Internet cafés, for example.

Some urbanists have come to accept these changes by theorizing that they are logical outcomes for the postindustrial society that America has become. Writers claim, for example, that current trends were set in the nineteenth century, with the building of the first suburban towns, which initially appeared as well designed "garden cit-

*Privatization drives city building in the twenty-first century: pylons of the new baseball stadium, downtown San Diego, California.* ies." They argue that America evolved as a frenzied, entrepreneurial nation of people who preferred fast transit and suburban houses with backyards. Dispersed morphologies were therefore inevitable, a product of American inventiveness in creating the technological means (highways, automobiles) to use peripheral locations.[1] Others argue that these trends are part and parcel of the shift in American urbanism toward a postmodern condition, caused by the changing nature of urban economies, social dynamics, culture, and spatial form.[2] Still others celebrate the advantages of virtual communities and cyberspace.[3]

Postmodernity in urbanism came into its own in the 1990s. Postmodernists brilliantly captured the essence of American cities at the close of the millennium—from the dispersed islands of gated communities to "edge cities," spaces built by global investors. They argued that these new trends called for a different set of filters through which to understand the new urbanism. Postmodern theory, they offered, emphasized multiple rather than singular ways of seeing the city, diversity as opposed to homogeneity, and local governance rather than centralized authority.[4] Postmodernity transcended the limitations of modernist planning, which had failed to embrace the political complexity of urban life in the twentieth century. Postmodernists were critical of an increasingly privatized planning process that favored a "user pay" mentality and greater roles for private consultants, lobbyists, or public relation firms in urban planning, in the midst of increasing corporate interests in the education process.[5]

Yet, postmodern analyses of the city still leave us with a vacuum. Postmodern theory may help us understand how to critically view the urban condition. But what do postmodernists offer as solutions to the urban crisis? In one of the best works on the subject, case studies are drawn from Las Vegas, Tijuana, Mexico, and the Hollywood film industry.[6] Are these prototypes of where cities should be heading? Where are the innovative design visions of the urban future? Where are the great twenty-first-century urbanists to replace Lewis Mumford or Daniel Burnham? What paradigms of urban design and planning will flourish in the new millennium?

In the spirit of the ancient Greek skeptikos, one wonders whether postmodern interpretations of the city should be accepted as inevitable. At the same time, we ought not imagine a romantic return to the preindustrial city—the medieval fortress town, or the Baroque streetscape. Neither should we pretend American cities will ever have the density and historic traditions of European urban centers. However, there is a clear need for an alternative vision of American urban space, one that embraces the traditions that defined America's urban evolution, while incorporating the best elements of inherited European urbanism. I believe those elements have lingered on the edges of our urban experience, but for political and historical reasons we have ignored them. Further, I would argue that the connection to Europe for American urbanism lies south of the border at the gateway to our Latin neighbors—that is, it lies in Mexico, and in Mexico's connection to Europe through Spain.[7]

Mexico has been an intimate part of North American urbanism beginning with the early settlement of this continent, although our history books and our scholarship do not always recognize this. Pre-

Columbian cities were the first planned settlements of North America. Mexico's modern connection to the United States is driven by its geographical proximity, and by the millions of Latino immigrants who helped shape the regional economy of the southwestern United States and who increasingly populate much of the continent today. Mexico's urbanism was shaped by indigenous forces, but the greatest influence on city building was exerted by Spain, which colonized and built most of urban Mexico over the three centuries from 1500 to 1800.

One of the central elements of Latino city building has been public space—town squares, plazas, markets, gardens, courtyards, and commercial streets. These elements have been important not only as physical design markers that anchor urban space but also as cultural and political forces that suggest a way of thinking about urban life,

*Plazas continue to be cultural anchors for Spanish-speaking cities of the world: Guanajuato, Mexico.*

and about the trade-offs between private rights and the public interest. Using the experiences of Spain and Mexico as filters, I will argue in this book for an urban design perspective that embraces the value of public space in American urbanism. Further, I will contend that politicians and policy makers need to make the creation and preservation of public space a much higher priority in planning for redevelopment and growth in the American metropolis of the twenty-first century.

This book is organized as a set of studies of the politics of public space and urban change in two Spanish-speaking regions of the world—Spain and Mexico. As I suggest above, the role of Spanish and Latino culture in American urbanism must be better understood. Mexico is an essential part of North America, both as a neighboring nation to the United States and as the largest contributor to its immigrant community. Moreover, Mexico is one of the United States' key trade partners, under the NAFTA agreement. This partnership guarantees a future of increasing Mexico-U.S. economic, cultural, and environmental integration. Americans need to know more about the cultural dimensions of Mexican urbanism as part of their understanding of urban space in North America; among other things, this will help strengthen the commitment to public space in the planning of U.S. metropolitan areas.

## CONTEMPORARY URBANISM AND PUBLIC SPACE

A salient feature of contemporary American urbanism is the fact that basic forms of public space—pedestrian streets, squares, plazas, promenades—are rapidly becoming either obsolete or unrecognizable. Most scholars generally agree that as the city has shifted from an era of decentralization to one of "despatialization," public life is reconfiguring itself in very different forms. Speaking of "cyburbia," and the "end of public space," one author contends that it is not that buildings or places are absent from the city fabric, but that the spaces in between are missing.[8] Traditional public spaces have lost their attraction, if not their role, in American cities.

We have entered an era in which the city as a physical place is being deconstructed into an array of forms that conform to the postmodern, antigeographical needs of a global society. Urban dwellers still travel through space, but they are increasingly less aware or less dependent on noticing its content.[9] Today, it is often only the spectacular spaces, the places with images that mirror those in the electronic space of television, that remain in the mental maps of urban dwellers.[10] Technology buffers urbanites from real space, both for reasons of global marketing and security. The result is that people are mainly engaged by public spaces that simulate something, rather than those that are historically or culturally embedded in the urban fabric. Contemporary urbanism—a world of shopping malls, skyways (aboveground street networks between tall buildings), freeways, TV screens, historic districts created by local chambers of commerce, and high-tech exurbs like Silicon Valley—has become ephemeral.

Yet, even as the traditional fabric of cities fragments into a mosaic of serviceable techno-residential suburbs and functional economic districts, the demand for public life remains high. This demand is expressed in the form of some 30,000 shopping malls in urban America, or by the proliferation of festival marketplaces, regional fairs, parks, theme parks, and other forms of public entertainment. Are these disparate spaces the only alternatives we have left to construct a public life in our cities in the twenty-first century? Are they the last building blocks we have to create livable inner-city communities? It is my contention that we can better respond to these questions by taking a detour through the public spaces of two urban cultures, Mexico and Spain.

*Ephemeral public space: the U.S.- Mexico border fence morphs into a public monument honoring those who die crossing the boundary at Tijuana.* As one explores the public spaces of Spain and Mexico, inevitably the historic importance of a specific form of public space—the plaza—must be confronted. "La plaza" is an indigenous element of Mediterranean urbanism. It was imposed forcibly on Mexico (and the rest of Latin America) either through oligarchic precolonial societies or via the colonial Spanish imperial political system. The etymology of the word plaza is worth considering: its origins lie in the ancient Latin word platea, which referred to a broad way or open space. By the medieval period, the Latin word had evolved to placea, or in Middle English plaece. Today the word place is commonly understood to refer to "a particular part of space, of defined or undefined extent, but of definite situation," but that definition is listed as only the third most important in the Oxford English Dictionary; the first definition given is "an open space in a city, a square or marketplace."[11]

This implies that the first openings in the fabric of cities—dating back at least to ancient Greek and Roman cities, and to the early medieval period—the first sites where the street grid gave way to some form of open space (probably a marketplace or gathering place), became the spaces that would distinguish one subarea from another within a city, the spaces that gave urban districts their original identity. In the twentieth century, the term place became a generic word used to distinguish one part of the urban fabric from another; it appears that this distinguishing element began as a public plaza.

## CITIES AND THE SENSE OF PLACE

One category of work in planning and urban design in the second half of the twentieth century involved the search for ways to rescue the "sense of place" in cities, since this treasured quality was being eclipsed by technological change. Some urban design scholars sought to analyze the physical and symbolic landscape cues that make cities more understandable to residents. One popular approach[12] identified five defining structural elements, three of which define urban places (the district, the landmark, the node), one that frames their boundaries (the edge), and one that defines the experience of moving through them (the path). Indeed, the field of environmental psychology tries to capture the experience of place and find uniform ways of measuring it (cognitive mapping, for example). More recently, the field of environmental simulation has utilized technology to simulate unique places for the purposes of preserving them in the midst of urban development.

But "sense of place" is, at best, a vague notion, difficult to measure, and highly subjective. Yet, seemingly everyone would agree that cities with meaningful spaces are more stimulating than those that are homogeneous. One can point to the importance of individual sensibility as a factor in creating a sense of place. Two states of mind have been suggested for city dwellers. "Ordinary perception" is the stream of consciousness that shuts out place and surroundings; it is the conscious state of typical city residents during their daily routines of moving around the city. On the other hand, "simultaneous perception" is a way of taking in one's surroundings and experiencing a place more completely.[13] The latter tends mainly to occur in the places with the richest built environment, such as a glittery theater district or a beautiful landscape. A goal of urban designers should be to create urban

spaces where users are jolted out of their ordinary state of perception into a state of simultaneous experience of the urban landscape.

History is one of the central pillars upon which sense of place is based. Cities are cascaded sets of landscapes created at different moments of history. The strongest sense of place may thus occur in places that are able to preserve these different layers.[14] But culture may also play a role. For example, the built environment of a non-Western city like Tokyo enhances the perception of place. The Western system of street addresses and gridded street layouts would be useless there. Most streets are nameless and individual houses do not have marked addresses. To become oriented in Tokyo, one must learn the ethnography of the city, by walking its streets, by talking with people—that is, by experiencing it, and learning its contents through habitual exposure.[15] The meaning of urban space shifted from the medieval period, when it was a means for promotion of human contact, to the Renaissance, when it conveyed aesthetic beauty, to the industrial period, when space lost earlier meanings and became merely a domain for circulation.[16]

Indeed, a pivotal shift in the field of urban design occurred in the

*Great public spaces jolt urban dwellers into noticing what is around them: civic plaza for the Louvre Museum, Paris.*

early 1970s, with the advent of postmodern design theory, which imagined new meanings for urban space. During the 1960s, critics of modernist cities argued that skyscrapers and freeways were destroying the sense of place in the city.[17] A decade later, a highly publicized book on Las Vegas argued that traditional notions of space and place were not the only means to achieve exciting landscapes.[18] Perhaps urbanists, the authors argued, were too obsessed with traditional enclosed spaces (like the Italian piazza), and too quick to dismiss the virtues of the highway and even of urban sprawl. For example, the urban highway strip was embellished with signs and symbols that creatively sculpted a new urban tableau tuned to the scale and needs of the automobile. Urban space and time boundaries were being redefined, moving the urban experience out of the ordered, hierarchical grid of modernism to a more anarchic, chaotic, inventive postmodern urban structure.[19]

## TIME, PUBLIC SPACE, AND URBAN SOCIAL TENSION

Change in the nature of public places can be tracked across time and through different political contexts. The two defining eras are the preindustrial period and the industrial/modern period (the nineteenth, twentieth, and twenty-first centuries). The transition from the former to the latter led to a crisis of public space.

Preindustrial cities have been characterized as having an "appearential order," a system where strangers identified one another based on visual appearance—clothing, hairstyle, and so forth.[20] Public spaces had multiple functions—water collection, news gathering, political expression. Daily use of public space brought strangers together in a space where appearance defined order. In industrial cities, the new order was "spatial"; territory became conditioned by social class. Strangers were defined in public space—their social rank indicated which zones of the city they could travel in. During the industrial era, urban property was defended with zoning laws; public space was managed by municipal codes, which prevented homeless citizens from loitering or sleeping in certain public areas. These laws created bizarre forms of order in public space; for example, in 1920s London a vast army of poor, homeless men were not allowed to remain for any length of time in any public space—local municipal codes literally kept them moving until 6 p.m., when charitable lodging houses opened for the evening. But even then, the homeless were allowed to stay for only one night, and then put back on the streets.[21] This kind of behavior made public spaces places of tension in the modern era, a world where urban strangers find it increasingly difficult to cope with one another.

One scholarly history of civic life argues that urban public space reached its height in the seventeenth century, began its decline in the eighteenth century, and has come crashing down ever since. Public space, in the post-Renaissance centuries, was theater—a place where personal identity was acted out in civic locales. In European cities public plazas were the spaces where citizens experienced their identity by engaging in politics, entertainment, or social gossip. The gradual decline of urban public life unfolded in three stages. First, in the late eighteenth century egocentric public places were created to celebrate kings and royal families, or to provide privatized squares for the rich. Public life also moved indoors, to cafés and theaters, or it shifted toward the isolation of the new parks. Second, in the nineteenth century people began to turn inward and obsess with self and personality, while public life became passive rather than active. Urban dwellers preferred to be spectators, for example, by sitting in cafés and looking out at the city. Third, public life significantly declined in the twentieth century; people failed to find meaning in increasingly alien public places and retreated further into the family space. They saw little chance for active public lives and further retreated into private spaces by the lure of electronic communication and entertainment in their homes and offices.[22]

This transformation of city life from public to private, between the seventeenth and the twentieth centuries, still left open the question for contemporary urban policy makers: what role should public spaces play within the metropolis? Several schools of thought emerged in the second half of the twentieth century. On one side were those who defended public life and the model of the pedestrian city. They attacked the failures of modernist freeway cities and called for more high-density urban places like New York City.[23] Their arguments were based on ethnographic observations of the quality of life associated with high-density streets and sidewalks, which they saw as the vital spaces of the modern city.

By the 1980s, however, others argued that the sheer force of technology, particularly communications technology, makes it less possible to plan for pedestrian-oriented cities. They believe the nostalgia for European-like cities is misplaced in the United States, a society of individual-oriented living spaces, where public life can be experienced in "virtual spaces," such as interactive media, radio talk shows, and cable television.[24] Futurist urbanists cast shopping malls as the new downtown business districts, and the new public spaces of contemporary North America.[25] They argue that since the format has caught on, developers and merchandisers will now become more innovative in making the shopping malls respond to the larger public life needs (recreation, public discourse) of city dwellers. Yet, many are critical of such a view, noting that such retail environments are artificial public spaces, in that they are controlled by private capital and principally designed for marketing and not for residence.[26]

It is possible to imagine two forms of public space: first, as a physical, material form, say a town square, with actual physical dimensions, and an architectural form. But that space is more than simply a physical space, it has a second form—a historically determined and politically created context. The town square can symbolize a democratic society, one in which people can freely gather in public spaces, as opposed to say a totalitarian society, where access to those spaces is highly controlled, and where certain behaviors are disallowed. This second form of space may be the most crucial to defend, since reliance on private interests for access to gathering spaces in the public sphere may end up being dangerous to a free society.[27]

### CULTURE AND PUBLIC SPACE

There is little question that the contemporary city is facing an urban design crisis wrapped in a larger social dilemma: how to reinvent an urban public life that promotes a sense of community and a feeling of identity with the urban environment? One critical dimension of this dilemma has not received the attention it deserves—the role of culture.

There is a strong culturally derived theme of antiurbanism embedded in American urban life. Its roots lie in the nation's history, but its expression appears in both subtle and less subtle antiurban messages and subtexts that permeate contemporary urban life.[28] For example, the print and visual media tend to portray the urban street as a negative place. Such terms as "street person" imply that the street is a dangerous locale, as opposed to the safe nested environment of privatized space like a shopping mall. Ironically, in much of the world, especially in the Mediterranean region, writers, designers, and urban dwellers view the street as "the river of life in the city." Yet, the American mass media often project an antiurban message: the street is the space where spectacular and dangerous events unfold. But not everyone accepts this. It has been observed, for example, that although the public may perceive homeless people as "undesirables," most members of this population segment are typically not dangerous, and can make positive contributions to urban life.[29]

Nonetheless, streets are dominated by narratives that define them as stages for gang activity or other threatening behaviors. Streets and open spaces encapsulate the public's "fear of crime" in contemporary American culture. They have increasingly been portrayed in American culture as "mean streets."[30] This perception has undoubtedly contributed to the growing privatization of space in American cities, the walling off of people into secure consumer spaces and gated residential communities. Underlying these changes may be an emerging, deep-seated cultural fear of strangers.[31]

The cultural/historical strain of antiurbanism in the United States is distinguished by an especially hostile view of informal public life. Other world cultures have signature "third places"—public gathering sites that have become celebrated cultural icons—for example, the Spanish plaza, the English pub, the French café, the Viennese coffeehouse, or the German beer garden.[32] But such places are disappearing in American urban culture. In their place the private home has become the dominant place of gathering.

This antiurban bias in U.S. culture reveals itself in the American attitude toward parks and green spaces in cities. In Europe parks evolved as part of a collective way to design convivial, community spaces for leisure. The English "pleasure garden," for example, was part of a movement to invent innovative places for such purposes. These included promenades, shopping streets, or town squares. The idea was that the city was a microcosm of the world. This was the in-

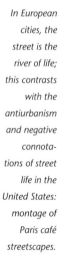

*In European cities, the street is the river of life; this contrasts with the antiurbanism and negative connotations of street life in the United States: montage of Paris café streetscapes.*

tention of early park designers in the United States, such as Frederick Law Olmsted. Yet, in the end, a more antiurban view of parks has prevailed, one in which they are seen as an escape from the evil of cities, even an escape to the country.[33]

Historically, the connection between public space and place can be traced to the public plaza, whose evolution over the centuries reveals varying cultural expressions at different points in time of the need for public life in cities. It is generally agreed that the first important urban societies—in India, Mesopotamia, and Egypt—did not utilize the public square as part of the design and social fabric of their settlements.[34] The first significant urban public places were found in ancient Greek cities, specifically in the form of the "agora," the civic embodiment of political life. The agora was a place of assembly, at first for political gatherings, and later as a location for the Greek market.[35] While the "acropolis"—the sacred, religious locale—was walled and closed off, the agora was an open, accessible space, and was seen as the symbol of the "polis," the locus of self-government of early Greek democratic city-states. At its best, the agora was a rallying point for speech and open-air citizens' meetings. In fact, the agora's origins are said to trace back to the practice of Greek warriors gathering in a circle periodically to discuss matters of common concern. The circle became a place of free speech. "Agora" meant assembly. As one scholar noted: "[B]y having access to this circular space known as the agora, citizens became part of a political system based on balance, symmetry, reciprocity."[36]

In its earliest form, around the sixth century BC, the agora was said to be an open-air space, spontaneous and richly adorned with public life.[37] In the later Greek/Hellenistic period, after the third century BC, Greek cities were more ordered, and the agoras were rectangular in shape, surrounded by buildings and closed off to traffic. This signified a less spontaneous and rich public life. As fancy gates and porticoes began to appear around the agoras, and as traffic was shut out, they reflected the weakening of collective power, and a corresponding decline of the Greek city-state.[38]

If the agora symbolized democracy in ancient Greek city-states, the Roman forum stood for power. The forum, in fact, is said to have evolved from the morphology of Etruscan towns and later Roman military encampments, where the geographical center was the axis of power. In Roman cities the main streets (cardo and decumanus) crossed here, and the most important institutions and buildings were on this central site (especially the "basilica," or combined court of justice and market hall).

The Roman model of urban form emphasized the creation of a central space—limited in size to give it more meaning. It is not surprising that the forum, or town square, was born along the Mediterranean, considering the degree to which both Greek and Roman urbanism embraced it.[39] There is evidence that, aside from its origins as a space of power, the forum played many roles in Roman cities: as a site of commerce, political discourse, the administration of justice, and dissemination of news. Commerce occurred around the forum in the market halls of the basilica. Shops were set up on the forum to teach language and rhetoric as part of commercial life, while the central storerooms for weights and measures were also located here. There were public-speaking daises on the Roman squares for engaging in political discussion. Public controversy could be aired here; its resolution might then move into the halls of the basilica. Meanwhile, much information was dispensed in the forum: election posters, sale contracts, wills, adoption notices. It was, in short, a media center.[40]

The idea of a town square, as developed in Greece and Rome, began to assert itself in the medieval towns of Europe, and would find specific, more elaborate expressions in the Renaissance period. From the ninth to the thirteenth centuries, European towns were either concentrated, walled spaces built around castles and monasteries, or fortress compounds (such as the French bastide). Within these towns of crowded, crooked, and narrow streets, the plaza or square was a space that organically appeared to facilitate certain functions: the gathering of water, the collection of church taxes, buying and selling goods, exchanging information, or entertaining. Many of the early squares were market squares, and typically they formed outside the walls of the town, at the gate. While market squares were the most common form of medieval plaza, there were also spaces that formed in front of churches or town halls, which were used for either celebrations (tournaments, processions, etc.) or civic purposes (judicial proceedings). Limited technology forced the public into medieval squares on a daily basis, and a sense of collective destiny and community prevailed in public life. After the Middle Ages, some public life would move from the plaza to the indoor world of theaters, cafés, stores, or the royal court.[41]

The Renaissance period, particularly in Italy, formalized the design of the town square. The Renaissance brought the discovery of perspective, scale, and proportion to the design of the Italian piazza. One is struck by the sense of order and uniformity that accompanies the arcade-enclosed squares of the sixteenth century in Italy. Some have suggested that the conscious, formal designs of the period mark the beginning of city planning, expressed through a connection between design and power.[42] In any case, the pure geometric forms of the 1500s gave way to ornate, theatric piazzas in the Baroque period that followed. The squares became showpieces for royal families; the superiority of royal power was expressed through architecture that was both monumental and beautiful. The piazzas of Rome, especially those designed by Bernini, typify the theatricality of the Baroque era. This "academic classicism" is repeated in the plazas of seventeenth-century France, and it later inspired designs of public spaces in another great European city of the time, London.[43]

The plaza was born and nurtured along the Mediterranean—in Greece, Italy, Spain, and later France. After labyrinthine streets and medieval towns, the plaza was embraced—as part of a higher, cosmic order—by the royal families of the Renaissance and Baroque eras. In Versailles in 1700 the royal architects found the ideal design of space, in which a town, palace, and gardens could be woven together into an abstract construction of power. The plazas of Renaissance and Baroque Italy, France, and Spain became monumental spaces of royal control. They set the tone for plazas built all over Europe as late as the beginning of the nineteenth century—from Trafalgar Square in London to Red Square in Moscow.

But, as one author wrote, "as progress spread, the piazza died."[44] By the nineteenth century, as the industrial revolution began to re-

*The most powerful influence on public space is time; the longer a place survives, the more it becomes an anchor of cultural memory: bridge across the Seine River, Paris.*

structure urban space, traditional public spaces dramatically changed. Some were simply abandoned; others would play different roles in the changing ecology of the modern city. With the emergence of stores and storefront design as part of the urban landscape, strolling along streets became a new kind of public experience, and commercial street corridors begin to replace the town square as the gathering spaces of an industrializing society.[45]

While these changes were transforming the grand traditions of public space in Europe, in the United States the industrial revolution arrived in a nation with a very young urban design legacy. The pioneers who settled the United States had brought the memory of European public spaces, and these found expressions in the colonial era in the form of fenced grazing areas or "commons" in the middle of New England towns, military parade grounds, or church squares.[46] As American cities formed at the end of the eighteenth century, and through the nineteenth century, it was clear that private land speculation, rather than civic planning, was the driving force. For the immigrant population streets, rather than squares, became the dominant public areas of urban life. By the second half of the nineteenth century parks were where people enjoyed leisure in the city, drawing on the new trend of the beer garden and pleasure grounds of cosmopolitan Europe.[47] The idea of the park as a work of art and as an urban social outlet flourished through the design and promotion of the ideas and park designs of Frederick Law Olmsted and his colleagues.

These parks meant that while an urban citizen could find a pleasant experience with nature, public squares where people met spontaneously and interacted would be absent from most U.S. cities. As a result, there are few truly monumental open-air public squares in the United States.[48] This fact does not necessarily bother American designers today. Indeed, one writer's comment about U.S. architects probably sums up the opinion of many: "[A]rchitects have been bewitched by a single element in the Italian landscape: the piazza. . . . They have been brought up on space, and enclosed space is easiest to handle."[49] It has been argued that centralized public space does not constitute part of the American form of "psychosocial expression"— individual, freestanding buildings at reduced densities, rather than collective spaces in high-density settings.[50] Privatized gathering space as opposed to community space is stronger in the United States than in Europe or Spanish America.

Yet, it may be that the urban plaza is misunderstood in the United States because it is seen as a physical environment or stage set, rather than a metaphor for playing out individual and community relations, as well as manifesting the local social order in space.[51] Thus, there is a need for spaces where the role of individuals in the community can be made visible. It may not take the form of a pure public square, but it needs an expression in the urban built environment.

These ideas have been put to work in the fervent decade of public space revival that evolved in the United States during the 1980s and 1990s. In one study of the design and uses of public space in New York City, rigorous field observation and measurements were used to determine specific strategies for making public spaces function even in a high-density metropolitan setting.[52] Meanwhile, landscape architects and urban designers began to look at public spaces more carefully. Some argued for better control and management of these public plazas;[53] others suggested studying not only the public spaces but also their

relation to immediate surrounding land uses.[54] Many different kinds of public spaces were carefully analyzed, including miniparks, "vest pocket" parks, neighborhood parks, college campus spaces, and day care spaces.[55]

Absent a richer historic tradition, the emphasis in the United States has been on innovative public spaces. For example, in large urban centers, like New York City, new plazas were created around corporate buildings, like IBM, Seagram's, and the Chase Manhattan headquarters. Equally, new public spaces were connected to large-scale civic

*In the United States the best public spaces are those that evoke a sense of place: Brooklyn Bridge, New York City.*

development projects, like Lincoln Center. There are few well-pre-served historic plazas in New York City—perhaps Rockefeller Plaza, completed during the Depression years, is an exception. Many believe that public space can continue to thrive because it provides stimulation to users; a sense of belonging, discovery, and meaning; a symbolic connection to the larger society; and a sense of the local character of place.[56] How these elements can be collectively preserved in cities remains one of the important tasks for public space planning in twenty-first-century America.

## THE ARCHITECTURE PROFESSION AND PUBLIC SPACE

One of the dilemmas of the contemporary architecture profession is that, too often, it fails adequately to address the design problems of spaces between and around buildings. Architecture embraces the building as the supreme measure of professional achievement. The global celebration of Frank Gehry's Guggenheim Museum in Bilbao, Spain, is an example of how the world came to worship one building. The media's virtual obsession with the museum came at the expense of any discourse about the spaces around it. We heard almost nothing about the city of Bilbao during the period of fervor over the appearance of Gehry's titanium-walled building/sculpture on the shores of northern Spain.

A narrow focus on buildings has not always been the essence of the architecture profession. Indeed, the rise of modernist architecture in the early twentieth century, under the leadership of prominent figures like Walter Gropius, Le Corbusier, and Frank Lloyd Wright, was distinguished by its attention to the connection between buildings and the well-being of the larger city. Modernist architecture was notable for its grand social vision, its excitement about the ways architects could contribute to building a better, more equitable society. Many of the modernist designers wrote and thought about the larger city, and about the spaces around their buildings.[57]

But at some point in the late twentieth century, U.S. architects began to doubt whether architecture could really solve the larger problems of cities—crime, poverty, the decline of inner-city neighborhoods, social inequality. By the 1970s the architecture profession had retreated from the modernist "grand social vision" model of design to a concern with "form making at the scale of buildings alone."[58]

This shift was especially noticeable in universities, where close ties between architecture and environmental studies/city planning began to loosen in the 1970s. New intellectual and institutional alignments emerged: architecture and design, elevated to the status of high art, on one side; urban planning and policy, tied to politics, government, economy, and social issues, on the other. This realignment led to a very different role for the architect than during the height of modernism. Since the 1970s, as one commentator has suggested, "[t]he expression and comment of an individual architect became more important in the design of buildings than perceiving the city as a whole, and architecture as collective, connective or shared."[59]

In the heyday of modernism, in "Professional Practice" classes in architecture schools, students were taught that the architect's role, both ethical and legal, when there was a dispute with a client or a general contractor, was that of "an impartial arbiter whose prime responsibility was to the quality of the environment, natural as well as man-made."[60] But this changed. "Today, an architect's sole responsibility in the U.S. and elsewhere, is clearly to the client—to the person who pays the bills. And much of the quality of our cities, our suburbs and our countryside has suffered dramatically as a result."[61]

While the shift in the professional conscience of architects may be the most important explanation of their subsequent declining interest in public spaces around buildings, there is another consideration as well. In architecture there has been a persistent tradition of viewing the architect as, first and foremost, an artist, a designer of spaces, who must rise above all other forces—zoning, politics, and so forth—that might neutralize his or her creativity. The myth of the "architect as artist" contributes to the isolation of architecture from urban policy and from the practical concerns about urban spaces around buildings. Frank Lloyd Wright often spoke of the "hand maidens of architecture—music, painting, sculpture."[62] This reinforced the ideology of the architect as a master craftsman and artist, his/her role elevated above the mundane matters of street maintenance, traffic control, or city planning.

Perhaps one reason for skepticism about the role of architecture in shaping cities is that some of the early attempts at urban planning by master architects were either embarrassing or substantively ill-advised. Le Corbusier, often called the "father of modern architecture," was a visionary when it came to understanding how to harness industrial materials to create light, modern, functional structures. But Le Corbusier's foray into urban planning theory was not so stellar. His 1930 book La Ville Radieuse (The Radiant City) envisioned a city denuded of its historic buildings, wiped clean of its neighborhoods with their traditions and sense of place, and replaced by a grid of high-rise buildings surrounded by open space and an interlocking system of freeways. Walkable streets were to be erased, superceded by the modernist geometry of a "machine age city." Le Corbusier theorized that neighborhood life could be translated into a new kind of futuristic architecture: vertical high-rise structures, in which each of the neighborhood amenities that formerly were aligned along the street would now be assigned to floors in a tower—the supermarket on one floor, the school on another, the bank on yet another, the community park and swimming pool on the roof.

Le Corbusier actually wanted to implement this plan for the center of Paris, surgically removing all of its historic buildings, its narrow alleyways, old stores and cafés, and the entire infrastructure of place, replacing these with high-rise towers. This could have destroyed one of the world's most valuable historic urban districts. As one critic noted, "The one thing nobody in La Ville Radieuse could expect to have was the 'esprit de quartier,' the sense of variety, surprise and pleasant random encounter that once made living in Paris one of the supreme experiences of urban man."[63]

Fortunately, Parisians, much as they loved Le Corbusier, the master builder, did not accept his urban design prescriptions for their city. Le Corbusier was reportedly immensely disappointed throughout his life that he was never able to actually implement his vision of cities, in Paris, but his disappointment "could not have begun to compare with the misery and social dislocation the Radiant City would have inflicted on its inhabitants had it ever been built."[64]

While the father of modern architecture in Europe was failing to produce an acceptable urban design model for the future, across the Atlantic Ocean America's greatest twentieth-century architect suffered a similar fate. To his credit, Frank Lloyd Wright, like his European counterpart, wanted not only to design individual buildings but also to create design solutions aimed at solving the larger problems of cities. For example, Wright invented a new kind of prefabricated, futuristic housing system—the "Usonian City." He wondered "how to mitigate the horror of human life caught helpless or unaware in the machine that is the city."[65]

In the 1930s Wright crafted a model for the future of cities—he called it "Broadacre City." The model predicted that growth would eventually cause cities to spread out and become horizontal, not vertical. Broadacre City envisioned multilevel highways serving dispersed settlements in farmlike settings. Gasoline service stations were assigned central roles as urban activity nodes. Wright believed automobiles would dominate and define the city of the future; thus, places where automobiles were serviced logically should become community and social service centers. Meanwhile, he celebrated new electronic technologies that would allow city dwellers to enjoy the consumption of social experiences—movies, opera, theater, concerts—in their own homes, experiences that previously would have brought them out into the public realm of the city.[66]

Wright never discussed whether this kind of home-oriented urbanism could destroy the spontaneity and stimulus that urban citizens had experienced in public spaces for centuries. Indeed, in Broadacre City, public life—the meeting of strangers in spontaneous, pedestrian-scale spaces—would disappear, replaced by home-based consumption of culture and information, or by automobile-oriented errands centered around gasoline service station nodes. Wright also speculated on new technologies that would dominate future cities—including bizarre vehicles that looked like a cross between a tractor and a minivan, and family helicopters called "aerators" that could hop about from place to place. He also predicted there would be drive-in churches.[67]

Was Broadacre City, in the end, an urban design model that could be taken seriously? Or was it "the embarrassing foible of an aging master"?[68] For one, Wright supremely underestimated the size of future suburban towns. Today, many millions of residents live in the suburban and exurban rings around cities, and with that, millions of cars circulate in these sprawling metropolitan regions. Wright's romantic Broadacre City model assumed a population in each town of only 7,000! He clearly did not anticipate the scale of suburbanization and the ensuing crisis of transport unleashed when so many cars are wedged into one urban region, and when there is no reasonable, large-scale transit alternative to move people across low-density spaces.

Wright's failure to predict the scale of peripheral suburban growth personally affected him. In the Phoenix metropolitan area, Wright bought land as far from the suburban town of Tempe as he could imagine. He believed this land, on which he built the architectural community school called Taliesin West, was well beyond the fringes of any future urbanization in the Phoenix metropolitan region. Wright was wrong. Today, all of the land around Taliesin West is either already urbanized, or slated for growth in the near future.

Broadacre City, from a public space perspective, failed to acknowledge the importance of pedestrian-scale, spontaneous public life. Wright seemed willing to abandon the aesthetic of the flaneur, the nineteenth-century urban dweller role introduced by the Parisian poet Charles Baudelaire. The flaneur is the urban stroller, who wanders through the city and enjoys the serendipity of meeting people or bumping into stores, bookstalls, food vendors, previously unseen art,

or any number of hundreds of unexpected stimuli that are embedded in the spontaneous urban landscape. Wright ignored the importance of density in older city spaces, the way a tight-knit fabric allows for social interaction, the aesthetic pleasures of cafés, restaurants, and street life. Broadacre City does not acknowledge the social, economic, and cultural advantages of the high-density downtown. It failed to predict that city dwellers would respond to suburban sprawl by creating movements to revitalize pedestrian-scale urban districts, and empower public places like streets, promenades, town squares, street markets, alleys, and other public spaces.[69]

The evolution of architecture toward a discourse that emphasizes buildings rather than the urban spaces around them is reinforced by the social tendency in Western culture to focus on objects. Objects are vehicles for consumption in a consumerist society, and they thus become the focus of a culture of advertising, media, and obsession with gratification through ownership of things. Things or "goods" are connected with people's self-image in a global consumerist world. This forms part of a "culture-ideology of consumerism."[70] As architecture shifted its emphasis to buildings after the 1970s, the mass media absorbed and reinforced this message. The role of the architecture critic was often reduced to viewing buildings as if they were subjects of high art—physical sculptures arrayed across the urban landscape.[71]

Perhaps it is not a coincidence that the view of architecture as high

*Frank Lloyd Wright weighed in on the urban design debate from his visionary architectural retreat in Taliesin West, on the edge of Phoenix, Arizona.*

art corresponded with the evolution of the postmodern architecture movement in the 1970s. Modernist architecture was criticized precisely because its concern with the larger issues of urban well-being came at the expense of the aesthetics of building facades. For some observers, modern architecture had become plagued by an impersonal, cold, purely functional approach. It was not sympathetic to historic context. It was not playful. Postmodern architecture evolved as a response to this imagined gap in the urban landscape. It emphasized the visual meanings and metaphors that buildings could evoke, celebrating the idea of the visual poetry possible in the urban cultural landscape, as well as the way that new buildings could still speak to past architectural styles.[72]

Meanwhile, the question of urban space, and the larger importance of architecture's role in the built environment, would be all but forgotten. Postmodern architectural discourse morphed into a high-level dialogue among intellectuals, writers, and architects about culture, history, metaphor, and symbolism in the urban landscape. In the end, however, the reinvention of architecture as a debate about art and the symbolism of building facades was unsatisfying and even dangerous to the responsibility of master designers who create spaces that people ultimately must live in. As one critic noted, "[T]he space of art is the ideal one of fiction. In it things are not used and they never decay; one cannot walk in a painting, as one walks along a street or through a building. Architecture and design . . . have everything to do with the body."[73]

People must live in the space of buildings and in the spaces around them. However, only a minority of architects and their critics began to see the importance of this point. Yet, there is an angst among this group, a need to worry about the spaces beyond their own buildings, and the future of urban spaces at a time in history when technological and cultural forces threaten to further anesthetize urban dwellers to the importance of the living spaces that surround them. When an architect or an architecture critic writes a guide to a city, it is refreshing to see that not only buildings are reviewed, but urban spaces as well. For example, in one architectural guide to New York City, public squares, parks, and other spaces appear as part of the city's important architecture.[74]

Indeed, some books on modern architecture have devoted entire sections to topics like "Public Places." In these works, authors explore everything from parks built over freeways to giant civic centers.[75] One study highlights the construction of the new Brazilian capital of Brasília, as a laboratory for exploring the problems of modernism and its inattention to spontaneous public life in a city. Brasília, it argues, is "an expensive and ugly testimony to the fact that, when men think in terms of abstract space rather than real place, of single rather than multiple meanings, and of political aspirations instead of human needs, they tend to produce miles of jerry-built nowhere, infested with Volkswagens."[76]

Like art, architecture in Western culture has tended to follow the dictates of cycles and "trends." In affluent societies, especially in status-conscious American culture, style and marketability create value. Marketing in the United States demands that products and professions have a "cutting edge," something different that will elevate them to high status in the public eye. Fashion trends tend to be cyclical and are typically labeled and classified into neat categories and then promoted through the mass media. To maximize attention, catchy names and hip phrases are utilized.

So, in the last three decades, it has been fashionable in architecture to be "postmodern," to reject the values of the modernist paradigm, replacing these with concepts like flexibility, multitasking, and playfulness, which emerge as the new rules of postmodern design. Buildings have to be colorful, playful, historical, and metaphorical in their message. This has had the effect of creating a new set of global architectural icons, celebrated postmodern designs like the Guggenheim Museum in Bilbao, Spain. These icons rise to the level of global stardom, like Hollywood actors or famous sports heroes. Along the way, questions of public life, the nature of urban space, and social change are forgotten.

A more recent example of trendiness in urbanism lies in the celebration of cyberspace and cyberarchitecture. Architects and writers speak of a parallel universe that connects the physical city and the electronic space of networked computers—an emerging harmony between the space of the Internet and the space of streets, town squares, downtown pedestrian zones, boardwalks, or festival marketplaces. This new discourse argues for a new kind of digital urbanism, in which the calling card is summed up in these words: "the network is the urban site before us, an invitation to design and construct the City of Bits."[77] In the end, these postmodern works reduce urbanism to a game of words, metaphor, and double meanings.

The digital revolution has had a huge impact on urbanism, and on the way people live in cities. But architecture and urbanism are still about people and built environments set in physical, material space; this is a distinctly different world from that of cyberspace. Both will continue to exist, and there will be significant interaction between these worlds; but in the end, they remain distinct domains—one electronic, the other material.

It is very clever for a scholar to write "My name is wjm@mit.edu, and I am an electronic flaneur. I hang out on the network."[78] But this form of narrative implies a false premise—the idea that somehow the Internet world is a place that will have its own architecture and city planning. This is not the case. Electronics remain electronic—bits of data that can be recorded, transferred electronically and reproduced on a TV screen, a computer monitor, a PDA, or a laptop. Beyond that, they do not exist in physical space. Whatever the future of cyberspace, there will still be material space to contend with. The confusion in this literature is that it seeks to impose a science that is sociospatial and material (architecture/urban planning) onto an electronic space that is neither. As one critic has frequently stated about cyberspace, "[T]he last time I woke up in the morning, there were still four walls, a floor and a ceiling. Physical space still matters."[79] You do not sleep in cyberspace, you cannot make love there, you cannot hike there, and you cannot drink coffee there (the idea of the cybercafé notwithstanding).

Cybercity advocates like to imagine how electronic media will reinvent urban life, yet they are often just speculating. For example, a book written in the mid-1990s suggested that several elements would digitally reorder urban space.[80] They included the virtual university, videoconferencing, and online art museums. A decade later, none of these key elements had significantly altered urban life, nor did they show signs of permanently displacing the original urban physical space experiences of university life, business meetings, and museums. The virtual university, once thought by some to represent the future of university education, has not taken off as fast as predicted. University administrators are learning that many elements of on-site teaching cannot be duplicated online. Students are learning that real classrooms have an intangible aspect that can never be replaced on a computer or in simulation.

Videoconferencing has proven to be a good tool for disseminating information and curtailing traveling costs, but many professions still value live interaction between people and professionals. The online art museum is an ancillary source of promotion of the work of museums, but it has not seriously interrupted the existence or growth of museums anywhere in the world. Indeed, the twenty-first-century trend is toward hiring top architects to create new and exciting physical spaces that will become global attractions to visitors. The most significant twenty-first-century trend in art museums is not the online museum, but the visceral material space of new iconic structures like the Guggenheim, which has attracted millions of tourists to the virtually unknown city of Bilbao in northern Spain, to the real physical space of this exceptional place. Unquestionably the Internet has helped promote the museum, but in no sense is it a substitute for the in-person physical experience.

Have "cyber-apologists" overromanticized the rise of computer technology, using clever narratives to create the metaphor of a new digital city? Is the digital city a real alternative to the physical city, or is it a different space—a space of electronic processes that allows for communication and exchange of information and ideas? To compare the information superhighway with actual physical systems of transportation is, in the end, an act of poetry, but not of science. One would hope that the science and logic of urban space is given more credit for its uniqueness and for the power of its inherently spatial and material form, its inherent organic ecosystem defined by the earth and its resources, and its inherent people–space dynamic.

There are, of course, subfields of architecture and scores of individual practitioners who embrace the people–land and people–space relationship. Architectural history is one important anchor for this. While some historians may place too much emphasis on the history of buildings as objects of art, others understand the importance of architecture and urbanism as measures, at different moments in time, of how people transform both the spaces and the landscapes that physically surround them.[81]

In this regard, one of the most important trends in architecture as a profession was the development of the field of "landscape architecture." Landscape architecture, by its very definition, has allowed one subset of trained designers to go beyond the building, focusing their energies on the land and space around it. Indeed, "landscape architecture" is defined as "the art of arranging land, together with spaces and objects on it, for safe, efficient, healthful, pleasant use."[82]

The landscape architecture profession was conceived by Frederick Law Olmsted, America's towering figure in the nineteenth-century design of parks and open spaces. Olmsted coined the term "landscape architecture" in the late 1800s. This was important because it marked a point in history when attention for designers was deliberately turned away from buildings and back toward the urban environment—in other words, "the portion of the landscape developed or shaped by man, beyond buildings."[83]

Landscape architecture is frequently misunderstood by outsiders, who superficially believe it to be concerned merely with plants and vegetation. But, in fact, it is a practice that covers everything from site planning to parks, housing, natural resources, gardens, soils, and geology. It is, in essence, architecture's attempt to reconnect the urban landscape to people. Within the larger architecture field, however, landscape architecture as a profession carries much lower status.

## GLOBALIZATION AND PUBLIC SPACE

In the study of cities and regions, globalization has become an important paradigm for understanding the breakdown in the traditional hegemony of the nation-state as the dominant force in the restructuring of cities. Scholars argue that the national has been eclipsed by what are termed "transnational practices," an amalgam of forms of control exerted by global corporations over societies at different scales.[84]

Consider how global companies manipulate consumer behavior through the design of consumer products. For example, products like fast food, soft drinks, and coffee are produced as uniform packages consumed in almost the same form across the planet. Once these products become cultural icons, global investors can control consumption through advertising. The homogenization of consumer products has been termed the "culture ideology of consumerism,"[85] and has garnered considerable attention from scholars of globalism.[86]

My argument is that global corporate interests seek to homogenize and package not only physical consumer products but also the larger spaces within which those products are consumed—stores, hotels, restaurants, malls, and so forth. This homogenization and globaliza-

*Consumerist landscapes invade streets and public spaces.*

tion of the built environment is reproduced in the changing landscape of public spaces in modern cities. It includes:

• shopping malls that are routinely enclosed and decorated in homogeneous styles—with color, comfort, and a feeling of safety and removal from the surrounding city
• simulated streets and festival marketplaces that offer "walkable streets" protected from the automobile
• artificial, air-conditioned interior spaces, such as the inside of giant hotel complexes, with monumental glass atria, stores, discotheques, restaurants, stately fountains, all allowing the city dweller to move off the streets of the real city
• recreational spaces such as theme parks, designed around fantasy motifs entirely removed from any real urban context, that tend to spill back into the real city, allowing the "theme park" concept to begin to seep into city building more generally.

In this book one of my objectives is to explore the impact of globalization on selected cities in Spain and Mexico. I am curious how global forces manifest in urban public spaces, and how cities are responding to these forces.

In Spain, the lessons of Madrid and Barcelona are instructive. Madrid, the national capital, has hitched its future to global trade and Spain's membership in the European Union. This is evident in the degree to which some political interests want to reinvent the historic core as either a tertiary (service) center, a giant office zone serving transnational corporations, or a global tourist center. Under these scenarios, traditional public spaces suffer and residential communities struggle to survive.

Barcelona's destiny is equally tied to the global economy, but it has made different decisions about the role of urban design and the downtown. Barcelona chose a different path—it decided that its image as a global center for investment could be enhanced by revitalizing its public spaces as part of a complete overhaul of its historic center.

In Mexico, the national capital, Mexico City, is an important place to explore the impact of globalization. Following the signing of the North American Free Trade Agreement (NAFTA) in 1993, Mexico City quickly established itself as the command center for capital investment in the Americas. Since political power is centralized here, much of the nation's wealth is also concentrated here, and this serves as a magnet for global investors. Mexico City encapsulates what we might call the yin/yang of globalization—it houses both the best and the worst of a global urban future. Its elite neighborhoods are among the most impressively designed urban communities in the Americas; its poverty is severe. Wealthy enclaves, from Polanco to San Angel, are set against a backdrop of smog, daily traffic gridlock, and increasing fear of crime in public spaces.

Oddly, despite these limitations, Mexico City continues to have a rich public life. Its streets and plazas are convivial. The core of the urban region continues to be filled with hundreds of thousands of people per day. Even major traffic arteries, such as Paseo de la Reforma, retain a strong degree of walkability and are surrounded by pedestrian-scale neighborhoods. These neighborhoods—Colonia Roma, Condesa, Polanco—retain a vital sense of place and identity, in part anchored by their lively streets, plazas, parks, and gardens.

Mexico City's historic center, filled with some of the most important public places in all of Mexico—including plazas, gardens, and courtyards—presents the greatest challenge to the nation's ability to preserve good public spaces. Yet, the hyperactive growth around the inner core is increasing the pressure on the center. Traffic and commerce are all converging around the center. Its functional nucleus—the great Zócalo—appears as if ready to burst open, like a gaping wound. Cars, buses, people, and pedicabs can no longer comfortably share the narrow gridded streets around the Zócalo. The center cannot hold.

Yet, in medium-sized cities like Querétaro, Mexico, the center is making a comeback. The story of Querétaro is like that of Barcelona, on a smaller scale. Querétaro's downtown charm and public life have accompanied its transformation as one of the important cities on the "NAFTA corridor," home to high-technology firms located along the highway from Mexico City to the Texas border.

Farther north, along the Mexico-U.S. border, we find a laboratory for understanding globalization. Booming cities on both sides of the international boundary are joined across the border through common transnational economic interests in factories, tourism, and trade. The cities along this frontier present an opportunity to explore how culture differentially impacts public space.

## PUBLIC SPACE REBORN IN THE NEW MILLENNIUM

It is clear that traditional plazas and public spaces cannot survive everywhere in their original forms, given the nature of the postmodern metropolis. Even in European cities many traditional plazas have been turned into traffic circles. Profit-driven demands on land make it more and more difficult to renovate historic squares. Often there is pressure from business interests to convert historic spaces to more profitable use. Meanwhile, existing, underutilized public spaces often have been taken over by drug dealers or criminals. Some public spaces, such as streets or transit lines, have become too fast moving and hostile to serve as functional public gathering spaces. Other commercial streets and promenades, when well designed, are suitable as community nodes. Some cities have redesigned streets for pedestrians. Corporate plazas are viewed by many as too privatized and lacking in spontaneity.

In the midst of the chaos of postmodern cities, new kinds of spaces are being created to attract capital back into cities, spaces that are fitted to the communications age of high technology and a preoccupation with instantaneity. The new spaces seek to reinsert the celebration of urban life in high-density settings, often in the form of what have been termed "spectacle spaces," including such places as Baltimore's Harborplace, Boston's Fanueil Hall, New York City's South Street Seaport, and San Antonio's River Walk.[87] As the twenty-first century begins, a new kind of public square is reemerging. It is a bizarre twist, a repetition of history, since almost exactly a century ago, in Vienna, Austrian modernists were calling for a new kind of city. Meanwhile, traditionalists were warning not only that sacred spaces like plazas and squares should be preserved, but that they should be central to urban planning in the face of the fragmentation that modernist influences would bring in the twentieth century. Today, in different parts of the world, public spaces are being prioritized in delimiting a design for the twenty-first-century metropolis.

For example, the city of Frankfurt, Germany, decided to anchor its neighborhood rehabilitation plans around a set of upgraded public spaces. The city hired an American filmmaker to study public spaces. In one case, it was thought that the main railroad station was becoming a high crime area due to its use as a loitering place by foreign workers. The filmmaker took more than 60,000 photos and found that foreigners were not loitering in the train station; they were lonely and simply used it as a place to meet friends. This realization led to reorganizing the downtown to allow the train station to become a more dynamic gathering place.[88]

In London, England, planners believe the future design of the United Kingdom's capital city must be centered around a plan that protects and connects its major green spaces and public squares. Designers have emphasized this point, using the example of Trafalgar Square, which they argue is made less usable by its inaccessibility to pedestrians, and its poor connection to other public spaces and to the waterfront.[89] In New York City, for more than two decades, various interest groups supported the completion of studies directed at understanding how to create functional public spaces. These studies led to the creation of a system of well-designed small public spaces in Manhattan, and of a group, the Project for Public Spaces, devoted to management of similar spaces for other cities.[90]

As we shall see in this book, in Mexico and in Spain, governments have built their urban redevelopment strategy around traditional squares and public spaces. In Mexico, three examples of cities with a system of public plazas and pedestrian streets are Guadalajara, Puebla, and Querétaro. Monterrey, the country's northernmost industrial urban center, created a downtown redevelopment scheme anchored by a grand public space called the "Macroplaza." Mexico City planners are beginning to look at existing public spaces as the potential anchors for downtown economic redevelopment.

Spain has asserted itself as a world leader in recognizing the importance of public space in the economic and cultural vitality of urban life. Barcelona, as mentioned above, may be the best example of all. In the mid-1970s Barcelona was becoming a sprawling jumble of high-density apartment block complexes. The city had evolved into an undistinguished mass of modernist high-rise towers and was losing its sense of place. Following the 1975 death of Franco, the city hired Oriol Bohigas, a designer from the Catalonia region, to direct its planning program. Bohigas pushed for a project-oriented redevelopment strategy that tied neighborhood rehabilitation to the concept of identity. Public spaces would anchor the redevelopment plan, and over the next ten years, some 160 civil projects of plaza redesign, monument building, or creation of green spaces were carried out, from the historic core neighborhood in the Gothic Quarter to the apartment block suburbs.

The above suggests that public space is a phenomenon that is attended to in distinct ways in different cultural settings, from Italy, France, and Spain to the United States. I propose that there is a connection between the original form of public space—the plaza or the agora—and its surrounding context, or place. This plaza-place connection is most deeply rooted in a connection between plaza and culture, since the traditions of public space were often maintained locally, particularly before the industrial revolution. Even in the modern period, there are distinct traditions and cultural modes embedded in the shaping of urban space. Public space, so largely tied to its context, must therefore be understood by examining its evolution and connections to surrounding neighborhoods.

The nexus between Mediterranean/Iberian Europe and the Americas, when it comes to public space, begins with Spain. By 1500, as Spain began colonizing the Americas, it had very distinct urban design traditions, many of which were exported systematically to the New World through strict rules on town building, passed down by the king to the colonists of Spanish America. Today, not only are Spanish cities like Barcelona considered fundamental cultural centers for understanding public space, Mexico's plazas and gardens continue to serve vital urban functions. The Laws of the Indies, which formally transplanted the Spanish vision of the city to the Americas, are one of the few examples of the institutionalization of European spatial design ideas in North America. In Mexico, vibrant public space is a product both of Spanish planning and local conditions. In the words of one scholar, the Mexican plaza "can be seen as a distillation of the national character—its love of conviviality and spectacle, its ability to make the everyday seem special, its energy and fatalism, the tight bonds that link friends and family."[91]

An important distinction can be made between what we might term "Mediterranean/Latino" city space and "Anglo-European" city space.[92] Mediterranean/Latino urban space is structured so that the settlement space comprises the main setting for life, with the dwelling representing one element within a larger whole. In the Anglo-European city, however, the inverse is true: the dwelling is the main setting for life, while the settlement space is merely a connective tissue allowing passage from one location to another. These contrasting cultural notions of urban form imply dramatically different roles for public space. One could argue that Spain's historic influence on urban design in Mexico, and Mexico's subsequent cultural integration with the United States in the twentieth century, will strengthen the connection between European and North American urbanism in the future. It is timely, therefore, to reexamine the Mediterranean/Latino case, if for no other reason than to imagine that, in a globalizing world, this form of urbanism has arrived at the doorstep of North America via Mexico.

## The City and Public Space in Spain

*Spain is a bridge between Europe and Africa. Its plazas are legendary; no country puts them to more intensive use.*
MICHAEL WEBB, *THE CITY SQUARE*

I am walking through the narrow streets of downtown Madrid, a few blocks from the Plaza Mayor. It is a cool, late afternoon in early December. The sun has already slipped behind the wall of six-story buildings, and this particular street is nearly dark. As I cross the street and head up the sidewalk, I am on the lookout for a small alley leading to a bookstore. An elderly woman has crossed in front of me and stopped at the portal to her apartment building. The street is empty, but for the two of us. She is busy fumbling for her key and trying to hold on to several packages. As I stride up the sidewalk, I fail to notice her and bump into her, knocking her packages over. In my home country, the United States, such an incident would normally elicit anger and fear on the part of the elderly woman. To my surprise, as I begin to apologize to her, she looks up at me with amused, kind eyes and merely says, "Oh, not to worry. Such things happen. Have a nice day."

As a visitor in Spain one is struck by the feeling that public life continues to exert a strong pull in its large cities. Pedestrian-streets, squares, and gardens are vital to business and to the urban quality of life. Spain's unique culture of public space can be best understood by exploring its evolution. The long, complex history of the Spanish plaza, and its companion promenades, café-lined streets, gardens, and parks, reveals why Spain has invested so much money and political will over the years to guard its architectural and public space heritage.

In Spain public spaces are not merely romantic niches commemorating the landscape of previous centuries; they are critical devices used to promote inner-city businesses, particularly in services and tourism. In cities like Madrid and Barcelona one finds a direct link between the location of public squares, promenades, and parks and clusters of supporting economic uses: restaurants, nightclubs, cafés, bakeries, beer halls, tapas bars, and wine cellars. During the summer, a booming business unfolds in a carnival-like setting, as commercial establishments move outdoors. Cafés and restaurants spill into the plazas and parks and streets. In the larger parks and along the boulevards, the tables and chairs parade for kilometers, creating a kind of permanent outdoor urban salon, or what in Spain are called *terrazas*.

In Spain's public spaces—the street, the plaza, the subway—there is a sense of order and tolerance, an unwritten rule that strangers have the right to maintain their privacy in public space. An event I observed in the Madrid airport illustrates this point. While waiting for my luggage in the crowded baggage area, I noticed three of Spain's most famous actors standing with a friend as their baggage arrived. While many travelers nearby also noticed them, not a single person approached them. Unlike in the United States, where the public invades the privacy of "stars," it appeared that Spanish citizens simply recognized that these movie stars had the right to engage in the civic act of picking up someone at the airport, without being trampled down by an admiring public.

The order and vitality of public life in urban Spain is, of course, subject to many of the same ill winds that have blown across public space in the United States—crime, pollution, noise. Yet, there is still a great vibrancy to urban public life, and there has been a resurgence of people coming into the downtown from the suburbs on weekends, to wander in the streets and parks and plazas. In this chapter I review some of the historic conditions that fostered the development of cities and public life in Spain.

### URBAN SPAIN THROUGH THE MIDDLE AGES

Before AD 700 there were few large cities in what is now Spain; this territory was mainly populated in small settlements, particularly along the coast where Phoenicians, Greeks, and later Romans established ports. Rome conquered most of the region and proclaimed it as Iberia, building settlements in the interior. The Roman Empire's greatest material legacy came in the form of infrastructure—mainly aqueducts and bridges. The arrival of the Moors from North Africa in the eighth century sparked the creation of the first important cultural prototype of urban form—one that would have a lasting impact in Spain. Islamic rule in Spain extended from the year 711, when the Moors conquered Spain, until 1492, when the last Moorish stronghold, at Granada, was conquered by the Christian kingdoms.

The Islamic city in Spain had three key elements: the *alcazaba,* a walled fortress compound, usually built on the highest point; the *medina,* usually also a walled settlement that housed the *mezquita* (mosque), as well as stores, baths, and market streets; and finally, the *arrabal,* or extension of the city outside the main gate, an area that was usually not walled. The morphology of these cities tended to be irregular and featured narrow, labyrinthine streets. The compactness of the Islamic towns made sense in the same way that similar concentrations did for the towns of the Christian north: it was easy to defend a concentrated community, and to build walls around it. Narrow streets also created shade, or allowed for the use of cloth shelters for shade in the hot, dry climate, especially in southern and central Spain. Islamic culture is generally regarded as a culture of privacy. There were few public outdoor spaces in Islamic cities. Instead the city dweller experienced the outdoors in the enclosed private patios and gardens of the Islamic home.[1]

Around AD 1100 one began to see in Islamic cities of Spain the appearance of small markets in the places where the narrow streets widened slightly. These breaks in the medieval urban fabric represent the first of what we might term "public spaces" of Islamic Spain. The markets tended to be specialized by product: tailors, butchers, shoemakers, or chemists had their own markets. Such a market was called a "souk" (*suq* in Arabic), and in Spanish this translated to "*zoco,*" possibly a precursor of the word *zócalo,* which is synonymous with *plaza* in Mexico.

Several things should be said about these cities where the first semblance of a market space appeared during the Middle Ages. Unlike the earlier Roman cities, or the cities evolving in the Christian kingdoms of northern Spain, Islamic cities were not administrative centers. They were viewed by their rulers merely as places for the masses to live and carry out their social and religious obligations. As a result, Islamic cities were not subject to strict building codes and municipal regulations: their form unfolded in more spontaneous ways, and rarely did one find uniform buildings, street widths, or other design elements.[2]

It is useful to consider the meaning that streets and markets held within the larger cosmic view of Islamic culture. In Western societies, and in the warm Mediterranean climate, the streets represented the extension of home, a place residents would seek out frequently, where they could enjoy fresh air, sun, and human interaction. This is especially true in the medieval period, where living quarters tended to be dark and cramped. But in Arab and Islamic culture, the lives of townspeople were devoted to Islam, as well as to the activities of industry and commerce, all carried out in the crowded, noisy center, where mosque, market, and shops were located. Homes were hidden away on side streets and alleys. The streets and alleys tended to be quiet and empty, and were said to be so little used that grass grew on them.

*The Islamic patio eventually gave way to the evolution of enclosed "outdoor patios," or plazas, in Spain.* For Arabs there was little public life on the streets. Women may have gazed onto the urban scene through hidden windows, but the outdoor space of daily existence—the places where parents interacted with children in the open air—was the interior patio, or an upper galley or patio where they could look out over the mountains. For wealthier families, the design of interior patios was quite magnificent—enclosed with grand Moorish arches, tiles, thick vegetation. Some scholars have even speculated that the idea of the enclosed outdoor patio contributed later to the notion of the enclosed, monumental plaza mayor.[3]

The Islamic urbanism of Spain defined the early street layouts of cities such as Córdoba, Granada, Sevilla, and Toledo. Even today one finds the Arab quarter, with its morphology of tight spaces, high walls, irregular street patterns, winding narrow alleyways, and a noticeable absence of open spaces and public plazas (except those inserted after the Islamic period, usually on the edge of the Arab quarter).

While Islamic urbanism dominated the making of the cityscape in southern Spain during the medieval period, a different set of circumstances was evolving in the so-called Christian north, centered around the regions of Asturias, Galicia, Cantabria, León, and Castilla. Here traditional walled medieval towns and cities grew, most notably Burgos, León, Salamanca, Valladolid, Zaragoza, and Ávila. Some of this region had been affected by the Camino Frances, a connection of "itinerary cities" linking French Christianity across the Pyrenees mountains to northern Spanish Christianity through a series of military towns, including Santiago de Compostela, Toledo, Burgos, León, and Pamplona. The French military town, or *bastide,* operated on a simple gridiron plan. The morphology of the town was entirely set up for defense. The walls were built in the twelfth and thirteenth centuries. Churches were sometimes phased into the building of the surrounding wall, as in the town of Ávila. Streets were lined with porticoes and supports. The tight housing designs necessary in a compact, walled settlement and the high-density streets did not allow for open markets, or widening of streets for markets. In only a few towns small open spaces were sited alongside churches.

In general, however, the first outdoor plazas in these medieval Christian cities evolved as market spaces, often held outside the gates of the town, usually near the main entrance, and usually on a weekly, rather than daily basis. The subtle shift from "market place," an occasional market vaguely located near the city gates in the period before the tenth century, to "market plaza," where definite known markets existed at the gates of medieval towns after the tenth century, gives a sense of how these outdoor spaces began to become a more permanent part of the medieval urban plan. Still, the markets remained largely outside the all-important walls of the settlement.[4]

These "market plazas" were given permanence by the royal families that controlled the towns. The king heavily regulated these markets, charging taxes, tolls, entrance fees, and fees for traveling along roads, or for crossing bridges to get to the markets. The larger markets began at some point in the twelfth or thirteenth centuries to operate on a daily basis. In 1180 such a market was found in Salamanca, Segovia, and Valladolid, and was called the *azoque,* which sounds like a version of the Arabic *suq*. By 1300 many of these market plazas in northern Spain had wooden buildings enclosing them, and public diversions began to be scheduled there by the king: singing troubadours, jugglers, dancers, poetry readers, and equestrian showmen. In the late medieval period, bullfights took place on the plazas. These squares were appropriate locations for a bullfight, since they were completely enclosed by buildings, creating a natural arena built into the fabric of the city.

By the 1300s the market plaza had become a vital part of the city, though still outside the walls in most cases. But now, a makeshift town was growing around the market, with buildings and the homes of those who engaged in commerce and industry: Jews, Franks, Moors. Meanwhile, inside the walls lived the royalty, nobility, ecclesiastical officials, cattle owners, and urban workers. In many ways, while the Christian north evolved apart from the Islamic south, cities in both regions were similar. In the north, the market plaza grew outside the walls, and a rough settlement formed around it. In the south, a similar process unfolded, with the *arrabal* outside the walls of the medina.

### RENAISSANCE AND BAROQUE URBAN SPACE IN SPAIN:
### THE AGE OF THE AUSTRIAS, 1500–1700

The Renaissance (1400–1600) marks the time period when Spain became politically unified. The Christian kings expelled the Moors in 1492, and Spain was "reconquered." During this period notions of the "ideal city" were born, inspired in large part by the writings of Greek philosophers like Aristotle, and by the dream of building a great city such as Rome. In an ancient document from the Catalonia (Cataluña) region, dated in the 1300s, a chapter is found entitled "What form should a beautiful and well-constructed city take?" The chapter goes on to speak of four quarters, two main streets, a vast and pleasing plaza with a cathedral on it, all spread across the flattest possible surface. A Spanish bishop, Rodrigo Sanchez de Arevalo (1404–1471), wrote a book titled *Suma de la Política* (Summary of Politics), and in it, he speaks of "how to find and build good cities."[5]

Clearly the Renaissance marked in Spain (as well as in Italy, France, and elsewhere in Europe) a new preoccupation with creating beauty in high-density towns and cities, a beauty thought to be greatest when achieved through design order and symmetry. These concerns were said to course through the notebooks of Italy's Leonardo da Vinci. In Spanish cities such thoughts led to recommendations to build wider streets and to create rectilinear spaces with larger, uniform plazas surrounded by well-designed buildings.

But the "ideal city" was the antithesis of the Hispano-Islamic city that had been built for defense, not for beauty, and thus lacked sufficient room for widening streets, and for opening the narrow winding corridors and alleys to allow the building of plazas. In the 1400s, campaigns emerged in some Spanish cities—notably Barcelona, Valencia, and Burgos—to widen streets, create new plazas, and beautify cities.[6]

On the sites of medieval market-plazas, the Spanish royalty decided to create monumental spaces of beauty and power: the plazas mayores. High-status families were ordered to build sumptuous palaces and homes around these central squares. Spain's best architects and artists were called in to design the ornate, uniform buildings that would enclose these plazas. They would serve two basic functions: first, representation, to symbolize the power of the king at the most

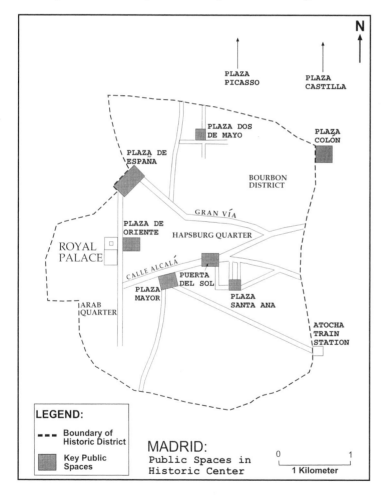

Madrid: Public spaces in the historic center.

important space in the town—the market; second, to give society a sense of belonging and a connection to the king through the celebrations and festivals held regularly on the main plazas.[7] Thus, one could argue that the plaza mayor never really functioned as a market space, so much as a center of celebration, a monumental space of spectacles to be viewed from the many balconies attached to the surrounding buildings. The notion of plaza mayor as theater makes sense when one thinks about the origins, the creation of a show for the royal families, replete with a built-in audience created in the built environment of adjacent structures.

Many and varied were the celebrations held on the great plazas of Renaissance Spain. In Valladolid marriages, executions, and ceremonial trials for the Spanish Inquisition (called autos-da-fé) were all held on the main plaza. In fact, the first such trial in all of Spain was held in Valladolid in 1559. Fourteen people were reportedly burned at the stake. Around the plaza were situated impressive buildings with as many as 330 doors and 3,000 windows from which to view events.[8] Other cities—Salamanca, Jaén, Badajoz—built impressive plazas of their own. Using Italian designer Alberti's model for plazas in Rome, Spanish kings and their advisers sought to construct porticoes around the plazas. These new design strategies emphasized order, regularity, and symmetry—thus giving the Spanish plazas a monumentality that they had not possessed before.

The height of Spain as a world power was reached during the Age of the Austrias, so named when Juana, the daughter of the Catholic monarchs, Ferdinand and Isabella, married the son of Emperor Maximilian of Austria. When their son, Carlos I, became king of Spain, the "house of Austria" was regarded as Spain's royal lineage. It would last for nearly two centuries. Charles I was elected Emperor of the Holy Roman Empire in 1519, and ruled over Spain, Naples, Sicily, Sardinia, Austria, the German states, and the "Low Countries" (Belgium, the Netherlands, etc.). His son, Phillip II, by the mid-sixteenth century ruled over an empire that rapidly colonized the Americas. Before the defeat of the Spanish Armada in 1588, Spain was probably the most powerful nation in the world.

During this period of the royal "Hapsburg" (Austrian) family, urban space in Spain took on a new form. Cities began slowly to abandon their medieval defensive functions, as they grew beyond the safety of castle and walls. The driving forces of growth often tended to be religious complexes (such as convents and monasteries) or hospitals. Where in the medieval period the rhythm of urban space was typically defined as a cluster of buildings, many of which were often connected within a walled compound, during the age of the Hapsburgs individual buildings became the main focus of aesthetics among architects. Meanwhile, the emergence of transport vehicles, such as horse-drawn carts, led to the appearance of transit streets. Local citizens' rights were newly recognized by the king, and town laws, or *ordenanzas*, began to appear. The city still remained relatively compact, with the walls often extended to accommodate new areas of growth. Beyond this lay the forests and royal hunting grounds.[9]

Royal leaders viewed the city both as a mystical form, requiring a vast infrastructure of religious buildings, and as the setting for an architecture of symbolic power.[10] This emergent symbolism was most dramatically expressed through the creation of a space of power: the plaza mayor. Before, the plazas were functional markets with a few buildings around them, but during the late sixteenth and seventeenth centuries, they became rigorously organized architectural spaces. Squares were no longer decorative afterthoughts—empty spaces near churches or buildings—but rather "spiritual" extensions of the churches or convents. The meaning of the building extended out into the public space before it.

Unlike the French *place*, which often served as a street crossing, the Spanish plaza mayor was an enclosed space that actually blocked traffic. On the Spanish plaza mayor one always found the municipal government building, fortifying the tradition of local rights and *ordenanzas* administered there. Glaringly absent from all plazas mayores were religious buildings, as the kings and royal leaders in Spain were careful to maintain their power above and separate from that of the Church. The churches were set back a block or two, usually with their own religious plazas.

The plaza mayor was an enclosed space where all of Spanish society could get together. In Islamic Spain the enclosed Andalusian patio facilitated the gathering together of members of the family; in sixteenth- and seventeenth-century Spain the enclosed patio became the enclosed plaza, and it was all of society, not just the family, that could get together in that enclosed space. It was the intention of the Spanish royal family to create an architectural space—the plaza—that signified their power and importance; it was also their intention that this space be heavily used by all city residents. To encourage this, a wide array of social activities was scheduled in the plaza: parties, masquerades, drinking, walking, bullfights, and of course, the all-important town market. In effect, the plaza became the transitional space between the private realm of the home and the public realm.[11]

### The Plaza Mayor

In 1561 the king of Spain, Phillip II, ordered that the court be moved from Toledo to Madrid. This obviously changed the destiny of the city forever, making it a capital city and center of commerce, and opening up all sorts of economic opportunities over the next several centuries. Physically, the expansion of Madrid implied by its becoming the seat of the royal court caused the city, by the early 1600s, to grow beyond the limits of the medieval-Islamic walls, and in 1625 a new wall was built around the city with some 13 main gates. The new city extended as far east as the Palace of Buen Retiro, near what would become in

*The iconic Plaza Mayor of Madrid is a celebration of the town square as an anchor of urban design identity in Spain.*

the twentieth century Retiro Park. On the western flank of the city, the Royal Palace served as a strong edge. The city consisted of long streets and buildings of two to three stories.[12] This was undoubtedly Madrid's greatest period of architectural triumphs, a time when the powerful royal family invested in the construction of spaces in the city—plazas—to celebrate royal power, while encouraging the idea of citizen interaction with the monarchy.

"To speak of Plaza Mayor and to think of the one in Madrid is one and the same thing."[13] Indeed, Madrid's Plaza Mayor has become an iconic space, a kind of museum of plazas. It is the place you go in

Spain to discover the model of plaza life for all of Spain. The Plaza Mayor reminds Spanish citizens that pedestrian life is not only possible, but desirable as well. The space transcends the neighborhood, transcends all of the city, and by transforming it into a museum, it becomes a monument, apart from the fabric of the city yet intimately connected to it.

Its origins are more humble, of course. Following the medieval period, a small settlement grew around the east gate of Madrid—a small market plaza, which came to be called Plaza Arrabal. By the late fifteenth century this was an active plaza that housed the vendors of bread, fish, meat, and all manner of agricultural products. It was also beginning to attract residential buildings immediately around it, and soon became a gathering place for citizens. By the 1490s the sale of products like shoes, wine, and oils was recorded on the plaza.[14] During the early sixteenth century the plaza continued to thrive as a market, and its uses expanded to include bullfights. In 1532 King Phillip II changed the name of the square to Plaza Mayor, and more parties and bullfights were held here.

It is known that in the early 1600s, King Phillip III wanted to "dignify" the plaza; there were others who sought to require that all homeowners on the plaza create uniform facades on their buildings. In 1608 the king hired the architect Francisco de Mora to elaborate a project to "regularize" the plaza. By then the king had clearly designated two uses for the plaza: to serve as the main daily market in the city, and to serve as the main setting for grand feasts and celebrations of the Spanish royal court. Interestingly, there was no relationship whatsoever between these two disparate functions—the one a habitual daily urban market, the other a baroque scene of pompous royal celebrations by what was, at that moment in history, the most powerful kingdom in the world.[15]

The dawn of the Plaza Mayor as a great Renaissance plaza came with the commissioning of its design in 1617. This was a period when similar ornate plazas were being built in other European cities: for example, the Place des Vosge in Paris (1605–1612) and Covent Garden in London (1631–1635). In 1619 the plaza was completed; it consisted of nine entrances, three archways, six hidden streets, 477 balconies. It held 3,700 residents and for major events could fit some 50,000 spectators.[16] The design was rectangular, with five stories rising above the porticoes on the ground-floor level. The architecture of the two main structures—Casa de Panadería and the Casa de Carnecería—consisted of towers or spires, designed along the lines of the Monastery at El Escorial, which at that moment was one of the most powerful, if slightly somber, pieces of architecture in all of Europe. A British writer's description of El Escorial could easily be used to describe the Plaza Mayor: "Rectangular and enormous, and implacably severe, unrelieved by any softness or foliage or decoration. . . . In the coldness and bleakness of this building, you may detect the aristocratic stoicism of Spain, something grandly ascetic in the character of the country, which often makes it feel otherworldly and aloof."[17]

The Plaza Mayor was a massive rectangular space. In some ways the size of the plaza was the most overwhelming element of all, and the surrounding five-story Renaissance apartments, with their wrought iron balconies, arched corridors, stone columns, and porticoes, merely served to enhance the grandiose image of the giant plaza. Madrid's Plaza Mayor was created as a space of grandeur and prestige—a showcase for the Hapsburg royal family. Its architecture of uniformity was typical of the Renaissance period. Here some of the most important events of seventeenth-century Madrid would take place: the canonization of the patron saint of Madrid, San Isidro; visits by dukes and duchesses from Austria; autos-da-fé for the Spanish Inquisition; the first great Spanish bullfights. Unlike in Latin America, the plaza mayor in Spain almost never had a major church on it; certainly the one in Madrid is notable for having no church or other religious building on it.

The theater aspect of the plaza cannot be underestimated. The rectangular and enclosed nature of the space, combined with excellent viewing from its balconies, made it a kind of natural theater. Furthermore, this was precisely the intention of the royal monarch: to create a space where citizens could feel a part of the royal monarchy, and yet be kept in their place. The space created by the king was where all important social events were carried out. But it was also used in more everyday ways, creating a ritual of plaza life that continued through the twentieth century. In other European countries this was not necessarily the case. In France, for example, some public squares existed only to glorify the king (the Place de Vosges); they looked as if a rural castle or palace had simply been moved into the city. No everyday activities took place there. Even more striking were the residential squares that emerged in England. In London the first grand squares were actually private spaces for aristocrats and wealthy families.[18]

The list of public events and spectacles that took place in Madrid's Plaza Mayor during the seventeenth and eighteenth centuries is impressive: bullfights; jousting; horse events; processionals; various games; autos-da-fé; executions; masquerade parties; carnivals; light and fireworks "night shows"; *encamisadas,* or frivolous celebrations of victories at war; royal births and weddings, where everyone wore long white shirts over their clothes; *parejas,* or parades, where horses danced to music; theater; dances; *verbenas,* or festivals on the eves of saint's days; and even riots and military battles.

### Plaza Santa Ana

To the south and east of the Plaza Mayor lies one of the most well preserved public squares in Madrid: the Plaza Santa Ana, named after a Carmelite monument built on the site from 1586 to 1611. The founding of the Carmelite convent was led by two leading figures in Spanish mysticism: Santa Teresa de Jesus and San Juan de la Cruz. Santa Teresa was a nun who believed in uniting action with contemplation, a

progressive position for the sixteenth century, when most mystics were thought to be dedicated to spirituality alone. San Juan de la Cruz, a disciple of Santa Teresa, wrote mysterious poetry about the dark recesses of the soul, and about the spiritual vacuum of human life on earth.

On this site was born one of the most creative cultural institutions of late-sixteenth-century Madrid, a specifically Madrileño form of spontaneous outdoor urban theater called the *corral de comedias.* This development would mark the beginning of an energetic period of creativity, the so-called golden age of great Spanish literature, painting, and playwriting. The *corral* was an outdoor theater born in the court-

*Plaza Santa Ana was a thriving center of theater life in the sixteenth century; it was later a favored haunt of literary giant Ernest Hemingway.*

yard of an apartment complex in Madrid in the late 1500s. It was said that the original such theater was called the Corral de Pacheca, which began in the afternoons with music, then a short skit introducing the author of a play, followed by the actual *comedia* (play). Between acts there were short farces called *entremeses*, and after the play there might be a postscript or slice-of-life scene called a *jácara*. Finally, at the end there would be dances. The scene around these *comedias* was spontaneous—the activities in the crowd were as much a part of the action as the play itself, and the crowd was known to get carried away, with fights breaking out over seats, or between rival authors and actors.[19]

The *corral* consisted of an open space with platforms on either end: one for the stage, the other for women spectators. Down below were standing and seating areas for men, and it was here that the fights would break out. Wealthy families occupied compartments or box seats along the sides of the space, and residents of the apartment complex overlooking the *corral* rented seats in the balconies of windows. The male standing-room spectators were called *mosqueteros* (musketeers), and it was their function to decide whether the play was good or bad—their derision or applause served as a form of critique or censorship of the era. Even the greatest of playwrights were known to have been derided severely in these *corrales*.[20]

This very distinct Spanish form of theater produced some of the greatest plays and writers in the history of theater, including Calderón de La Barca, Tirso de Molina, and Lope de Vega. The Plaza Santa Ana is a space that embodies this period of creative history.

## BAROQUE CITIES AND THE EARLY INDUSTRIAL AGE, 1700–1900

Madrid's Plaza Mayor was the quintessential Renaissance space: monumental in scale, perfectly uniform (i.e., the enclosing sides were symmetrical), an ideal theater for the royal powers. The use of perspective in design allowed city builders to conceive of urban space through a single point of view. This led to a new kind of standardization in design. Baroque urban design and architecture displayed these new tendencies; for example, in the uniformity of decor in the great royal towns and residences built in the period, such as at Versailles, St. Petersburg, or Aranjuez (Spain). The designs were highlighted by ornate scenography, revolving around the king and the palace.

It has been argued that during this period, while there was some consciousness of social needs, most city building unfolded within the realm of art.[21] Much of the urban expansion in Spain in the 1700s took place at the whim of the king. The inner circle of royalty wanted mainly to beautify the cities, creating grand royal palaces and gardens on their outskirts. For example, during the period of Carlos III, a student of European as well as Spanish designs, urban development looked toward Paris and sought to mimic its salons, promenades, fountains, city gates, and parks.

In the 1800s urban form was dramatically altered by technological progress, demography, and politics. The availability of steel brought new designs for bridges, buildings, and railroads. Train stations or commercial galleries could be built in a space covered with a steel frame. By the end of the century there were trams and electricity, and cities were growing. Madrid and Barcelona each had half a million residents by 1900.

The nineteenth century saw a shift from Baroque to neoclassic designs, followed by an attachment to "romanticist" architecture. Urbanism in Spain in the nineteenth century began to move away from the Baroque emphasis on perspective to more rational principles. Growth had long since moved beyond the walls of the earlier cities, and in the outer regions had become quite chaotic. The nineteenth century in Spain, as in other parts of Europe or elsewhere on the globe, was a time of discovery and technology, but in cities it was a time of experimentation. Never before had Spain seen such large industrial centers, and such population growth. Now it was necessary to determine how to plan urban expansion beyond the confines of the old historic cores.

But before that could be done, in the nineteenth century Spain would pass through several periods of political change and instability. During the early part of the century, under the rule of the Bourbon King Ferdinand VII, Spain's colonies in the Americas were beginning their march toward liberation from the mother country. Meanwhile at home, Spain was fighting for its own liberation from the control of France. This was the period of the Wars of Independence, which began with the revolt of May 2, 1808, in Madrid, later immortalized in the paintings of Goya, and ended with the Spanish victory at Bailén later that year. Once Ferdinand had power returned to him by Napoléon, he abolished the constitution and declared an absolute monarchy. Meanwhile, the cities of Spain under royal domain entered a period of neoclassic urbanism, in which the designs of the past were recreated with modern materials. Ornate five-story apartment buildings lined the city streets just beyond the historic centers of Madrid, Barcelona, and most large Spanish cities.[22]

The middle of the nineteenth century saw a series of internal battles over political power (the Carlist Wars), which ended by 1876 with the eventual restoration of the Bourbon leadership by Alfonso XII, considered the last relatively powerful Spanish king. The period of the restoration brought to Spain a continuation of modernization of its cities, in the form of road and railroad construction and urban expansion.

How to expand at the periphery was the big question for urban Spain, a nation wedded to its historic urban core. In the middle and later part of the nineteenth century, two important schools of thought about urban growth emerged. The first consisted of a set of ideas often referred to as the "great *ensanches*," or new suburban grids, just beyond the historic core. In Barcelona in 1859, and in Madrid in 1857, city planners developed a scheme to expand just beyond the edge of the city using a new technique of quadrangular street grids within a rigid site plan. These rectangular grids would be crisscrossed by diagonals, which would carry the major transit—mass transit and, later, automobiles. The rectangular grid would support residential densities of three to five stories, and within the grid would be small neighborhood parks. Barcelona's *ensanche* was the most extensive and well designed of all urban growth plans in Spain, and it had the distinction of attracting some of the most innovative turn-of-the-century residential architecture in Europe, under the leadership of Antonio Gaudi and his modernist design colleagues.[23]

In fact, the turn-of-the-century period produced more than its share of visionary urbanists in Spain. One man who stood out was Arturo Soria, from Madrid, who, unlike those who embraced the *ensanche* plan, believed that the old urban core could not support modern city life at all. The *ensanche* planners projected the grid around the existing core, assuming that the historic center would continue to anchor the city, and that the new suburbs would still feed off the old center. A second group, led by Soria, was convinced, however, that the future of urban Spain lay in the development of autonomous linear garden cities built within a rail line–driven morphology.[24] His vision was in accord with other garden-city thinkers of the late nineteenth and early twentieth centuries, from Patrick Geddes in Scotland to Lewis Mumford in the United States.

In 1892 Soria began to piece together his vision of the Ciudad Lineal, the linear city. He formed a private entity, the Companía Madrileña de Urbanización (Madrid Urbanization Company). His company, however, was not in the business of land speculation; its purpose was to market housing units along a trolley line east of downtown Madrid. Unfortunately, Soria was able to market only enough land and housing to cover about 5.2 kilometers along the projected 50-kilometer trolley line, which would have theoretically housed some 30,000 inhabitants.[25] The project was dependent on small investors, and never went further than the original 5 km of trolley, which at the turn of the century connected to downtown Madrid on both ends of the linear corridor. Today remnants of the Soria project are few: a tree-lined boulevard of the same name, a stop on the subway named after the urbanist, and a few buildings that survived the high-rise apartment and office block developments across the district in the twentieth century.

## PUBLIC SPACE IN EARLY INDUSTRIAL MADRID

In Madrid the transition from Hapsburg to Bourbon royal family control coincided with the expansion of the city's boundaries toward the periphery, and in particular toward the royal park in the east called the Parque del Buen Retiro. Bourbon Madrid is not really a particularly well defined space within the historic core area of Madrid; it is blended in with earlier and later periods. The Bourbon period is probably most notable for the beginning of Madrid's connection to the outer world, the beginning of "Europeanization," through both the influence of the French court and the increasing interaction with Germany, Italy, England, and other European cultures.

By 1800 the population of Madrid had reached 200,000, and the nation was about to enter a period of political instability, foreign occupation, and a series of civil wars between those wanting to end monarchical rule and those wishing to preserve the status quo. Madrid was influenced by Napoleonic planning, through the force of his appointed king, José (Joseph) Bonaparte, who brought notions of French plaza-gardens and the French boulevard. In the second half of the nineteenth century we see the impact of the early schemes for modernization and industrialization, with the development of the *ensanche* plan for laying out apartments in rectangular grids in suburban areas arrayed around the historic center of the city.

The evolution of public spaces and plazas during the period 1700–1900 very much reflects the nature of political authority and the dominant modes of thinking about urbanism of the period. Let us consider several important urban plazas that evolved during this two-century era preceding the modernization of the twentieth century.

### "FRENCHIFICATION" OF THE PLAZA MAYOR

There were three great fires on the Plaza Mayor—in 1631, 1672, and 1790. The last one was so damaging that most of the plaza had to be

rebuilt; the original design standards were kept, while the material structure was improved. During the Bourbon era in Madrid (1700–1900), the use of the plaza for celebrations was largely curtailed. The Bourbon Kings imposed a more French view of plazas—as formal spaces of royalty. In the early 1700s bullfighting was eliminated on the Plaza Mayor. By 1749 a separate space for bullfights, called the "Plaza de Toros," was created on the eastern side of Madrid, near the Puerta de Alcalá (Gate of Alcalá). By 1800 many would describe the French Bourbons' impact on the life of the Plaza Mayor as one of "very intensive repression."[26] Most major events, other than such patriotic occurrences as the official reception of foreign dignitaries, no longer took place on the main plaza. Executions had been moved to other locales. The Bourbons went so far as to change the name of the space to Plaza de la Constitución (Plaza of the Constitution) in 1820. The next year they started calling it "Plaza Real" (Royal Plaza). In 1829 the wedding of King Ferdinand VII was held on the plaza. The last big event was the 1846 marriage of Queen Isabella II to Francisco de Asis, a French Bourbon, and the companion wedding of two other royal figures. This wedding featured the last bullfight on the plaza. More than 100,000 people attended the festivities.

*By the nine-teenth century the Plaza Mayor had become a symbol of French royalty.*

In the middle and late 1800s, various civil wars in Spain had their impact on the Plaza Mayor in Madrid. Riots took place on the plaza, and its name was changed at one point to Plaza de la República. The Romantic era also brought a change in that trees were now planted on the plaza. During the last decade of the nineteenth century, trolley lines entered the plaza, and ran around its perimeter.[27]

## PUERTA DEL SOL: THE PLAZA OF HISTORY

In the early 1800s, as Madrid passed through a period of turmoil and foreign occupation, events were often set on the Puerta del Sol, which became a stage for much of contemporary Spanish history. As early as 1622 the writer Lope de Vega had speculated about the murder of an important noble, the Count of Villamediana, on the square, and the talk among the plaza gossipers (*mentideros*) about the murder. But in the nineteenth century a crescendo of historic events began to build on the Puerta del Sol. Napoléon Bonaparte, continuing his ambition of territorial control, had sent his brother José to govern Spain in 1808.

The Spanish uprising against the French was met with a massacre on the plaza; in the words of one writer: "The struggle, or one should say the bloodbath, was appalling in the Puerta del Sol."[28] Many crucial historical moments in nineteenth-century Spanish politics came to pass on the Puerta del Sol. The Constitution of 1812 was proclaimed here. Opposition to the king and a liberal revolt by Riego was announced on the Puerta del Sol in 1820. In 1836 journalists told of people running through the Puerta del Sol yelling, "Viva la Constitución" ("Long live the Constitution").[29] During the Carlist Wars of the middle and late

*The Puerta del Sol is perhaps the most famous historic place in Spain; many important events occurred in this public space.*

nineteenth century, and political proclamations were presented on the plaza. A president, José Canalejas, was assassinated on the Puerta del Sol in 1912.

The Puerta del Sol continues as a locus of popular demonstrations today. In the midst of the civil disturbances and Carlist Wars, the Puerta del Sol was also a center of technological transformation. The first gas lamps of Madrid were installed here. The first trolley lines centered around the plaza, as did early electric lighting ventures, and later, the first telephone systems, asphalt road construction, and the first subway line.

### THE ROYAL PLAZA: PLAZA DE ORIENTE

It has been said that the essential mission of the Plaza de Oriente is to offer a public space on the eastern flank of the Royal Palace, a space that is both functional (allowing the public a glimpse of royal life) and aesthetic. It is also said that to understand this plaza, you must understand the relations between the royal palace and the city.[30]

The Bourbon period is the last period of royal power in Spain, and it is the time when Spain lost its hold on what was once the largest colonial empire in the world. The history of Bourbon control of Spain is the history of gradual decline of a royal family. Although the modern Spanish king, Juan Carlos, partially rescued the image of the royal family through his successful democratization of Spain in the 1980s,[31] the Bourbon period is remembered mainly as one of disappointment and political instability.

The Plaza de Oriente, a plaza fronting on the Royal Palace, is thus an appropriate public space to represent Bourbon Madrid. The palace here was built on the site of the original Moorish alcazar (fortress) overlooking the Manzanares Valley to the west. Early in the Bourbon period, in 1734, the alcazar burned down. In 1764, during King Phillip V's reign, the new stone and granite Royal Palace was completed, a product of the designs of Ventura Rodríguez Rodríguez and several prominent Italian designers. Gardens and patios and other additions continued to be added in the years following. The sumptuous classical palace was a great landmark on the west side of Madrid overlooking the valley and the Sierra de Guadarrama beyond.

Because the Royal Palace had its own plaza—the Plaza de Almería, to the south—early in the nineteenth century the idea of creating a more public plaza to the east of the palace surfaced. It was actually promoted by a foreigner, the king José Bonaparte. José Bonaparte believed that Madrid generally needed more small- and medium-sized plazas; he later was nicknamed, somewhat derisively by Madrileños, as the "Rey de Plazuelas" (King of Small Plazas). José Bonaparte commissioned the clearing of land and the design of the Plaza de Oriente, whose name comes from the idea that the plaza would be located on the "east" (*oriente*) side of the Royal Palace. Some people find this name confusing since the plaza is on the western edge of downtown Madrid. In any case, the design and construction of the Plaza de Oriente began in 1818, but due to political uncertainty and disputes over leadership, it was not actually completed until 1881.

During the years of its construction, other changes occurred around the site that added to its vitality. In the 1820s construction was completed on the new royal theater, or Teatro Real, opposite the Royal Palace. It was mainly used for music, specifically for opera, and has since taken the name Teatro de Opera. Around the plaza, buildings were constructed on either side of the opera building, creating the shape of an arc. In these buildings opera singers frequently lived or stayed as guests. The actual plaza was designed with a central garden, fountain, and such landscaping as was in vogue in French and Italian gardens of the time. A series of marble statues were designed for the roof of the Royal Palace, but instead of being placed there, the statuary was arranged around the central garden of the Plaza de Oriente.

## SOCIAL PROTEST AND PUBLIC SPACE: PLAZA DOS DE MAYO

The Plaza Dos de Mayo is truly a neighborhood plaza. It is used by many layers of society around it: students at a nearby school, neighbors walking the dog, chatting with friends, taking an evening stroll, or just passing through on the way to the market. During the 1970s and 1980s its community, Maravillas, has also become one of the centers of nightlife among Madrid youth. Many bars, cafés, and clubs have opened, and the plaza has become a kind of reference point for young people coming into the city from the outskirts of Madrid.[32]

The site itself was the location of the Maravillas convent, which was built here in 1616. In 1723 part of the palace was destroyed in a fire, and in 1807 the remaining property was converted into the major artillery supply depot and command post of the city. This would prove to be an important development, as events of only one year later unfolded. Spain had become an important element in Napoléon Bonaparte's strategy of courting European allies and seeking global hegemony.[33] When neighboring Portugal refused to comply with this Continental System, Napoléon reached an agreement with Spain: Spain would support France against Portugal; the French would occupy Portugal. Napoléon sent a force there in 1807, but he also moved troops to Spain, saying they were in transit to Portugal. But in February 1808 the French occupied Barcelona and Pamplona. The next month, they entered Madrid. Meanwhile, with the Spanish royal family outside the country quarrelling among themselves, the crown was ceded to Napoléon, who sent his brother José to rule in Spain.

Popular unrest grew, and on May 2, while the French had 40,000 soldiers outside Madrid, a crowd in the city decided to storm the French-controlled armory on the hill above downtown. A number of Spanish officers joined the revolt, and when they were reinforced by soldiers from a nearby volunteer barracks, the rebels attacked and quickly occupied the armory. The French troops crossed into Madrid from the east and south, killing civilians and occupying all of the city except the Monteleón palace and surrounding hill. When the French troops finally attacked the hill, hundreds were killed on both sides, until the Spanish finally surrendered. There were mass executions the next day, immortalized in a later painting by Goya.

The uprising of May 2, 1808, has become a symbol of nationalism and patriotism throughout Spain. What is interesting is to observe how this historic event came to shape a neighborhood and the public space that carries the memory of the event. In 1840 some of the streets in the Maravillas neighborhood were renamed to commemorate the uprising of 1808, and in particular its heroic soldiers—Velarde, Daoiz, Ruíz, and the young woman Manuela Malasaña, who had been active in assisting the revolt, as well as another heroine, Divino Pastor. By 1860 the artillery quarters were abandoned, and Madrid was in the process of a new stage of growth and modernization. The artillery buildings were sold to a private owner who wanted to develop the site. The property owner negotiated an agreement with city officials to put in streets, draw up a site plan for development, and build a public square; in return, the city would pay for demolitions, sewage, and other public service installations. The plaza was to be built around the original archway of the old Monteleón palace, as a reminder of the events of May 2, 1808. It would be called Plaza del Arco.[34]

At the same time, one of Madrid's most prominent writers of the period, Angel Fernandez de los Rios, writing about the future of the city, proposed that on the hill of Maravillas a large garden square be built around the old arch.[35] In 1869 part of the old Convent of Maravillas was demolished, freeing up space to create the plaza, and three years later the rest of the convent site was given to a school, which continues to occupy the site today. During the 1880s buildings around the plaza were constructed, giving the space a uniform enclosure.

This seemed to set a tone for the neighborhood, which during the nineteenth century evolved into a place where people with alternative ideas came to live. It was known as a center for *tertulias* (social gatherings), cafés, and meeting places at the turn of the twentieth century. One nearby local café, the Café Comercial, was a legendary meeting place for anti-Franco leftists. It had been founded much earlier, in 1867, and its reputation grew. Some leftists who met there between 1931 and 1936 were later picked up by Franco's secret police and killed.[36]

## CITIES IN TWENTIETH-CENTURY SPAIN

Both the *ensanches* and the Ciudad Lineal suggest that at the turn of the century Spain was experimenting with innovative ways to accommodate population expansion while preserving the inner-core neighborhoods and the downtown. Spain's urbanism in the 1900s is intensely debated in its two largest cities, Madrid and Barcelona. The centralism of centuries of absolute monarchy remains paramount—the two largest cultural centers will experiment with and implement new trends in urban design and planning, which the rest of the nation will then use in its towns and cities.

Madrid has been the driving force of twentieth-century urban Spain. It was a city originally created in the most artificial of conditions—on

*Madrid has seen its share of political unrest, which remains embedded in the landscapes surrounding the city's streets and squares in the form of graffiti.*

the inhospitable, arid, upraised Meseta, the central plateau of Spain. Madrid was a quintessentially royal city; it grew, not so much because of its natural advantages (even its early supplies of water began to dissipate with massive growth in the twentieth century), but because of historical momentum. The Bourbon kings simply inherited a well-entrenched capital from the Hapsburg dynasty and stayed with it. By the twentieth century, Madrid was too big. But it had anchored the nation for so many centuries, it was difficult for anyone to tamper with such an arrangement. A powerful culture of urban workers and leaders, as well as a political system of decision makers, was deeply embedded in this Castilian metropolis on the Meseta.

The 1900s in Spain was not an easy period for the nation to experiment with urban planning and design projects. The century began on the heels of Spain's 1898 loss of the last vestiges of its overseas empire—Cuba, Puerto Rico, and the Philippines—to the United States. Then, after staying neutral during World War I, Spain experienced considerable economic instability, and around the nation, popular insurrection began, especially in Catalonia. In 1923, running out of options, the Spanish king permitted General Miguel Primo de Rivera to establish a dictatorship. By the early 1930s the instability had worsened, with two sides forming: the liberals who wanted to establish a democratic republic, calling themselves "Republicans"; and the right wing, aligned with conservative wealthy interests, the military, and the Church—all of whom wanted to preserve the institutions of the past—calling themselves "Nationalists."

In 1936 the Spanish civil war began, and it lasted for three long years, at the end of which Spain was devastated. Major battles were fought in the large cities, and a campaign of revenge and destruction by the victorious Nationalists further disrupted urban Spain. Little significant planning for growth took place, and as the population of city residents continued to climb, spontaneous urban life began to show signs of withering. Spain's cities were badly in need of good planning, especially the larger ones, including Madrid, Barcelona, Bilbao, and San Sebastián. In 1946 Franco hired an urban planner named Bigador, whose Plan Bigador burdened Spain's urbanism, for the moment, with Franco's urban design fantasy of imperial fascism.[37] Franco's "ideal falangist city" never really caught hold in Spain. In the meantime, the absence of effective planning created problems in the existing cities on two levels: first, growth occurred outside the prescribed suburban nuclei; and second, green spaces disappeared due to speculation in land by those in favor with Franco.

Not until the 1960s did Spanish planners shake off the paralysis of the early years of Franco's regime and begin to engage in serious planning. In 1963 an ambitious metropolitan plan was created for the Madrid region, and many other cities followed suit. Unfortunately, by then, a legacy of planning drawn from Le Corbusier, the French modernist, had taken hold in Spain. The new urban model of development emphasized high-density apartment block projects, with an absence of serious social programs, good public spaces, or efficient transit systems.

By the 1970s, in cities like Madrid, the transportation crisis and the environmental crisis were firmly lodged. Rapid rural-to-urban migration added an additional housing crisis. During the 1960s and early 1970s the government aggressively built high-rise modernist apartment blocks on the periphery of the large cities. Millions of housing units were constructed to resolve the crisis of homelessness and of shantytown constructions (*chabolas*). Between 1961 and 1976 (the year after Franco died) the National Housing Plan led to the construction of 4 million dwelling units in multistoried blocks all over Spain.[38] Gone were the shantytowns; in their place, Spain, almost overnight, produced several of the most crowded and environmentally troubled metropolitan areas in western Europe.

Barcelona, along with Madrid and Bilbao, was one of the examples of a city that had grown too fast, and without order. Its historic character was endangered by dull, high-rise block complexes that blanketed the periphery. These developments were even threatening to choke the historic core. So chaotic were the sprawling apartment slabs with their lack of a sense of humanity that one architectural observer described Barcelona's 1970s morphology as a "disastrous mess."[39] By the 1990s architecture critics in Spain remained skeptical about the nation's urban future. They compared the country's urban policy to the voyage of Icarus, the figure of mythology, son of the architect Daedalus, who perished when flying too near the sun, and having the wax that fastened his wings melt. Was Spain, they wondered, also flying metaphorically too near the sun?[40] Could Spain find the urban planning imperatives it needs to preserve its legacy of good public spaces in the twenty-first century?

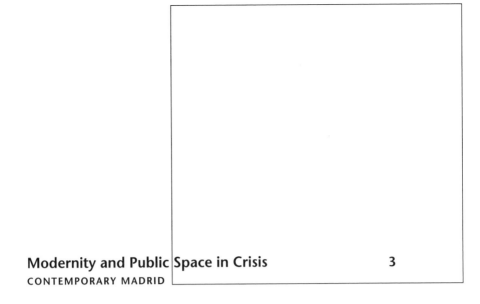

## Modernity and Public Space in Crisis
### CONTEMPORARY MADRID

*In the Puerta del Sol, you are seized by a curiosity which never wearies, a desire to amuse yourself, to think of nothing, to listen to gossip, to saunter, and to laugh.*
HUGH THOMAS, MADRID: A TRAVELLER'S COMPANION

Urban design was inspired by the modern architecture movement in post–World War II European cities. That movement, for all its aspirations of urban social improvement through design, left behind a legacy of placeless communities. Modern architecture's great flaw may ultimately lie in its embrace of a contradiction between space and place.[1] The father of the modern architecture movement, Le Corbusier, was a strong believer in the Bauhaus school's principle that art should function according to the laws of physics. The center of attention for the designer was the building as an object. Bauhaus advocates believed that solutions to twentieth-century urban social problems lay with buildings and machines. Cities were viewed as clusters of objects in space.

In urban Europe the most visible elements of the Corbusian "machine age" city were the vast apartment block cities and new towns that sprawled around the historic cores. The tower block apartments typically hovered above open spaces that remained vacant, or at best, were covered over with a few trees, mere afterthoughts beside the architect's true obsession—the building. In the end, the modernist city became a chaos of such objects, which the introduction of zoning could do little to correct, since zoning did not ultimately deal with either the content or the design of space, but merely with densities and categories (residential, commercial, industrial) of its use.

Madrid—Spain's largest metropolis and the nation's capital—offers an illuminating case study of a city that embraced Corbusian modernism in crafting its twentieth-century identity. Notwithstanding its traditional urbanism of high-density, narrow, inner-city streets and gregarious, crowded plazas, modern Madrid embraced the architecture of sprawling high-rise suburbs. The city became an icon of modern architecture; its urbanism was an experiment in the op-

*Tower block apartments such as this one typified the explosion of modernity in late-twentieth-century Madrid.*

timism of modernity embraced by an emerging national capital in a new modern century. In Madrid, however, architectural modernity would ultimately collide with political reality. Madrid embodied a test for modern architecture—could design solve social problems in the midst of a political crisis (the Spanish civil war and its aftermath)? Madrid's twentieth-century urban landscape serves as a record of the city's response to the crisis.

As early as 1910 Madrid's dominance as a national political and economic center brought hundreds of thousands of new migrants to the city. The pressure to physically expand outward provoked an early urban strategy called the Plan de Extraradio, a series of radial transit lines that guided growth outside the urbanized core. This plan was badly needed, since by then Madrid consisted of three zones: the traditional core, the *ensanche* (a gridded late-nineteenth-century growth zone around the historic center), and the "extraradio," or peripheral outskirts. In the peripheral zone, new construction was spanning out in a chaotic and unplanned pattern, often leaving new developments without access to services such as water or sewerage. Large-scale migration into the city was heavy in the first decade of the twentieth century. The *ensanche,* with its orderly rectangular grid of streets and urban services, was too small and its properties too expensive to absorb the new, largely lower- and working-class arrivals. These newcomers found housing in the unplanned outskirts, which soon became saturated with inhabitants. As a result, by the early twentieth century, Madrid was a study in contrasts: the historic core; the orderly, rectangular *ensanche;* and beyond that, the wildly irregular, unplanned suburbs.[2]

In 1929 a second crack was taken at planning Madrid—via the "Rationalist Plan" of Zuazo and Jansen, which sought to extend the urban area beyond the *ensanche,* by connecting to small rural settlements. Satellite towns surrounded by green spaces mirrored a planning trend that had spread across Europe during the same period. But, an era of unrest soon intervened—in the form of the civil war. Following the war, in the late 1930s, the victorious leader, Francisco Franco, began to turn his attention toward the planning of his capital city, Madrid. Franco's plan was to convert the capital into an "imperial city" with monumentally scaled buildings and processional highways. Madrid historians claim it was never seriously implemented as a comprehensive planning strategy.[3]

Meanwhile, Madrid grew rapidly, with towns forming beyond the nucleus of the 1929 plan and green spaces disappearing, partly due to speculation in land by officials close to the Franco government. In 1963 the outer edges of the city became even more chaotic, as spontaneous clusters of shantytowns began to form on the periphery. This sparked the development of the Metropolitan Area Plan. It sought to organize suburban growth, provide a transport beltway to move automobiles around the city, and revitalize the old historic core, by protecting sites and buildings, and by rerouting car traffic away from the center, which had become far too congested.

Notwithstanding the good intentions of the 1963 plan, it was a case of "too little, too late." Within two decades Madrid became an urban area in crisis.[4] By the 1990s population exceeded 4 million in the region, with nearly 3 million people concentrated in the urbanized core. The city became the dominant economic and industrial center of Spain; a vast proportion of industry, banks, government ministries, and high-tech office buildings was concentrated in Madrid.[5] Economic growth in the 1980s and 1990s brought a glut of physical expansion into the Madrid region, without the proper planning and design guidelines to control it. The result was a city awash in physical chaos—poor land-use controls, overcrowding, traffic congestion, and insufficient infra-structure (highways, mass transit, housing). Madrid was too spread out, a polycentric metropolis with growing social polarity.[6]

This rapid growth was built on the massive rural-to-urban migra-tion of the 1960s and 1970s. By responding to this shift during the years that followed, with the construction of massive numbers of housing units in the modernist tradition (high-rise, block apartment complex-es), the government solved a numbers problem (people without hous-ing), but created an urban design crisis. Sprawling apartment block suburbs exist everywhere in Spain, but Madrid is the most glaring ex-ample of continuous building of objects in space, without planning for that space. Rapid growth generated a host of diseconomies—from air pollution, traffic, and noise to poor public services, insufficient open space, and excessively high housing costs. Physically, the city became fragmented and distorted. The historic core was torn apart and "ter-tiarized"—its residents pushed out as investors bought up historic buildings and converted them to offices.

Observers criticized the speculative real estate boom of the 1980s and 1990s and the explosion of automobiles in the city. For example, in the early 1990s Madrid was labeled "an urban area badly treated by its citizens and those who govern it. In the realm of architecture, to write about Madrid is to cry."[7] Among other mistakes, the city was fragmenting the urban core with underground parking lots and tun-nels "with an excavation syndrome that goes unheeded."[8] Observers lamented a city whose center was being invaded and destroyed by automobiles and tertiary (service) users, while its periphery was di-vided into dormitory suburbs for immigrants in the south and for the wealthy in the north.[9] Madrid had too many block apartment and resi-dential suburbs, while its center was overrun. It became a freeway city, oriented toward big, highway-dominated development—"more like Dallas than like Paris."[10]

Twentieth-century Madrid expanded well beyond the walls of the old Bourbon city, at first in the gridded blocks of the *ensanche*, around the urban core, then along radial transit lines. After 1960 Madrid embraced the U.S. model of suburban expansion and automobile-oriented suburbs along the freeways. Most of the growth from the 1970s through the 1990s was planned around the first beltway, the M-30.[11] Madrid's growth will continue to infill along its highway corridors.

## THE CRISIS OF PUBLIC SPACE

Given the above, it is not surprising that Madrid's system of public space was damaged during the half century of growth between 1950 and 2000. As the pace of urbanization intensified early in the twentieth century, planners and private interests then shifted growth toward the periphery, and Madrid's public life was forever transformed. The reasons for the resulting public space crisis in Madrid can be summarized in three words: planning, profit, and automobiles.

The crisis of planning in Madrid today is epitomized by strategies that are not necessarily in the city's best interest, but that have defined its growth over the last five decades. First, as mentioned, Madrid's growth was steered toward the periphery, in a series of concentric rings oriented toward automobile highways. Second, it was thought that massive housing shortages could be quickly resolved by building high-rise block developments on the outskirts of the city. This "rationalist" city-planning strategy dominated Madrid for most of the mid-twentieth century.

During the 1990s the city administration made a commitment to improving traffic congestion by controlling circulation and encouraging the use of automobile–mass transit (park-and-ride) interchanges on the periphery. This arrangement allowed users to drive from their homes to points on the edge of the city, leave their car, and arrive in the center by subway.[12] Still, the legacy of suburban planning remains the apartment block complex. It has been said that the high-rise block is antithetical to Mediterranean urban space, which historically embodied a dialectic between good public squares concentrated in the center, and private homes with interior patios.[13] In Madrid, the tower blocks did not allow space for private interior patios (the balconies as they are designed are poor substitutes), and neighborhood public spaces were virtually neglected or poorly designed.[14] As one observer wrote about the new suburban neighborhoods developed in the 1980s and 1990s, "[S]e encuentran sin otras plazas que las ocasionales de garaje" (They are found with no open spaces other than the occasional garage).[15]

The real estate booms of the 1980s and late 1990s vaulted the profit motive into the forefront of urban growth. It became profitable to speculate in land, particularly on the urban periphery, but also in the center. In both areas, developers and investors were more conscious than ever of optimizing profit on land. Some landowners shifted their land into more profitable uses. Open space and public space were the big losers, since they typically were the least profitable categories of private land use. Cities try to buy land cheaply, but private owners know there is no rent to be had from plazas and public spaces.

In Madrid, as elsewhere, the automobile has had much to do with the decline of public space and public life. The flight to the suburbs shifts the scale of people's lives; they spend their time driving from suburb (home) to central city (work). They are part of an emerging individually defined, isolated, car-oriented lifestyle. Automobiles demand space as well, for parking and for access (roads, freeway off- and on-ramps, etc.). This results, in turn, in either the elimination of plazas, their transformation into traffic circles, or their perforation by underground parking lots and subterranean passes. In Madrid by the

*A giant waterfall was designed to neutralize the noisy proliferation of automobile traffic around Plaza Colón in post-1970 Madrid.*

mid-1970s public plazas had taken on new functions, shifting from places of social reunion and relaxation to spaces of traffic circulation.[16] Dozens of Madrid's public plazas were turned into traffic circles. Tens of thousands of vehicles circulated through these plazas on a daily basis. Other town squares, while not serving as traffic circulation nodes, served as urban parking lots for hundreds of vehicles. Still others were used to cover underground passes and automobile tunnels. In short, downtown, historic Madrid was being remade for automobiles. The public plazas were judged to be archaic, and thus could gradually be recycled into automobile-servicing sites.

In modern cities the private automobile is antithetical to urban public space. This is especially striking in cities like Madrid that were once pedestrian oriented. Motorists tend to believe that as citizens they should have access to all areas of the city. They imagine their rights of circulation as similar to the rights of pedestrians, who, in a democratic state, presumably are free to move about the city. But by their increasing presence all over the old central city, automobile users are, in effect, reducing its accessibility for pedestrians. Boulevards, promenades, and plazas either disappear or fade into oblivion, as the rush of cars dominates space. Roads with high-density traffic make the simple act of crossing a street to get to a plaza a dangerous activity.[17] Politically, it has become difficult for elected officials to advocate publicly the protection of public space, or the limitation of automobiles in certain streets, or in certain zones of the city. "Who will be the mayoral candidate in our country who actually believes he can be elected and be willing to incorporate into his electoral program a drastic limitation on the use of public space by private automobiles?" says one Spanish scholar.[18]

A leading architecture critic in Spain has written this about Madrid: "[T]he automobile declared war on the plazas of the past, and urbanists on the plazas of the future."[19] Some gestures have been made both in the city and in the suburbs to create new plazas, but many such attempts have not been accompanied by adequate site studies, ignoring context and thus creating designs without meaning or abstractions that get lost in their space. In their place the only viable public spaces in Madrid are often the supermarket, the airport waiting room, or a discotheque, places where people meet spontaneously in an unpretentious space.

One study of public spaces in Madrid suggested that although many attractive plazas, parks, and promenades still exist, they are not used to the extent that one might imagine, given the surrounding densities of people and their need for open spaces.[20] For example, in the best weather, the number of plaza users in central Madrid averaged between 50 and 100 per plaza in sampled spaces. The main users today, according to this study, are people who wish to take advantage of the plaza's "free" availability, as opposed to recreational spaces where one must pay—gyms, health spas, sports events, recreation parks, shopping malls, and so forth. Thus, the users of traditional public plazas are often elderly residents, or lower-income families with young children. Also, the study found that a growing population of marginal groups of people (unemployed, homeless, drug users) is now competing for use of the inner-city plazas of Madrid.[21]

There has been a decline in public life in Spain, particularly in the larger cities like Madrid. The principal loss is that of open discourse—in the streets, the plazas, and the promenades. This decline encompasses the disappearance of the *tertulia* (social gathering) and its replacement with visual media (TV, movies, computers) or radio, where discourse is passive and occurs primarily in private space (the car, the home). Discourse is also subject to the hand of the government, which regulates communications, transport (airports, highways), and even public spaces. The spontaneous public life that once existed—in the street, the plaza, or the café—has been offset by something new: high technology, privatized forms of leisure, and recreation.

The combination of lost public life and privatized public space has led to the fragmentation of cities, a decline in civility, and a lack of public discourse. As one walks the streets of Madrid, incidents of violent behavior or incivility are almost always connected to the drivers of automobiles. For example, during a period of six months of residence in the historic center of Madrid, this writer observed only a handful of violent confrontations, and they all took place among drivers of road vehicles. The two most violent incidents confirm this point. In the first, a car trying to turn grazed gently against the bumper of a taxi. No damage was done, but the cabdriver leaped out of his vehicle, and verbally attacked the driver, taunting him to come out, and seeking to engage in a fistfight. In the second incident, a car was illegally parked in front of a bus stop. When the bus pulled up in front, it nearly hit the car. The driver got out, stood in front of the bus, and in a rage, began madly to pound on the windshield in front of the driver. He seemed possessed, and riders on the bus became quite upset. Meanwhile, on the adjacent Plaza de España, city dwellers were peacefully reading their newspapers on park benches, elderly couples were holding hands and walking around the fountains, and mothers chatted while their children played soccer. The plaza, only a few meters away from the feuding motorists, seemed a world apart.

### THE POLITICS OF THE APARTMENT BLOCKS

During the 1950s and 1960s, rural-to-urban migration in Spain created a massive shortage of housing. It has been said that one out of every seven Spaniards moved during that period.[22] The technocrats, who became powerful in the Franco government after 1957, wanted to build an economically advanced but politically reactionary society in Spain.[23] One way to do this was to create an urban proletariat of homeowners. The government put together an ambitious housing scheme, called the National Housing Plan, that would build high-density, massive apartment block complexes on the outskirts of the major cities. Franco's ministers wanted to boost the image of the state by getting rid of the shantytown eyesores (called *chabolas*) that were forming on the urban edges. From 1961 to 1974 the government either built or facilitated private-sector construction of apartment block towns inspired by the modernist architects. Over 4 million housing units were built nationwide, mainly in stark tower blocks, set within vast wastelands of open space on the outskirts of Spanish cities.

The giant working-class and middle-class suburban apartment block towns were filled with migrants from some of the poorest regions of Spain—Andalusia, Estremadura, and Castilla la Mancha. To own a unit (called a *piso,* or floor), families were forced to double-up, or live in very overcrowded conditions. Despite these problems, however, the housing shortage was largely resolved by the late 1970s, aided by massive government subsidies. In Madrid it was estimated that some 35,000 shacks were still being removed as more housing came online during the boom of the 1980s. Problems of affordability remained, but generally the demand for housing was met by the government.[24]

Many Spaniards, especially those from middle-class families, adapted to the high-rise housing lifestyle because the tower block apartments offered amenities (playgrounds, garages, and swimming pools) that lower-density buildings closer to the city did not offer in the 1960s and 1970s. More recently, some developers have put together low-rise housing block schemes, including those in the dormitory suburbs in the south of Madrid and new "chalet" developments in the northwest part of the city. Yet, Spaniards have generally viewed the "suburbs" as a place for the middle and lower classes. Those who could afford to have favored living closer to the city. The trend toward upper-class suburbanization, so typical in North America, may be taking hold in parts of Spain, but it is offset by the difficulties of commuting home for the long lunch break, or by what one author calls the Spaniard's "compulsive sociability," the desire to wander the streets or meet in groups in cafés and restaurants. Furthermore, many wealthier families who moved out to Madrid's suburbs in the 1970s and early 1980s have since moved back into the city's center out of boredom.[25]

If Spain solved its quantitative housing needs during the 1960s and early 1970s, it did not solve its qualitative ones. From 1961 to 1976 Spain went from being a nation where most people lived in rural towns and small cottage-scale houses to a nation of urban dwellers living in high-density tower block apartments. By then, according to one expert, more of the nation's population was living in high-rise blocks than any nation in Europe.[26]

What kinds of neighborhoods were created in the spaces where high-density block apartment complexes were built? The apartment blocks and towers of Spain's *suburbios* faithfully translated the Corbusian vision of modern urban design from two-dimensional drawings to the three-dimensional world of real suburban space. In the new high-rise slab cities, little attention went into designing livable space around the buildings themselves. Many residents in these places complained about the absence of good public spaces—plazas, alamedas, or promenades—some of which had been originally promised, but never built.[27] In the rush to provide so much housing, so quickly, the government never put much energy into the planning of the vast spaces within which the tower cities were situated. The design of those spaces had been left in the hands of the individual designers of the high-rise buildings, and as so often happens, their concerns lay with their buildings as objects in space, rather than with the spaces around their buildings.

The modernist high-rise complexes at best distorted, and at worst erased, the traditional elements of urban space such as streets, plazas, and parks. In Spain modern architecture and "rationalism" had become exceedingly popular approaches to design as early as the 1930s. The apartment block became the paradigm of machine architecture, in a sense the paradigm of modernity, and its expression flourished in larger Spanish cities, especially Madrid, in the form of open block apartment buildings, theaters, markets, or coliseums.[28]

Unfortunately, even the neighborhood associations that formed in the 1960s and 1970s to demand housing from the government failed to lobby for good designs in the large spaces around the buildings. Neither did they push for more and better public space. Surveys of various tower block communities around Madrid show that while large parks exist, good public spaces (plazas, promenades, etc.) for walking and socializing do not, and that residents find the spaces around their high-rises alienating and confusing.[29]

As more attention has turned to the failure of the modernist high-rise cities, observers have increasingly been critical of the basic lack of design criteria and planning in the public areas. The morphology of open block structures themselves, it has been argued, is antithetical to Mediterranean urbanism—which is anchored by the private home with interior space (garden, patio) and the vital public plaza.[30] When government does intervene, to pave surface roads and to install equipment such as streetlights or drainage facilities in the areas between the buildings, this is then credited as "planning for public space."[31] These spaces must be redesigned with attention to creating a sense of identity in the neighborhood. Unfortunately, within the city of Madrid few public planning or design agencies pay attention to the quality of life of public spaces, other than parks.[32]

One promising trend can be seen in the work of the regional governing agency, the Comunidad de Madrid, in developing a plan for revitalizing public spaces in the rural towns at the edge of the metropolitan region. These towns are the receiving zones for the next waves of urbanization as Madrid expands outward. Many of these small towns are medieval or Baroque in origin, and possess historic plazas and well-preserved ancient buildings nested in high-density spaces, which provide an anchor for urban redevelopment schemes. In 1986 the Comunidad de Madrid put together a plan for remodeling and strengthening public space in 178 municipalities lying on the outskirts of the city. The published plan studied these different towns and came up with an eight-point strategy for revitalizing and upgrading spaces: 1) to better delineate public spaces; 2) to preserve surrounding architectonic elements; 3) to reorder traffic around the public spaces; 4) to make the spaces more accessible to users; 5) to remodel with "hard plaza" methodology—that is, use simple design elements to make the plazas available for flexible and special uses (markets, fairs, etc.); 6) to provide or account for sun, shade, trees, benches, lighting, and fountains; 7) to provide for maintenance of plazas and public spaces; 8) to incorporate citizen participation into design and remodeling planning.[33]

From this ambitious plan the Comunidad de Madrid began its first set of interventions between 1987 and 1992. Thirty-one projects were undertaken in four different types of towns: historic centers, medium-sized towns, high-density towns, and small towns. Most of the projects were completed by 1993. They consisted mainly of revitalized plazas and promenades, historic streets and boulevards, traffic circles, gardens, and small parks. The thrust of the plan is to preserve the public spaces in the centers of these small towns before greater urbanization hits, by clarifying and better articulating them. The goal, then, is prevention of what happened in the high-rise superblocks—the alienation of public space.

## THE DECLINE OF PUBLIC SPACE NEAR MADRID'S HISTORIC CENTER

As Madrid grew toward the periphery between 1950 and 2000, its historic center continued to suffer serious problems of traffic congestion, overcrowding, housing shortages, and increasing crime. Once the locus of some of Europe's greatest public spaces, Madrid's historic center began to experience a public space crisis. While many Madrileños continue to use the historic center, the long-term viability of its streets and plazas is unclear. Indeed, many of the public spaces created in and around the historic center in the late nineteenth and early twentieth centuries have been particularly vulnerable to decline. A survey of some of these spaces confirms their shaky status as public places.

### IMPOSED SPACE AND LOSS OF IDENTITY: THE PLAZA COLÓN

The Plaza Colón, on the eastern edge of the historic core of Madrid, can hardly be called a plaza at all. It lies along the most important tertiary corridor of the contemporary city, the Paseo de la Castellana, the main artery for automobile movement through the urbanized core. The overwhelming experience of this space is one of busy traffic. In fact, the corridor is so congested that aboveground pedestrian access to the plaza is impossible; one must use underground tunnels, and then cross side streets to get into the square.

The plaza's name alludes to a troubled identity. In 1885, after the end of the Carlist Wars and the failed First Republic, and during the Bourbon restoration under King Alfonso XII, a 14-meter-tall Gothic pedestal and a 3-meter-high statue of Christopher Columbus (Colón in Spanish) was installed on the site. The Bourbon royal family wanted to remind Madrileños of Spain's glorious past. What better way to do so than to build a statue honoring the discoverer of America. But most Madrid citizens were not in favor of the building of the statue; it was really an idea pressed by the royal family.[34] Columbus was not a native Spaniard, much less from Madrid.

During most of the first half of the twentieth century, Plaza Colón was a severely underutilized public square. In 1969 the city decided to install a garden on the east side of the plaza, naming it the Gardens of Discovery, a tribute to the Americas and, of course, to Columbus. The main feature of the Gardens was a wall-like, abstract sculpture honoring the discovery of the New World. The sculpture consisted of a series of large stone monuments, evoking the indigenous theme of stone architecture of the Americas. In 1977 the Gardens were officially inaugurated by King Juan Carlos of Spain. Later, the city of Madrid realized the Gardens were not sufficiently enlivening the space, so it also commissioned the design and construction of a subterranean Cultural Center, which lies just below the statue of Columbus, and houses an auditorium and theater for cultural activities, conferences, shows, and lectures. A giant subterranean waterfall just outside is so loud that it effectively drowns out the sound of eight lanes of automobile traffic on the neighboring Paseo de la Castellana. Behind the waterfall a mural depicts the voyages of Columbus.

In the end, this space lacks any identity. The demolition of surrounding historic buildings—the palace, the old neoclassic mint building (Casa de Moneda), and a series of original eighteenth-century apartments (where the writer Benito Pérez de Galdós lived)—erased most historic references. The plaza has become a "spectacle space"[35] where the cultural center, the waterfall, and even the gaudy statue of Columbus are meant to create a sense of excitement and thus attract daily users.

Yet Madrid's citizens have never really taken to this space. Since the late-nineteenth-century appearance of the statue of Colombus, citizens came to believe that the Plaza Colón was imposed upon them by the wealthy royal family. For them, the theme of "discovery," as

*In the twentieth century some plazas could no longer survive solely as people places; colossal sculptures became popular.*

a global event that lies behind the birth of this plaza, seems forced.[36] Perhaps the plaza is also simply too large (some 140,000 square feet). Anecdotal interviews suggest that most people do not have strong attachments to the plaza, and many tend to come there on a much less frequent basis than to other plazas, even large ones (the Plaza de España gets more regular visitors). Thus removed from the urban fabric, disconnected from history, this space can be experienced as an abstraction—the idea of Columbus, or of discovery—but not as a real place, because there is little here to make it a lasting place in the urban dweller's wanderings.

### THE SPACE OF GLOBAL TOURISM: PLAZA DE ESPAÑA

Built in 1911, the Plaza de España is distinguished by a marble statue of world-renowned author Miguel de Cervantes, and by two adjacent grandiose bronze equestrian sculptures of his literary heroes, Don Quixote and Sancho Panza. One of the most visited places in Spain, the large square is overrun on a typical day with tourists from as far away as Japan, Russia, or the United States.[37]

On the third centenary of the death of literary giant Cervantes, Madrid officials decided to build a monument to the author and to the "inter-Iberic twenty nations joined by the nexus of language."[38] The idea for the monument was to promote the image of "official" Spain, allowing the plaza to have a role as a conveyor of political and cultural propaganda.[39] In 1918, with the Cervantes monument fully installed, the Plaza de España was converted to a garden.

The essential character of the plaza today is its nexus as the center of innovation in global skyscraper technology. In 1948 the Edificio España was built on the east side of the plaza. At the time it was a 26-story, shockingly massive hulk of a skyscraper. Franco's government began advertising it as "the tallest building in the nation and in Europe," as a way of aggrandizing Franco and Spain.[40] It was a strange neoclassic monument to the age of skyscrapers. Some have noted its attempt to incorporate uniquely Spanish architectural elements into its design—it has a bit of architect Juan de Herrera's monumental El Escorial monastery in its look; yet, the pseudo-Baroque features seem lost or trivialized on such a large building. The interior is highly classical—with Grecian columns and red-and-black marble walls, not unlike the interiors of other Fascist-built edifices of the period. Several years later, from 1954 to 1957, Madrid's second most important skyscraper was built, also on the Plaza de España, this time on the north side, directly at the corner alongside the Edificio España. The new sky-

scraper, the Torre de Madrid (Tower of Madrid) was a more function-
alist, dull, International-style building made of reinforced concrete,
and constructed with the latest technology. In its time it was advertised as the "tallest reinforced concrete skyscraper in the world" by the
Franco regime.[41] It housed a hotel, administrative offices, and active
commerce.

For the next three decades these buildings, the Edificio España and
the Torre de Madrid, housed most of Madrid's key offices of international tourism, commerce, airlines, real estate, film, and construction,
as well as multinational corporate offices like U.S.-based General Electric or French, German, and other private interests. During the 1960s,
as Spain's economy grew, many important Madrid offices continued
to locate around the Plaza de España, as it had become a prestige address. One of the first modern high-rise hotels was built at a location
half a block off the plaza. Banks, insurance companies, and financial firms moved their offices here, and luxury residential apartment
buildings were erected. The national telephone company, Telefónica,
located here. Underground parking was built and underground tunnels allowed traffic to pass through without interrupting the plaza.
Meanwhile, this also became one of the major traffic intersections in
the city, the westside equivalent of the Plaza Colón. Here, the Gran
Vía, an important turn-of-the-century artery, cut across the urban
landscape, and met with a major westside north-south axis called the
Avenida Princesa.

A great deal of noise and air pollution plagues the plaza, due to
very heavy surrounding traffic. There is also heavy use of signage for
advertising everything from airline companies to insurance, resulting in considerable visual pollution. The Plaza de España is another
twentieth-century plaza that has become more spectacle than genuine
place with connections to its past. Gone, for example, are many of the
theaters and cafés of the early 1900s.

It has become a fragmented space; it is dominated today by modernity, by high-rise office buildings, by the new high-tech building
on the southeast corner, and by the numerous international tourism
companies (Air France, AeroMexico) whose signs dominate the visual
cityscape around the plaza. It has become the plaza of global tourism
and global finance. In the center the old icons still stand—the great
statue of Miguel de Cervantes and those of Don Quixote and his side-
kick, Sancho Panza. Here is the symbolic gesture where visitors come
to know Spain, through one of its great symbols, the idealistic knight,
patriarch of tradition. Don Quixote serves as a convenient icon for
Spanish tourism, a symbol easily digested by foreigners in a world of

increasingly rapid images and sound bites, the perfect advertising image for the country in the electronic media age.

Perhaps it is also fitting that the Plaza de España lies at the end of one of the longest commercial corridors of modern Madrid, the Gran Vía. The Gran Vía flows metaphorically into the Plaza de España. Along its many blocks numerous movie houses reflect the global media; most notably, a parade of cinemas advertise the films of Sylvester Stallone or Arnold Schwarzenegger, alongside international boutiques, fast-food outlets, and restaurant chains.

*Aerial view of the Plaza de España.*

It is characteristic of Madrid's public space crisis that many town squares created near the historic center in the post-1950 period never really caught on as vital public places. Notwithstanding the good intentions of municipal government, these small parks or plazas have become "lost spaces," sparsely utilized by the pedestrian population of downtown Madrid. Two excellent examples are the "artist squares" dedicated to two of Spain's greatest modernists—Pablo Picasso and Salvador Dalí.

Plaza Picasso was created as a sunken public space in the midst of Madrid's most important new high-tech commercial and office complex—AZCA (an acronym for block "A" in the commercial zone of a certain avenue)—along the Paseo de la Castellana. AZCA was considered a high-tech service node for modernizing Madrid, an agglomeration of high-rise office buildings, banks, major department stores, and more recently, housing complexes. The project was begun in 1966 and completed in the 1970s. During its evolution world-class architects were brought in to design landmark buildings including the white aluminum Picasso Tower, one of the tallest skyscrapers in Europe, designed by Minoru Yamasaki, architect of the former World Trade Center towers in New York City. Also in the AZCA complex was the glass-block Corte Inglés, a department store; the cubist Windsor Towers; the reddish oxidized aluminum BBV bank building; the circular Torre Europa (Tower of Europe), and the cubist, white-block Sollube Building. AZCA was symbolic of Spain's economic explosion and the expansion of its global markets in the 1970s. The complex is dominated by vanguard architecture, mainly of the International style—reinforced concrete, steel, glass, and aluminum—a huge metaphor for Madrid's emerging connection to the world economy. It is the most important financial-economic space in the city, and truly the kind of infrastructure that "global" cities build when their economies can support large-scale, high-tech tertiary and quaternary sectors.

The center of this mammoth complex of high-rise buildings, commercial space, and multistory parking garages was originally reserved for an opera house and theater, but that project was never realized. Instead, the city and the developers installed a giant sunken plaza-garden, some 177,000 square feet in size, making it the second-largest public space in the city (after the Plaza de España). The idea was to provide a relaxing outdoor space, sunken to be set apart from traffic and offices, a place where workers and residents could mix. Plaza Picasso is a well-manicured, lushly landscaped rectangular space, with more than 200 trees, and rather excessive seating space, considering the limited number of users observed here at different midday times and dates.[42]

The explanations for the virtual abandonment of Plaza Picasso are varied. First, the workers mainly arrive by car, and can reach their offices from the parking garages without going outside. Thus, there is often no reason to leave the complex to pass through the gardens. Second, workers interviewed claimed to be in a hurry, and rarely take time to rest in the plaza. When they go out to lunch, they typically go to restaurants. Third, the buildings surrounding the plaza are modern and impersonal; one does not feel safe and comfortable here— one feels isolated and overwhelmed by the skyscrapers. As one observer noted: "This pretended plaza, as big as it is, is nothing more than the sum of patios behind buildings that ignore it, and prefer to orient themselves toward the perimeter streets."[43] A Madrid architect makes the point thus: "The problem of AZCA is, first, that it is such a large investment, it's overwhelming to the pedestrian. It has so many levels and underground spaces, you lose your way when you are underground; this causes one to feel depressed here. There are unused stores and marginal spaces, too. This is, in the end, an example of a plaza that has the right conditions—commercial activity, residential activity, gardens—but poor design. Even after you get to know the space as a user, you feel burdened by it. It remains uncomfortable."[44]

It may not be altogether surprising that a plaza named after Picasso should fail to function well in Madrid. Just as Picasso was not from Madrid, the plaza does not connect to its surrounding neighborhood. It is a global plaza that sought to thrive on the spectacle of the skyscrapers, shopping centers, and high-technology motifs. But the spectacle is not the plaza; it is the exciting buildings—tall, menacing towers, cylinders, cubist boxes, and other innovative geometric forms that seem to beckon passers by to join the global city. If there is any place in Madrid that behaves like a new global financial center, it is AZCA, and people are drawn to it. But within the complex, the public plaza is somehow lost. It is artificially created, as are most plazas at first, but here the community has not found a role for the plaza. It remains isolated and disconnected.

Like the Plaza Picasso, Plaza Dalí was named for an icon—the surrealist Salvador Dalí—of the modernist period. And like the Plaza Picasso it honors an artist who was not from Madrid. Dalí was born and lived in the Catalonia region, near Barcelona. Plaza Dalí was inaugurated in 1986. It is a large pedestrian space (some 78,000 square feet) on a parcel of land that sprawls in front of the Palace of Sports, the first major indoor sports arena in Madrid, built in 1960 on the site of what was previously an old bullfighting arena. It lies on the edge of the fashionable, nineteenth-century *ensanche* neighborhood of Salamanca.[45] Around the Plaza Dalí lie a major department store (Corte Inglés) and a number of neoclassic six-story residential buildings with commercial space on the ground floor.

This plaza is a space of leisure and recreation from which to contemplate the playing of sports or the buying of consumer goods. In the midst of this stands a monument designed by Dalí. It consists of a giant granite sculpture, three stone pillars holding a third stone cross bar, some 36 meters in height. In front is a bronze sculpture of Isaac Newton. According to Dalí, the stone sculpture is a monument to architects and the first builders of cities, while the bronze sculpture honors the physicist and the perpetual relationship between art and science.[46]

Walking through the plaza one experiences a distortion—the plaza is trivialized by the adjacent oversized, gaudy department store—the

*Sculpture on the Plaza Dalí, Madrid.*

Corte Inglés—and by its white-box facade, as well as by the bland, cylindrical concrete and glass Palace of Sports. In the words of one Madrid architect, "The Plaza Dalí is a bad public space. It's an uneven space, like AZCA, designed badly in conception. It's like a circus. This plaza fails on every level: activity, form, size, everything."[47]

Once again a spectacle space is created to attract potential consumers. The space becomes another postmodern "nonplace" plaza, with references to global art, or more typically to symbolic icons, which, like Disneyland, erase the importance of the actual place, substituting the fascination with spectacular imagery, the abstract, and the mass media.

### THE HIGHWAY SPACE AND THE TWIN TOWERS: PLAZA CASTILLA

This tiny public space (a mere 3,000 square feet), adjacent to a traffic circle on the northern end of the Paseo de la Castellana, has become a small museum space to be viewed from the road, a spectacle space along the highway strip celebrated by postmodern writers.[48] The Plaza Castilla is overwhelmed by the four lanes of traffic that pass through a tunnel that runs under it, or by the two lanes of service roads that follow alongside. It is not an enclosed space; on the contrary, it is completely open to the automobile, bus, and taxi traffic that whizzes by it all day. In the distance, along the Paseo, tall, boxy, modern, brick or masonry apartment buildings line up as they would have on a Le Corbusier drawing.

Most significant for the plaza are the two tall, "leaning" office towers that rise across the entrance to the Paseo from the north. These buildings, called the Towers of Europe, were designed as office centers for trade activities between Spain and the European Community, which had accepted Spain as an official member in 1986. The Plaza Castilla would be the "gateway to Europe," another example of a late-twentieth-century plaza with a global theme. The offices of global trade and investment would loom over the Paseo and look down upon the plaza with its monument to Madrid politician José Calvo Sotelo.

Perhaps also symbolic of Spain during the 1990s, the investors behind the Torre Europa, including Banesto (Bank of Spain), became involved in a financial scandal, and for a period of several years construction on the skyscrapers was shut down. Thus, a time of global finance and investment was also accompanied by global-scale administrative disasters (not unlike the U.S. savings and loan debacle), and these problems left an imprint on the urban landscape. During the early 1990s the unfinished "leaning Towers of Europe" were a daily reminder to Madrid residents entering and leaving the city each day of the problems and risks of globalization.

## THE POLITICS OF CONTESTED SPACE: THE PLAZA DE ORIENTE

It is symptomatic of all contemporary cities that historic spaces in the downtown become politically charged, as downtown is redeveloped, modernized, and changed to fit the needs of a modern city. In Madrid perhaps the most controversial space in the 1990s was the Plaza de Oriente, a plaza-garden next to the Royal Palace, at the western edge of downtown overlooking the Manzanares River.

The Plaza de Oriente is a classic "dominated square," in that its existence owes to the fact of the Royal Palace's imposing presence.[49] This plaza became a political battleground in the early 1990s. A multimillion-dollar mixed-use remodeling project was proposed by one of Madrid's leading architects. It would include underground parking, some shops, and a well-preserved plaza. Many residents believed the project was being promoted partly because this powerful architect lived nearby and had personal interest in promoting the space. Others wondered why the government should spend so much money on a plaza that glorifies Madrid's monarchical past, but not its democratic future. The Socialist Workers Party of Spain (PSOE) opposed the remodeling on the grounds that it was a large expense that could be allocated to more immediate problems affecting the city, such as housing

*The "leaning towers"— two world trade office buildings that remained unfinished during a financial-political scandal— dominated the Plaza Castilla in the mid-1990s.*

shortages, gridlock, aging infrastructure, and environmental pollution. The PSOE also believed the space worked as it was, and ought not be tampered with. Many of its members were vehemently opposed to the building of more tunnels and underground parking because they believed such projects would only serve to bring even more cars into the downtown.[50] Madrid, they argued, had a much greater need for a better system of mass transit that connected to suburban automobile parking lots and thus fostered rapid, efficient mass transit into the historic core of the city.

Two clear factions formed. The redevelopment plan's supporters praised the chief architect and promoter:

Miguel Oriol is seen as a representative of the right. Spaniards have trouble accepting someone who is rich, handsome, and from the right wing. He comes from a well-known, wealthy family. Most of the arguments against the redevelopment are not rational. Some people on the right talked about putting in a shopping center underground, but not Miguel Oriol. The idea was used against him.[51]

On the other side, opponents were equally vehement:

The plaza debate has really been the obsession of one architect who has come to convince many politicians and administrators to help realize his dream, which is to create a theatrical plaza, a processional space at the side of the Palacio Real, introducing a subterranean pass for the traffic on the main street, and parking lots and shopping underground to finance the operation. My opinion is that it's a false problem. The Plaza de Oriente doesn't have at the moment any significant problem. Traffic circulates in front of the Palace naturally. And this is not one of the most important processional axes in the city. The Plaza connects the Royal Palace with the Theater of the Opera, but it is not a major axis.[52]

Symbolically, Plaza de Oriente's role as a public space was historically complicated by the fact that the square had been built under a foreign king, José Bonaparte. The formal details of the garden on the plaza—the uniformly manicured hedges and trees—add to the royal ambience and remind one of the gardens of nineteenth-century royalty in the "age of romance." At its best, the Plaza de Oriente appeals to the Spanish public's sense of history and offers the public symbolic access to royal life, a place to contemplate the royal plaza, and a feeling that the king is accessible, and that the royal family is important to

Spain's well-being and future. Royal life is portrayed as being part of Spanish culture, and the public is invited to partake of that culture, to sit and contemplate the palace.

Today the space is also defined by the opera building, which was either under construction or being remodeled for a good portion of the post-1950 period. It is a building that Spaniards cherish, but it has a history of structural problems, the result of which, over several decades, was the impression that the plaza was permanently under repair. As a result, despite its size (some 116,000 square feet) and its ample seating space (nearly 500 linear feet, enough for more than 150 people), the use of the plaza at peak times is often limited to a few dozen people, a very low number when compared with the other Madrid plazas of similar size. For example, the Plaza Mayor's peak use is above 400; Puerta del Sol's is more than 400 as well.[53] One would think this would be an attractive place for open space users in the downtown area, and for people strolling in the evenings or on weekends. It is part of a system of open spaces with views over the river and the Sierra de Guadarrama. One can also observe the royal guards from the plaza, and on days of diplomatic visits, bright flags are flown here, and the plaza becomes a place of royal celebration.

Because of its sparse utilization, the politics of remodeling attracted more attention during the 1990s. The Oriol plan would enhance the plaza as a pedestrian space. By digging a subterranean tunnel for the main street, Calle Bailén, an underground parking lot would be created for plaza users, as well as a cultural center with a café. Its opponents included the liberal PSOE (Socialist Workers Party) as well as other planners and architects. They argued that it might not be a bad thing to allow motorists to drive aboveground past the Royal Palace. Placing them underground deprives them of the view of this grand architecture. Furthermore, as one architecture critic argued, allowing cars access to roads that run alongside the plazas keeps crime levels down by providing a constant source of surveillance.[54]

But proponents countered by noting that the underground development would free up the space above for pedestrians and would create a connection between the plaza and the historic Royal Palace.[55] It would eliminate the noise and pollution from heavy automobile traffic on Calle Bailén and the large number of tourist buses that park along the plaza while their clients visit the palace. It would create an outdoor public space that could be connected to the surrounding pedestrian streets and other public spaces, and help anchor the adjacent residential neighborhood. Its principal advocate, Miguel Oriol, summarized his vision in this way:

When I moved to this building [his home adjacent to the plaza], I began to realize the problems of this plaza: first, the people who visit the plaza have to face too much traffic to cross Bailén Street; second, the palace facade has become soiled and unsightly; third, the noise is excessive here; and finally, there is a lack of respect for the noble facade of the palace. I saw that we needed to recuperate the union between Madrid and its palace, which the people love very much.[56]

Oriol was concerned about the destructive presence of vehicles:

The trees and gardens are contaminated by pollution from the cars. My design is to create an underground parking space to move all the vehicles off the plaza, and to allow traffic to go under the space by building an underpass for Bailén Street. This would remove the car from the destiny of the plaza. People who want to drive past to look at the palace would be motivated to come by mass transit and walk through the zone. By placing parking and circulation under the plaza we would get rid of all the traffic, congestion, stop lights and crowded intersections. This would allow us to achieve a better use of space not only for Madrid, but it would set an example for the rest of the country. By servicing the incoming cars underground, you leave the above space for the neighborhood.[57]

Oriol's opponents continued to hammer away with several counterarguments. First, traffic on the space is not really that bad; it is exaggerated by the developers, they claimed. Second, the city needs to spend money on higher priority public spaces; the amount of resources needed is not justifiable. Third, the tunnels and underground excavations would cause problems for surrounding garden spaces, while the subterranean parking would create pollution and attract criminal elements. Fourth, the project would destroy an attractive driving route for autos. Fifth, more parking equals more cars in downtown. And finally, revitalization funds should focus on residential growth, not underground parking.[58]

What is striking about this debate is that the arguments about design and planning are part of the more fundamental political differences between Socialists and Conservatives. Socialists tend to believe that downtown should be preserved in the best interests of the "public good"—enhancing quality of life for local residents and users, and creating equity in the use and distribution of open space. Conservatives typically believe urban space should be developed for profit and to enhance the symbolic and cultural power of Spain and its government.

## PLAZAS AND LOST POTENTIAL FOR REDEVELOPMENT IN MADRID

One of the arguments I have made in this book is that public space must be viewed in its historical context: as a part of a distinct segment (place) within the larger urban fabric. Public spaces are not merely islands of land uses that float freely detached from the urban landscape. They are set in a context, and it is that context—the history of a particular slice of the city—that gives public space its meaning. Correspondingly, it is public space that often crystallizes a place's meaning, injecting memory back into the urban landscape, as urban development transforms surrounding buildings. It is the give and take between public space and surrounding cityscape that creates rich city neighborhoods and an enhanced quality of life.

Thus, for Spain, we can say that the plaza is not merely a space. It is part of a place, connected to an era, a set of events, the unfolding of a history, and the shaping of a built environment. What remains to be understood is how the plaza connects with the shaping of the built environment in different moments in history, under varying circumstances, and in different contexts of urban space and politics. This process is, of course, undisputedly connected with the shaping of plazas at different moments in time.

The core of downtown Madrid, created mainly in the Hapsburg period, is not entirely prepared for the twenty-first century. City leaders have not adequately envisioned what role they want the downtown to play, and how its public spaces can contribute to that role. The historic center is significantly fragmented, mainly by various layers of infrastructure—wider roads, traffic circles, underground parking garages, and subterranean tunnels—designed to allow greater access for motorized vehicles. The result is that downtown has become immensely congested—with cars, buses, trucks, and pedestrians. Public spaces have either been demolished, or redesigned to serve the automobile. The city has not adequately considered how the plazas and other public places can play a role in economic redevelopment and land-use planning. Such an exercise is crucial if Madrid's greatest public spaces—the Plaza Mayor and the Puerta del Sol—are to be better utilized.

Early in the twentieth century, proposals were made to open one side of the enclosure around the Plaza Mayor and allow access to automobiles. This would have destroyed one of the great enclosed plazas in all of Europe. Fortunately for historic preservationists, that proposal was defeated. In the 1940s, with Franco in power, trees were cleared away, and the plaza became a vast open paved expanse, save for the statue of Phillip III in the center. In the 1950s the trolleys were cleared from the plaza; from 1966 to 1969 a subterranean road and parking area were built, and by 1969 all automobiles were cleared away from the plaza. During the 1970s and 1980s not very much was done to the Plaza Mayor by Madrid planners. City leaders had their hands full with the problems of traffic congestion and circulation, and with planning growth on the periphery. The historic core was protected from unsightly development by the city, but no strategic plan appears to have been crafted for the Plaza Mayor. In planning documents of the time no mention is made of the downtown public spaces and plazas as a significant element of the city's historic preservation and economic or architectural well-being.[59]

This lack of insight on the part of planners has left the Plaza Mayor, probably the major focus of downtown, increasingly cut off from its surrounding context. In a sense it is like the Monastery of El Escorial, an isolated world unto itself. When you visit the square, it is as if you had walked into a museum. You are transported to another era in a self-enclosed historic space. The space is powerful and evokes feelings of memory. The Spanish author Ramón Gomez de la Serna describes a visit accompanied by the American novelist Waldo Frank, who on walking into the plaza commented that his Jewish ancestors had probably been sentenced to death here. The author writes: "This great plaza still encapsulates fear, and one thinks that in the mailbox in the center, here is where confidential letters to the inquisition are placed."[60]

However, this great plaza, one of the most celebrated in all of Spain, and well known throughout the Americas, has such an exalted history, its value to the downtown is immeasurable. And its potential is unlimited. It already has a set of well-entrenched rituals that make it popular as a destination for local residents: the Sunday philatelic market; an engraving and print market on Saturdays; seasonal fairs, such as the Christmas fair; musicians and troubadours; diplomatic entourages; special masses; visits by schoolchildren; summer theater; and the annual festival of San Isidro, the patron saint of the city. Around the perimeter of the plaza a host of economic institutions keep the space surging with activity: restaurants, tapas bars, hotels, tourist shops, hat stores, stamp stores. In the warm months there are outdoor cafés with colorful orange and yellow umbrellas, with enough seating for over a thousand people. This emerging privatization of the plaza space makes some economic sense, but the municipal government must also consider that full privatization could turn Plaza Mayor into a more isolated tourist space, an island in the heart of a deteriorating downtown.

## THE PUERTA DEL SOL

The Puerta del Sol is the quintessential example of a public place that draws its power from the people and institutions that have embraced it over time. This is one of the great organic public spaces in all of Spain, not a planned, controlled space, but one that has been molded by the will of the people. As one writer observed long ago:

> During the first days I could not tear myself away from the square of the Puerta del Sol. I stayed there by the hour, and amused myself so much that I should like to have passed the day there. It is a square worthy of its fame; not so much on account of its size and beauty, as for the people, life and variety of spectacle which it presents at every hour of the day. It is not a square like the others; it is a mingling of salon, promenade, theater, academy, garden, a square of arms and a market . . . you are seized here by a curiosity which never wearies, a desire to amuse yourself, to think of nothing, to listen to gossip, to saunter, and to laugh.[61]

*The cultural importance of the Plaza Mayor of Madrid has remained strong: Sunday philatelic market.*

The greatest chronicler of the Puerta del Sol was the turn-of-the-century writer Ramón Gómez de la Serna (1888–1963), who devoted nearly one-quarter of a 400-page book about Madrid to the Puerta del Sol. The author describes details of the history and social ecology of the Puerta del Sol and vicinity, including various cafés, who frequented them, the nature of its vendors, and what they sold. For example, he writes of vendors selling pipes, buttons, ties, and optical goods; of a blind singer of picaresque ballads, and of entrepreneurs who sold dogs. When a cornice falls from a neighboring building directly onto the square, and no one is hurt, Gómez de la Serna writes: "Can a better sign be given of how Providence defends the people of the Puerta del Sol?"[62]

The importance of public plazas in Spanish culture is affirmed by a popular writer's allocation of a generous portion of his or her book to an hour-by-hour narrative of a typical day on the plaza. Gómez de la Serna portrays the Puerta del Sol as a cultural anchor of Madrid urban life. The plaza is given an exalted status. Its unique ecology, its secrets, its quirks and traditions are an essential part of Madrid's urban culture. A day in the life of the plaza is layered into a series of time periods and microecologies. First, dawn—fish trucks passing through, followed by street cleaners; then, early morning—monks out for a stroll, newspaper stands being opened and set up, milk vendors preparing their carts for the day's work. By 8 a.m., the scene shifts again—military men and manual laborers on their way to work; cafés coming to life, flocks of doves overhead. In the next hour the first breakfast is served amid the chaos of traffic. From nine to eleven o'clock in the morning people on trolleys head to work, or trucks deliver vegetables, fruit and bread. From 6 to 8 p.m. is the time of the paseo, or early evening walk around the plaza. Then, from 8 to 9:30 p.m. is the "hour of appetite" when couples walk and look for a meal, while trolleys whisk past the square.[63]

A strong cultural identity persisted over the centuries. "The numerous cafes and luxurious restaurants along the Puerta del Sol were crowded practically for all twenty-four hours. Milk actually flowed and honey was replaced by cubes of shining white sugar which were littered on the floor ... The incongruity of an oriental bazaar in the heart of a European city, crowded with people of western habits, was so very captivating."[64]

The plaza continued to have spontaneity, even as Madrid metamorphosed into a center of modern industry, technology, and commerce. The most important department stores of the twentieth century, including the Corte Inglés and the Galerías Preciados, clustered around the square, as well as along its pedestrian-filled streets running north toward the square of Callao. The plaza became a place to celebrate New Year's Eve, with the custom of striking the clock on the square (built in 1867) 12 times at midnight while eating 12 grapes. This tradition is very much alive in all of Spain today, and in fact, the Puerta del Sol is the symbolic place of congregation to observe the arrival of the New Year, just as New York's Times Square serves this purpose in the United States.

During the Franco dictatorship (1939–1975), while Madrid felt the presence of the dictator, the city continued as before, and the Puerta del Sol remained its most dynamic and spontaneous public space. Writer V. S. Pritchett, visiting Madrid in 1950, wrote: "After midnight in Madrid, when one has just finished dinner, one goes off into those packed, narrow streets lying off the Puerta del Sol in the middle of the city. They are streets of small bars, crowded with men roaring away at each other, drinking their small glasses of beer or wine, tearing shellfish to bits and scattering their refuse and the sugar papers of their coffee on the floor."[65]

In 1951 the Puerta del Sol was remodeled. The trolley lines were removed, and two fountains were installed. The square had evolved into the crossroads of Madrid—10 streets and avenues fed into it—as well as a cultural center of downtown. Most of the square was rapidly becoming tertiary (service oriented), and there were few residences directly on it. The main building on the south side—the old neoclassic post office (Casa de Correos)—was used by the Ministry of the Interior. It was rumored that Franco's secret police tortured and killed its opponents here.[66] Thus, on the square where Spain had sought to oust a despotic foreign ruler (Napoléon) in 1808, a century and a half later, the main building was being used to keep a dictator in power.

By the post-Franco period (late 1970s, early 1980s) the debate surrounding the Puerta del Sol had accelerated. There were those who supported opening it to more traffic circulation, something that became politically popular in Madrid. Alternately, architects, planners, and historic preservation activists favored closing the plaza off to traffic and expanding its pedestrian utility. In 1985 the city completed its plan for revitalization, creating two spaces within the larger space of the plaza: to the north would be a separate pedestrian space, with fountains, newspaper stands, subway entrances, and easy access to pedestrian streets that fed into the plaza. To the south would be the main road, Calle Alcalá/Calle Mayor, which would continue to be used for crosstown travel. Where before the pedestrian and automobile spaces had mixed, now they were more segregated, and planners hoped this would facilitate the plaza's use for both purposes.[67]

There is no question that the Puerta del Sol is a thriving pedestrian-scale space; yet, the street running across the plaza, Calle Alcalá/Calle Mayor, is also one of the most heavily used crosstown thoroughfares in central Madrid. In a city where the center remains an important activity node in daily urban movement, and where many travelers need to move across town, the Puerta del Sol is caught in the middle. For reasons of traffic circulation, it would be difficult to bar vehicles from this transit artery. This part of the city really needs to protect space for pedestrians, but as mentioned above, every planner and politician in Madrid will tell you that any mayor who pursues such a policy, even though it may be the correct urban planning solution, will be booted out of office in the next election.[68]

*Pedestrian life thrives on Madrid's Puerta del Sol.*

In the end, the reason the Puerta del Sol must be protected is its importance as a center of local culture, politics, and spontaneous citizen expression. As the crossroads of movement, and as an early market plaza that attracted important buildings to the zone around it, the Puerta del Sol has become the most utilized public square in Madrid, and the most dynamic. Thousands of people cross through the plaza every day. Perhaps it is the quality of surprise, of the unexpected, that makes this mix exciting—the drama of one's experience there not being precisely planned. It is a space that simply evolved on its own, with adjustments along the way, to the point where people experience pleasure and stimulation by moving through it. Union and syndicate groups hold their demonstrations here; it symbolizes a collective spirit that underscores Spanish history. The square has enormous symbolic importance, embodied not so much in the memory of specific events but in the idea that the Puerta del Sol is a place of collective spirit. The daily flow of people across the plaza serves to nourish that spirit, perhaps often on a subconscious level. How do you preserve this condition through urban design and planning? That is the ultimate question to ponder if historic Madrid is to be better designed in the twenty-first century.

### POLITICAL CONSTRAINTS FACING PUBLIC SPACES
Madrid embodies the spirit and politics of modern Spain. Its problems in urban design and planning are thus symptomatic of challenges facing the larger society—how to become democratic and modern while protecting culture and history at the same time. In Madrid, as well as in all of Spain, urban design must contend with the power of place, that sense of history that is conveyed in a locale, and that could become a tool for promoting its preservation and redevelopment. This spirit of place is reflected in the words of a well-known Spanish writer from Madrid: "There are nights when I could not digest the truth of evening, without passing for a moment through the Plaza Santa Ana."[69]

In Madrid and most cities the challenge of urban redevelopment lies in creating not only new forms but also new content. You cannot simply copy or even reconstruct form; you have to worry about content. As one architect notes, "When you create a new form, you have to realize that content will only come little by little. In the United States we are impatient, we put in a plaza, and we expect it to fill up immediately. In Mediterranean culture, there is more patience."[70]

The government of Madrid would like to think it can address these dilemmas with policy changes. According to the 1995 General Plan for the historic district of Madrid, among the main goals were : 1) renovation of selected public places where changing bus routes and parking can free up space; 2) a new model of traffic circulation for the inner city whose objective is to slow down auto traffic and provide peripheral parking lots to encourage more mass transit usage; 3) diminish the number of vehicles in the downtown by 5 percent, in order to recuperate the streets and plazas for people. But some say the government is missing an opportunity to do something worthwhile. Notes one critic:

> The last five years of Ayuntamiento [city administration] policy have been largely years of building underground parking and two level overpasses or tunnel crossings, transforming the city into a great swiss cheese. . . . It facilitates the passage of cars through the city, but makes it increasingly difficult for pedestrians to get around. The alternative and only viable policy is the elimination of automobiles in the center of the city. This is what a lot of European cities are doing, with success. It makes them more habitable, but it requires a changing urban field; it calls for people to restrict their use of their private automobiles as a way of getting to work during the week. This will be difficult to do. And no politician will dare to take this on because it is always catastrophic politically to support such as position.[71]

Observers criticize the right-wing government that dominated Madrid in the early 1990s, because its approach to urban planning was substantially development oriented. It favored urban expansion, mainly in the suburban ring. Madrid became a metropolis based in its peripheral belt. The big development projects were the completion of the M-30 and the beginning of the M-40 highways, and in the future there will be the M-50. All of the major growth is taking place along the edges of the M-30 and M-40. This pattern of growth is like many American cities—enclaves of development attached to the major highways, with ample space for parking, usually accompanied by a development (a shopping center, or some other nucleus) acting as a motor for economic growth.

In Madrid, the post-1960 political environment generated an urban planning culture that favored the automobile and suburbs. The historic center was neglected as Madrid became a decentralized metropolis, command center for the nation's integration into the European Community, and to the larger global economy. Downtown is becoming a center of office space. Automobiles have virtually free access to the narrow historic quarters. In the next chapter we shall see that under a different set of political circumstances, the role of public space in downtown redevelopment can be quite distinct in Spain. Regional culture and history can inform a different political response to the role of public space in urban design—as the example of Barcelona will make clear.

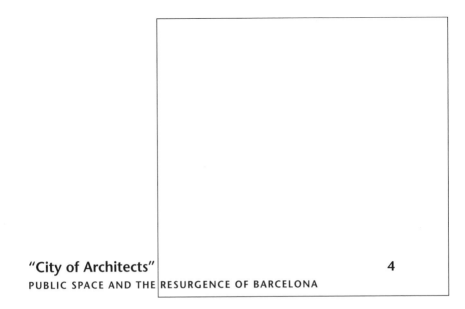

## "City of Architects"

4

PUBLIC SPACE AND THE RESURGENCE OF BARCELONA

Two decades ago the city of Barcelona was in a state of disarray. Freeways choked the downtown with traffic, while rows of high-rise block apartments and factories blanketed the placeless suburbs in a manner similar to the Madrid experience described in the previous chapter. The Gothic Quarter and nearby historic districts were in a sad state of deterioration. The waterfront, lined with abandoned warehouses and factories, was cut off from the city and lay virtually in ruin. One prominent city planner reported that in the 1980s he drove his car down toward the Mediterranean Sea near the old port; when he and several officials got out to survey the scene, they were forced to flee back to his car, as a pack of large gray rats chased them down.[1]

Twenty years later Barcelona has become one of the most celebrated urban design success stories in the world. Galvanized by the 1992 Olympics, which the city hosted, and by the conscience of its forward-thinking leadership, it transformed its waterfront, improved traffic circulation patterns in the city center, revitalized historic districts, built or redesigned more than 100 new parks and public spaces, and generally enhanced its appearance and well-being. One British architecture critic said of Barcelona: "It is the only truly great success in large-scale urban planning since the Second World War."[2]

While Madrid is an example of a Spanish city that modernized but was unable successfully to revitalize its system of public space, Barcelona stands in stark contrast. Located in the northeast region of

Catalonia, Barcelona is Spain's second-largest metropolitan area. It is a region whose history and culture are steeped in design. This led one Catalan journalist in the mid-1990s to coin a Barcelona slogan—"City of Architects."[3] In a mere two and a half decades since Franco's control ended, Barcelona crafted a dramatic redevelopment strategy anchored around the use of public space. Barcelona's spectacular reconstruction in the 1980s and 1990s was facilitated when the problems of downtown redevelopment were folded into a larger strategy of economic development, neighborhood planning, and urban design. Drawing upon the virtues of its past, Barcelona reinvented itself to fit into the global economy. In this chapter I will explore the role of public space as a critical component of the urban design and redevelopment strategy for Barcelona's late-twentieth-century metamorphosis.

## BARCELONA'S EVOLUTION

Barcelona began as a small port in the fifth century BC. Known as Barcino (for Hamilcar Barca, the father of Hannibal, the Carthaginian general), it later fell under Rome's domain, and was built up as a walled fortress with 68 towers.[4] Like much of Spain it passed under Muslim rule during the early Middle Ages, with the Roman street grid and other developments partially destroyed. By AD 1300 Barcelona was once again a thriving port, distinguished by its trade market (*llotja*) and by the growing dockyards (*drassanes*).[5] During this era the Catalan Empire dominated the Western Mediterranean; Barcelona was its primary urban center. By the late fifteenth century Barcelona's fate was forever changed, as it came under the hegemony of a unified Spanish kingdom through the marriage of King Ferdinand and Queen Isabella. The dynasty known as the Hapsburg royal family would rule Spain for the next two centuries.

Several key urban infrastructure projects forged Barcelona's identity during this time. The opening of the medieval wall in the fourteenth and fifteenth centuries expanded the Ciutat Vella (Old City), adding a new neighborhood—El Raval. This led to the construction of a third wall around the new addition to the city. In the gap left by the torn-down medieval wall "La Rambla" was born; its name is derived from the riverlike drainage of rainwater that courses through it and into the Mediterranean. While in its early incarnation the Rambla served as a moat and sewer along the city wall, it soon became, in the words of one scholar, "the first urban space of grand dimensions for strolling, leisure, fairs, and periodic markets."[6] Because the Rambla once defined the edge of the medieval town, important commercial activities had always clustered along it; this later led to the location of the main city market, or Boquería, here. Gradually the Rambla attracted important land uses—convents, a university, aristocratic palaces, and an opera house. The Rambla was viewed by eighteenth-century politicians as a strategic military tool—a wide avenue that could provide access for armed forces in the event of a riot or other security problem.[7] There is

little question that the formation of the Rambla established an important tradition of urban public life in this Mediterranean port, a tradition that would continue into the twentieth century.

Barcelona's modern period began in the middle of the nineteenth century. Catalonians were fed up with the Bourbon monarchy; they saw the walled city as a metaphor for the restrictions imposed on their lives by the royal family. Barcelona's greatest urbanist thinker and activist, Ildefonso Cerdá, emerged at this time. Cerdá was trained as a civil engineer, but his vision of the city went beyond engineering, incorporating politics, social equity, economics, and culture. His 1867 work, *Teoría General de La Urbanización,* may be one of the greatest early works on modern cities ever written. In Spain Cerdá is commonly referred to as the "father of the science of urbanism."[8]

Cerdá's ideas had an important impact on the design of public

*Narrow streets and pedestrians in Barcelona's historic Gothic Quarter.*

space in Barcelona. His 1859 plan for the expansion of the city into a zone called the "Eixample" (addition), a geometric hierarchy of gridded streets and blocks systematically interrupted by different forms of open space. Cerdá emphasized the importance of social hygiene, planning, and equity. His design called for very wide streets (60 feet across), large blocks (1,200 square feet), and buildings of no more than 57 feet in height on two sides. The plan anchored each block with a central patio as open space, and it ordered a minimum of 100 trees per block. The corners of blocks would be cut at a 45-degree angle, forming open squares at intersections. Every 400 blocks would form a neighborhood, which would have its own schools, hospitals, parks, and day care centers.

Sadly, the ideas of Cerdá were not fully implemented after his death in 1876. Developers began to destroy the planning designs of the Cerdá scheme. Buildings were erected over open spaces, encroaching on the block patio gardens, or on the two sides of the street not designated for building. Building heights were increased. The average square footage of blocks increased from 710,000 in the time of Cerdá to over 3 million by the late twentieth century.[9]

Despite these changes, the preservation of the Eixample leaves one of Barcelona's greatest urban-planning legacies at least partially intact, and its emphasis on hygiene, social equality, and open space is an important reminder of some critical influences on the modern city. One positive adaptation of the Cerdá plan was the building of private streets—called *passatges* (passages)—lined with wealthy homes and gardens, which illustrate the proper ratio between built space and open space that Cerdá had intended for all residents of the Eixample. Some of the larger commercial boulevards have become Barcelona's most important linear public space corridors. The Passeig de Gracia, for example, is a natural extension of the Rambla, and one of the great avenues for strolling in the city.

Several grand urbanist enterprises marked the transition to the twentieth century in Barcelona. As more industry relocated in and around the city, wealthy entrepreneurs sought bigger and more impressive buildings. The Universal Exposition of 1888 inspired Catalan architects and artists to search for a regional style, a Catalan architecture. This led to the emergence of a growing commitment to new building styles generally termed *modernismo*. The style tended to combine modern materials with historic designs. Antoni Gaudí and a collection of talented architects and artists transformed Barcelona's cultural landscape in the first decades of the twentieth century. Their stunning designs contributed to a spirit of public celebration of archi-

tecture in the new century. The streets of the Eixample that displayed the work of the modernists became exciting public spaces for viewing great architecture. In the 1930s, a group of Catalan intellectuals and architects formed their own group, the GATPAC (Artists and Catalán Technical Group for Progress in Contemporary Architecture), further amplifying the public discourse about urban design.[10]

Meanwhile, an impressive new park system was being put into place. The Universal Exposition of 1929 yielded a rich outpouring of new designs for promenades, parks, and plazas. The old fortress (Ciu-

*One of Barcelona's many pedestrian corridors, or "passatges" (promenades), leads to architect Antoni Gaudí's iconic Sagrada Familia.*

dadela) was torn down and converted into a great neoclassic park. The land on Montjuic, the mountain overlooking the harbor, was formally designated as open space, and other new parks were added, including one designed by Gaudí himself—the Parc Guell.

The Spanish civil war and subsequent ascendance to power of Francisco Franco in the decades of the forties, fifties, and sixties ushered in a period of decline in innovation in urban planning in Barcelona. Ironically, this was a period when the city most needed the great tradition of progressive urban design, since there was massive rural-to-urban migration into the city, and a rising demand for solutions to urban overcrowding. While Franco's government was busy turning out monumental infrastructure—highways in particular—irregular housing shanties were growing on the periphery of large cities throughout Spain, as mentioned in Chapter 3. Barcelona's periphery was no exception. As in Madrid, the solution to the housing crisis came in the form of massive residential *polígonos,* tower block residential complexes on the outskirts of the city. Meanwhile, densification of the inner city continued, traffic increased, and a sense of chaos reigned.

## URBAN RECUPERATION, 1976 TO THE PRESENT

The story of Barcelona's recovery is a complex one that begins with the death of Franco in 1975, and the subsequent transition toward a Spanish national democracy. Franco's demise was one of a confluence of macro forces and events that would set the stage for the dramatic transformation of the Barcelona metropolis. The late 1970s and early 1980s marked a period of European (and Spanish) economic revival. Spain's entry into the European Community's trade bloc in the mid-1980s was another especially critical factor, which unleashed a new era of increased trade possibilities, higher credit ratings, greater potential for attracting global investment, and greater national confidence in the economy. By 1982, with the election of a Socialist government in Spain, it was clear that regions far from Madrid (the capital) would finally be given more support from the national government in generating locally based programs of economic development.

This became immediately apparent in the Catalonia region. Barcelona was in the position of having a relatively strong economic and industrial base. The national transition toward democracy was met by a similar political transformation in the Barcelona metropolitan region. During the first decade of transition, between 1976 and 1986, two mayors—Narcis Serra and Pascal Maragall—understood that a good redevelopment strategy for Barcelona was not isolationist; it was built

around embracing both Catalonia and the rest of Spain. These mayors' strategies to promote foreign investment through large-scale projects like the Olympics were bolstered both through local networks and by selling the idea to national politicians in Madrid.[11] Their vision was of Barcelona as the future capital of "the north of the south of Europe,"[12] a center of industry and cultural innovation, with strong regional economic and transport linkages to the French cities of Montpelier, Marseille, and Toulouse, as well as to ports along the Mediterranean coast.

Equally impressive was the vision of local politicians and leaders in understanding that to grow economically, Barcelona had to reinvent itself as a city. Mayor Maragall stated that "cities are places for invention, for creativity, for freedom."[13] He told a writer at *La Vanguardia*, the major newspaper of the region, that "the principal attraction of the city is its urbanism, that is, the ensemble of public works that it has taken on and completed."[14]

Barcelona's resurgence began with the appointment of a Catalan architect, Oriol Bohigas, as the head of Delegación de Servicios Urbanos (Office of Urban Services), the city planning department. Bo-

*Barcelona is a walker's city; people in public spaces, in summer or winter, are a defining force in the city's culture and history.*

higas developed a close relationship with the new mayor (Maragall) and crafted a planning strategy built around three central principles: first, an emphasis on tangible projects, rather than "plans" that would gather dust on the shelves of urban bureaucrats' offices; second, the placing of neighborhoods (*barris*) at the center of all redevelopment; and third, the promotion of regional decentralization, allowing certain activities to relocate to nodes away from the immediate central business district. Taken together these three principles contributed to the renaissance of the city in little more than a decade and a half.

The tangible projects element of the Bohigas strategy centered around a set of key structural changes in the city: reorientation of traffic away from the center, through the construction of two new beltways; installation of underground parking spaces; reclamation of the waterfront; recycling of abandoned spaces into parks, plazas, and other public spaces; and filling those spaces with public art and sculpture. By moving traffic out of the historic center (Ciutat Vella), the city was free to engage in a massive program of rehabilitation for the historic quarter. This redevelopment would concentrate on controlling the circulation of cars and people through the historic quarter, while strengthening the identity of the quarter's four principal neigh-

*The slogan "Design sells" became an important theme in Barcelona's re-development in the 1980s and 1990s: beachfront sculpture, Barceloneta.*

borhoods—Raval, Barrio Gótico, Barceloneta, and the Casco Antiguo (medieval core). New and improved public spaces would greatly assist in fortifying neighborhood identity. Further, the proper design of those spaces, and their connection to each other, would help achieve the most important objective: spatial control over the one million visitors who descend upon the central city on weekends during the high tourism season.[15]

The emphasis on tangible programs produced over 160 new projects in a decade, ranging from commercial street improvements to new parks, plazas, and industrial sites converted to public facilities. These projects reveal a dominant feature of Barcelona's transformation—the focus on design.[16] As one former city planner stated about Barcelona's redevelopment strategy, "[E]veryone recognized that design sells."[17] The thinking in the government was that by designing great public places for people to meet and circulate, the city would both improve the quality of life for its citizens and enhance its competitiveness in the global economy. Barcelona's attraction to international companies and global consumers (including tourists) was partly a matter of image. Its image began with the natural environment but was refined and given substance by architecture and urban form. So, the civic leaders decided, what better way to uplift the city's image than to improve and beautify the public spaces where people mingle and gather.

The city embarked on a campaign to create new and spectacular public places, as well as redesign older ones. Public monies were used to build new promenades, gardens, parks, plazas, playgrounds, public monuments, and other gathering places. A former slaughterhouse was recycled into a magnificent park, embellished by one of the last great sculptures of Catalan artist Joan Miró. Factories and quarries were transformed into neighborhood parks and community centers. Artists, sculptors, and architects were brought in to create colorful works of public art throughout the city.

The successful effort to reclaim the waterfront was given a great boost by the Olympic redevelopment project. The 1992 Olympics attracted more than $2 billion for infrastructure development, with one of the major emphases on rebuilding the waterfront. What Barcelona's planners did was argue that sports facilities should not be the ultimate goal of the Olympic investment (as was the case with the Los Angeles Olympics in 1984). Rather the hosting of the Olympics would be used to supplement and complement the overall urban redevelopment strategy. Thus, while the Olympic monies helped build the Olympic Village along the waterfront, it also provided a catalyst for a larger wa-

terfront renovation project that included five new seafront parks, five
kilometers of public-access beach, a waterfront promenade, and space
for offices and new residential development. The Olympics added fuel
to an innovative planning and development program that had already
been created by activist planners, architects, and neighborhood leaders beginning in the late 1970s.[18]

During the late 1960s and early 1970s, the poor quality of life in
the periphery of Barcelona, as well as an emerging housing crisis, ig-
nited a set of social movements in the poorest *barris* (neighborhoods).
These movements were driven by spontaneously created political
forces called Asociaciones de Vecinos (neighborhood associations).
Community-based groups represented a powerful political lobby as
Barcelona's urban planners began to rethink their strategies in the
late 1970s. The General Metropolitan Plan (1976) called for decentralization of the city, and redefinition of its spatial order in response to
changing conditions. The emphasis was on redevelopment through
the delivery of more services to the peripheral, lower-class neighborhoods. Some planners argued that the problem at that point was
not the housing, but the quality of life in those *barris*.[19] This explains
the Bohigas strategy of building new parks, plazas, promenades, and
commercial redevelopment in the poorer zones of the city. Many of
the 160 new projects mentioned above were located in the working-
class communities.

*Barcelona's
reclaimed
waterfront
redevelopment
was aided by
the 1992 Sum-
mer Olympics;
it included
several kilo-
meters of public
promenades,
plazas, and
small parks.*

Neighborhood improvement overlapped with the larger goal of decentralization. The idea was that Barcelona's redevelopment needed to
recover the city's traditional sense of neighborhood. As one writer put
it, "the center should not be showcased at the expense of the periphery; run-down and shapeless places all over town should be brought
back . . ."[20] A cost-effective way to do this was found in Oriol Bohigas'
public space projects, which would not be concentrated in the tourism
sections of the old city, but rather dispersed throughout the working-
class *barris*. These would then be the focus of what Mayor Maragall
referred to as "a set of urban spaces—parks, squares—of high urban
and design quality throughout the city."[21] The decentralization strategy
was further reinforced in the late 1980s with the introduction of a new
planning strategy called Areas of New Centrality. This strategy defined
12 urban activity centers that would be emphasized as new "business
districts" to take the pressure off the Old City–Eixample core. Four of
the "areas of new centrality" were Olympic zones, while the others were
decentralized, high-density activity areas including the port, rail stations, cultural zones, and commercial corridors.[22]

Decentralization also involved reorganizing the territorial, economic and spatial structure of the region. The city of Barcelona, according to its planning department, must be part of a "metropolitan
network of cities," where the city is embedded in a regional network
of 26 well-connected suburban towns and cities. The government
emphasizes "recentralization" of existing outlying towns, especially
where new high-tech industries can be located. At the same time, such
a territorial strategy is only workable if the political, economic, and
historic "nerve center"—the city of Barcelona itself—is adequately
outfitted with appropriate infrastructure to connect with the ring of
cities around it.[23]

Planners and economists see the Barcelona coastline as an important development catalyst for the region. Two rivers—the Besos and
the Llobregat—flow from the hills toward the waterfront, and into the
Mediterranean. State and local governments are committed to rehabilitating the rivers, both of which have been ecologically degraded.
They also wish to redevelop the towns and cities along them, which
ultimately will connect to the city of Barcelona. For example, south of
the Olympic Village, a large-scale housing and economic revitalization project will convert the run-down industrial district and working-
class neighborhood of Poble Nou into a vital economic center, a second "Olympic Village." The Besos River subregion will be ecologically

reconditioned, its decaying industrial uses converted to a park, with housing, light industry, and office space around it. A new port and waterfront open space at the mouth of the Llobregat River will enhance this environmentally troubled industrial district.[24]

## GLOBALIZATION AND URBAN DEVELOPMENT

The 1992 Olympic Games became the catalyst for more than urban redevelopment; they became a means by which Barcelona began to be resituated in the international marketplace. One government study showed that the city needed to "take maximum advantage of the investment in infrastructure and image developed for the Games to definitively situate Barcelona and by extension, Cataluña, in the international agendas and financial circuits."[25] The strategy for Barcelona centered around two objectives: (a) to market Barcelona in a way that attracts high-level business, tourist, and institutional groups (conferences, meetings, etc.); and (b) to create a "Barcelona trademark," a set of products and services that international investors would want to purchase.

To achieve this international marketing goal, city leaders crafted an urban development approach around the following seven strategies that would make Barcelona:

1) a first-class manufacturing center for Europe, especially in the areas of design and industrial systems development;
2) a distribution center for merchandising in southern Europe and the Mediterranean;
3) one of Europe's six largest tourist centers;
4) a major convention center city, among the six largest in the world;
5) a center of higher education, particularly in the areas of architecture, design, engineering, and business management;
6) a city of medical services, health, nutrition, pharmaceuticals, and food;
7) a European financial center based on new products to replace those that the city would lose as a result of globalization.[26]

If one examines these seven globalization strategies, it becomes clear that Barcelona's "trademark" image was central to their success. The trademark was immensely fortified by the international attention garnered by the 1992 Olympic Games, which were a huge organizational and managerial success. Further, the Olympics served as a con-

duit to promote the visual beauty of Barcelona as a place to visit, hold conferences, or do business. City leaders successfully utilized the comprehensive physical improvements—many in new or recycled public spaces—of the Olympic investments to enhance their permanent image. In fact, the attraction to global businesses today lies squarely in Barcelona's "quality of life" image. Truly, many investors have come to realize that Barcelona has emerged as one of the most attractive cities in Europe in which to live, and do business, and this impacts their decision to invest here.

These changes in image and design partly filter back to the success of the seven global marketing strategies. For example, the first objective, to make Barcelona a first-class manufacturing city, is built around the premise that the competitive edge in manufacturing lies in design—of furniture, factories, and work spaces. These are also some of the new products that underlie objective #7, making the city a European financial center based on new products. Further, to become one of Europe's largest tourist and convention centers (#3 and #4), the city would need a spectacular design. In doing this, it would attract students from all

*The plaza at Olympic Stadium in Montjuic symbolizes Barcelona's aspirations to become a player in the global economy.*

over the world to its great universities, many to study the design professions, thus fulfilling objective #5, creating a global center of higher education. Finally, Barcelona's image as a clean, well-designed city serves an important role in enhancing its ability to be a distribution center and a city of health and nutrition services.

It is important to point out also that the international tourism strategy revolves around the concept of "urban tourism" as opposed to "mass tourism." Where mass tourism tends to bring in tourists into controlled locations, "urban tourism" envisions a broader strategy of integrating more educated visitors into the everyday life and spaces of the city. This strategy involves attracting not only traditional tourists but also those who take advantage of a work trip combined with a few days of tourism. This expands the tourism sector to include a vast array of business trips, conferences, and conventions, and thus a variety of combined travel arrangements.[27]

To put in place these global strategies, Barcelona city leaders realize they must commit funding to create a better global infrastructure. This includes an expanded airport, new highways, high-speed rail, and telecommunications. This will allow Barcelona to better connect itself to the rest of Europe, and by extension to the global market. Investments in the city's physical plant—in rehabilitation of the historic core, the waterfront, and hotels—also enhances its attraction to global tourists.

### PUBLIC SPACES AS ANCHORS FOR REDEVELOPMENT

It comes as no great surprise that, in the 1980s, planners, designers, and innovative urbanists in Barcelona thought public spaces could serve as anchors for the city's restructuring. Like Madrid and many other European cities with roots in the medieval and Renaissance eras, Barcelona's identity is tied to its high-density, pedestrian-scale historic center. But Barcelona's unique cultural and historical attachment to its public places goes beyond the typical European city. Barcelona's leap to even greater heights in public place–making was made possible by a group of important urban design thinkers who felt liberated in the unique Catalonian culture of independence. The result is that, in the words of one observer: "Barcelona is a walker's city, despite its inflexible grid. Its 'natural' patterns pertain to the square and the barri, not the beltway and the ramp. One of the things that strike the foreigner there—behind the smog, the din and the traffic—is the social importance assigned to strolling and the reality of its pedestrian etiquette."[28]

There may be no single explanation of how and why Barcelona chose *espacios libres* (free, open, or public spaces) as the centerpiece for urban revitalization. Perhaps essential is the idea that, by the 1980s, while there were significant social problems in low-income neighborhoods, the housing construction programs of the 1960s and 1970s, under the Franco government, had solved the immediate problem of shelter, for the most part. So, if the Catalan government was going to intervene on behalf of the poor communities, what was needed was some other way to deliver tangible products, aside from housing. Oriol Bohigas and others believed that *barri*-centered projects would improve the image of neighborhoods and, at the same time, enhance their identities. Public space improvements had the practical effect of adding to or improving the quality of life through green spaces, while providing a symbolic morale boost to a neighborhood in decline. It would, of course, be cheaper to spend government funds on these "collective spaces" than on individuals within the neighborhoods. And since, in the Mediter-

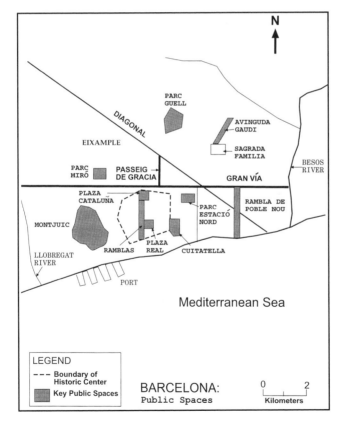

*Barcelona: Public spaces in the historic center and vicinity.*

ranean climate, people tended to gather in the outdoors, these public improvements would be heavily used.[29]

Bohigas and his successor, a city planner named José Acebillo, cast their nets widely in choosing neighborhoods and public space sites. One strategy was to recover the street as a community promenade. Various working-class neighborhoods had their own Ramblas; the planners chose to redesign them, making them more attractive to users and businesses. A second strategy aimed at rehabilitating older run-down plazas and parks. A third objective was to recycle lost corners of the city into new public spaces. Abandoned factories, slaughterhouses, and quarries were turned into parks, gardens, or squares.

Of the half dozen prototypical public spaces found in cities—mini-parks, plaza-gardens, squares, playgrounds, civic promenades, and large-scale parks—every one of these categories received attention in Barcelona during the 1980s.

There was also a very clear effort to incorporate art in designing public spaces. Most notable was the "sculpture in public space" program started in the early 1980s under the group led by Bohigas.[30] All of the artists, both Spanish and foreign, participated in the program by agreeing to work at a fraction of their regular fees. The scheme became so well known that hordes of international artists expressed interest in participating, and soon its fame spread. The sculpture in public space project yielded impressive results. Among the most popular sculptures one finds a giant still life of cubist shapes inside a glass box under a continuous flow of water, a monument to Picasso on a street named for the Catalán artist (near Parc de la Ciudadela); a lake with carved marble blades and fins (Plaza Soller); and an earthen park with colorful mosaic ceramic decorations, including one called "Fallen Sky on a Hill" (Parc Estació de Nord).

The overpopulation and deterioration of the quality of life in the Eixample district further bolstered the decision to choose public space as a focus for the redevelopment strategy. The Eixample had the highest density of any neighborhood in the city (including the old historic quarter). By the 1980s the increase in traffic congestion, density, building heights, and commercial activities made this zone virtually unlivable.[31] Many of the key public spaces chosen for redesign lay in or near the Eixample. They included new promenades like the Avinguida Gaudí or Avinguida Taradellas, small passages like the Passeig St. Joan, parks such as the Parc Miró and the Parc de L'Espanya Industrial. Also, planners decided that blocks within the Eixample would have to have controlled building heights; the city would also require that interior patios become garden spaces.[32]

### THE POLITICS OF "HARD PLAZAS"

One of the challenges facing Barcelona planners was how to inject new public spaces into the fabric of a congested, high-density city. One approach was to recycle obsolete spaces into new uses. For example, as mentioned above, former factory sites, slaughterhouses, parking lots, convents, quarries, and other abandoned structures or vacant spaces were turned to new public uses in the 1980s and 1990s. Once it was determined that a space would be transformed into a public plaza or promenade, the next key decision lay in how to design a new space and make it work within its existing context. During the 1980s, as the city of Barcelona unleashed its new project-oriented planning program, a generation of young architects was brought in by the administration to design new urban spaces. Many of these architects and designers were part of a new vanguard of progressive designers who were influenced by global trends in postmodern architecture as well as the regional tradition of avant-garde designs tied to the surrealism of Dalí, the cubism of Picasso, or the modernismo of Gaudí.

One idea that emerged out of this convergence of past and present, of old and new design and planning approaches, was the "hard plaza." This style emphasized a "minimalist" approach to new town squares, promenades, and other spaces, which left them largely unadorned, and minimally treated with concrete surfaces, austere trimmings, and furnishings often in the form of metallic sculptures or concrete benches. The idea was to eliminate trees, grass, flowers, and other vegetation, partly because of the expense in maintaining such spaces in a semiarid climate.

One prime example is the Plaza Real, a former Capuchin convent that was demolished and recycled in 1848 into a traditional enclosed neoclassic plaza. Its graceful buildings, symmetry, and appropriate scale, combined with flower gardens and stately palm trees, made it, by the mid-twentieth century, one of the most popular and well liked plazas in Barcelona. But in the early 1980s Bohigas and his planners and architects determined that the plaza had become too chaotic—

with cars parked inside, telephone booths everywhere, and illegal housing on the roofs of surrounding buildings. They were determined to remodel the plaza and simplify the space, returning it to its former graceful state. Some observers regarded this plaza as the first test for the new "hard plaza" design strategy.[33] Bohigas and company removed the flower beds, the cars, and most of the furniture on the plaza, preserving only the palm trees, and converted the remainder of the plaza into a paved, hard space.

*The "hardening" of the traditional Plaza Real attracted an initial outcry among critics.*

A huge outcry against the paving and redesign of the Plaza Real soon emerged, organized by residents and accelerated by local newspapers and other media. Some of this protest was fueled by the removal and replanting of the giant palm trees, which the concerned public believed would not survive the overhaul. The criticism grew to the point where the architects began to feel pressured. Many responded bitterly to what they believed was an unfair campaign to discredit their work. "The commotion that was raised was absurd," said one designer. "They accused us of carrying off the flowerbeds, but said nothing about our conserving the palm trees. A plaza is one thing; a park is something else. We shouldn't confuse the two. I think we all agree that the Campo of Siena, or St. Mark's Square in Venice are among the most beautiful spaces in the world. However, it's also true that they are hard spaces."[34]

Once the public saw that the palm trees would live, the uproar quieted down, but not for long. Another controversy emerged in the early 1980s, and it too centered around a controversial new public space, the Plaza de los Paisos Catalans, that was designed as a hard plaza. The space was next to the main inter-city train station, the Estación Sants. The adjacent space had been a parking lot for many years, but more importantly it had become a haven for illegal activities. Bohigas described it as a "lawless space like the pre-urban version of the Wild West."[35] Bohigas handpicked his team of architects rather than holding the more common juried competition. Apparently, Bohigas thought the space was going to be controversial, and he wanted to avoid another public uprising.[36] He did not succeed.

Bohigas instructed his design team to create a public place where none existed, but to do it inexpensively and without obstructing the flow of people into the train station. He asked the architects to "build without building, to design on a vacant space, but to keep the space vacant," one observer commented.[37]

The design team spent a year working furiously on the project. Their ideas very much followed the notions of the architectural vanguard that was in vogue in Barcelona in the 1980s. The new style tended to emphasize intellectual solutions to spatial problems, and thus to organize designs around conceptual and abstract elements. The architects felt that the surrounding context for the plaza was "the mechanical and automobile chaos of the end of the century."[38] Their design was a postmodern, minimalist study in abstraction and hardened space. It consisted of a vast open paved gray square interrupted only by a 900-square-foot steel canopy and pergola and lines of wooden benches. It immediately drew an angry response from observers. Neighbors complained about the lack of vegetation and flowers. One political party seeking support in municipal elections offered to have the plaza destroyed if their candidates were voted into office.

This plaza is a study in conceptual architecture that is ultimately not practical as a public space. Neighbors do not use the plaza; it is often empty at times when other spaces in the city are filled. It lacks many of the appealing elements of good public spaces—trees, fountains, food vendors. On the other hand, the plaza did create a "defensible space," a space that is open and easily monitored and therefore relatively free of illegal activities.[39] Also, it was built inexpensively, and is relatively cheap to maintain.

*One of the many public space redevelopment projects under Director of Planning Oriol Bohigas was the transformation of the train station Plaza de los Paisos Catalans; the new space epitomized the "hard plaza" trend.*

### RECYCLED SPACES, RECOVERED PROMENADES

The Bohigas strategy was aimed at recovering and liberating more public space in a city that, compared with London or Paris, was lacking in open spaces and pedestrian places. The planners adopted a flexible approach, identifying diverse places where space could be either created or improved. The strategy of recycling was critical in this process. The recycling that received the most public attention was the transformation of the formerly industrial waterfront into a zone of beaches, restaurants, galleries, and office buildings.

Many older factories were located in what had become residential neighborhoods. The Parc de L'Espanya Industrial is one such place. On the site of a former textile factory, a dramatic green space, artificial lake, and architectural sculptures have been built. The park lies in a very strategic section of the city, adjacent to the Sants train depot and surrounded by high-density residential apartments and commerce. It is a tranquil space amidst a very busy part of town. The park pays homage to the former industrial uses by preserving the school that originally served the factory workers' families. It is accentuated sculpturally by rows of massive towers that look like they might have been watchtowers for the old factory complex.

Similarly, on the site of another former factory in the southern portion of a working-class neighborhood, Nou Barris, an entire square block was remodeled into a giant square, the Plaza de la Palmera. One of the original chimneys from the factory has been preserved as part of the plaza design, an important icon connecting past and present. The plaza is surrounded by 12-story residential block towers, made from red or tan brick; the buildings house working-class and middle-class residents. The green-and-orange awnings add color to the surroundings. The plaza is more like a neighborhood park, subdivided into several functional spaces—a children's playground, a tree-lined promenade with wooden and iron benches, and an open sand field. A parking lot lies under the space, and food stands line its perimeter. Given its gargantuan size, the park is lacking in flora, and thus exhibits the influence of the aforementioned "hard plaza" philosophy. A tall palm tree anchors the plaza and gives it its name. One is struck here by how well this former factory site has been transformed into a heavily used neighborhood space.

Another recycled space lies on the site of a former slaughterhouse. This abandoned space was transformed in the mid-1980s into a plaza-garden called the Parc de L'Escorxador (Slaughterhouse Park), or more commonly, the Parc de Joan Miró. It lies in a very strategic place—on the eastern edge of the Eixample district, and just north of the Plaza de España and the entrance to Montjuic Park. It is part of a system of fluid public spaces running from the Plaza de los Paisos Catalans along one of the pedestrian promenades, the Carrer Tarragona, and into the Plaza de España and Montjuic Park. The signature landmark here is the 60-foot-high, multicolored tile sculpture designed by Joan Miró, one of his last great works for the city. Also, there are shaded pergolas and walls of trellised bougainvillea surrounded by palm trees. It is one of the city's majestic garden spaces.

Two other recycled public spaces are the Parc de L'Estació del Nord and the Plaza Soller. The former lies in the area of the abandoned railroad station (since converted to a bus depot) and near the Parc de la Ciutatella, the old fortress park to the west of the historic quarter. This park is relatively simple—green grass and trees, but it is notable for its sculptured shapes of turquoise and light blue ceramic tile, especially a giant serpentlike structure on a small hill for children to climb on. The sculpture celebrates Miró and Gaudí; the park celebrates designers, architects, and sculptors. Its feeling of emptiness suggests again the influence of the "hard architecture" philosophy. The Plaza Soller lies in the working-class district of Nou Barris. Built over a full city block in the 1980s, it is neatly divided into two spaces—a tranquil green space with running water, and a vast, paved hard plaza for community gatherings, dances, music festivals, and young children on bicycles.

Another way of recycling space is by converting streets used for vehicular circulation into pedestrian promenades. More than any other city in Spain, Barcelona has taken its "Rambla" tradition seriously. Where in the capital city of Madrid politicians can be voted out of office for even suggesting the closing of a street for pedestrians, in Barcelona such discussions are more favorably received by city dwellers. Bar-

*Parc de Joan Miró (also called El Escorxador [the Slaughterhouse]) is one of the truly majestic recycled public spaces in Barcelona today; the site was originally a slaughterhouse.*

celona has several celebrated promenades, including the Rambla of the historic quarter, the Passeig de Gracia, and Guell Park. But there have been more than 15 successful pedestrianization projects since the 1980s, many of them neighborhood commercial corridors converted into walkable promenades, with revitalized commerce, and other new land uses. One of the best examples is the Avinguida Gaudí, which runs from the Sagrada Familia, Gaudí's great unfinished design project and a landmark of Barcelona today, to the Hospital de Sant Pau, perhaps the greatest single work of modernismo, by Luis Domenech i Montaner. Observers have noted that these redevelopment projects don't merely change the street, they alter the streetscape, bringing better designs and more profitable commercial and institutional spaces into lower- and working-class districts.[40]

Three excellent examples of "invented promenades" are the Vía

Julia, Rambla Prim, and Rambla del Poble Nou. The Vía Julia is actually a place where a street was created out of nothing.[41] It lies in the center of the Nou Barris district, where Bohigas and his colleagues felt the neighborhood needed a commercial promenade to give it identity, and to strengthen the local economic base. Despite the changing elevations from one end of this 10-block-long corridor to the other, the designers were able to create a continuous flowing space. Two tall sculptural elements enliven the site. In the center lies an abstract iron

*Barcelona's Rambla remains an iconic space, perhaps the single greatest walking promenade on the planet.*

sculpture, shaped like a protractor, that is the landmark visual image of the space. Along the new corridor dynamic commercial activity has gradually found a foothold. There is little question that this promenade and street have rejuvenated the neighborhood.

The Rambla del Poble Nou is an eight-block-long corridor in the center of the working-class Poble Nou district. This is a mixed residential and industrial community. The Rambla here runs toward the sea and is lined by multistoried buildings, with shade trees, outdoor café seating for hundreds, restaurants, boutique shops, and offices. It is a clean, well-maintained space and appears heavily used by locals. Equally impressive is the Rambla Prim, which lies to the west in Nou Barris. This 12-block-long park/pedestrian corridor is lined with tall brick buildings (9–10 stories) and shade trees. It was designed and completed in the late 1980s. The central characteristic of all the Ramblas of Barcelona is that the walking space is at least two or three times as wide as the car space; this is true in both Rambla del Poble Nou and Rambla Prim.

### SUMMARY

Barcelona thus brings us full circle in Spain. In a nation of great public space tradition, Madrid chose to place the future of the city in the hands of national political figures bent on using the symbolic power of modern architecture to create images that foster nationalism. Nationalist architecture and urban planning do not necessarily make for the best citizen-oriented design, however. In Madrid we see a clash in progress—the traditions of public space and design fighting the forces of privatization, commercialization, and freeway decentralization. In Barcelona we encounter a different reality. We see that while the city can decentralize, it can also craft a creative strategy for invigorating the sagging inner-city economy. This strategy focuses on reinventing downtown and its public spaces.

In the next chapters we shift our attention from Spain to the Americas. Spain colonized both North and South America for over 300 years; during this time the building of cities was strictly controlled by the royal family in Madrid. The Renaissance and Baroque colonial cities of Latin America owe their construction to the models of good design in vogue in Spain at the time of their conception. But how were the values of Spain transmitted to the New World? And how were those ideas and values assimilated into the actual building of cities? To what extent do these notions survive in the early twenty-first century? We will consider these questions using the example of Mexico, the most populous Latin nation south of the United States.

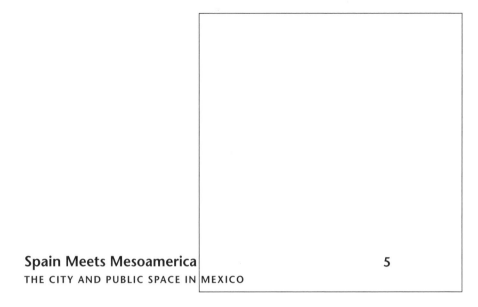

## Spain Meets Mesoamerica       5
### THE CITY AND PUBLIC SPACE IN MEXICO

*All things begin and all things end in the Zócalo, say the Mexicans;*
*and there is only a white sheet of stone blazing in the hot sun.*
ROBERT PAYNE, *MEXICO CITY*

In the early sixteenth century Spain was the most powerful nation
in the world; the king of Spain, Carlos V, crafted an imperial strategy
for colonizing the territories of the Americas. One of his representa-
tives, the Spanish conquistador Hernán Cortés, landed his fleets on
the eastern coast of present-day Mexico, swept across the vast mountain chain rising to the central plateau, and stormed into the Valley
of Mexico. By 1521, when Cortés lay siege to the great city of Tenochtitlán—center of power of the postclassic Aztec Empire—two completely different cultures, from opposite sides of the Atlantic Ocean,
were thrown together. Both cultures had become urban, although in
somewhat distinct forms.

Cortés and his Spanish soldiers defeated the Aztecs and their leader
Moctezuma, then vandalized or burned much of the great metropolis
of Tenochtitlán. They destroyed and disrupted its mosaic of floating
islands, canals, land causeways, temples, and pyramids sitting upon
Lake Texcoco.[1] But the Spanish colonists, called upon by their king
to build a new city—Mexico City, the capital of New Spain—over the
ruins of Tenochtitlán, fused elements of the urban cultures of Spain
and Mesoamerica. Colonial Mexico City was designed with the ideals

of Renaissance Spain, but it was actually built upon a physical landscape whose outlines and dimensions, whose plazas and open spaces, were distinctly Mesoamerican. One of the great examples of the mixing of Spanish and indigenous cultures in Mexico (and most of Latin America) was realized through construction of the first great city of the Americas, Mexico City.

It is noteworthy that in 1500 these two cultures, Spain and Mesoamerica—separated by an ocean and positioned in entirely different orbits—were entrenched in similar moments in their urban evolution. Spain was emerging out of the medieval period where the Graeco-Roman traditions of urban life had declined and cities stagnated, moved inside walls, and remained dark and enclosed. The Renaissance brought life back to Spanish cities; it refocused on the inherent qualities of space, and cities began to flourish as centers of new ideas, commerce, and economic development. Meanwhile, in Mesoamerica, the city was becoming increasingly more central to indigenous life, not only as a ceremonial place but also as an economic and political nexus from which to control surrounding territories.

If the city and urban life became central to both Spain and Mesoamerica, so did open space. The plaza lingered in the medieval cities of Spain, but after 1500 it began to flourish. The Plaza Mayor was a Renaissance creation born in Spain, but perfected in Latin America. In Europe the plaza and other public spaces grew from the Greek city-state's emphasis on the collective place (the agora) where citizens could participate in decision making. The Romans elevated the plaza to a place of political power (the forum) within the city. Spain inherited the Roman concept of the city, and by the time of the Renaissance her powerful kings were ready to build a New Spain, an empire across the ocean, whose engine would be a system of cities and towns. At the microscale these cities would be anchored by the spatial nucleus, the central place of power—the Plaza Mayor. But Mesoamerican cities already had their plazas, vast ceremonial spaces for the rituals of human sacrifice to the gods of sun, rain, or war. Mesoamerica also had already created the marketplace as an outdoor public space, where thousands made a daily or weekly ritual of traveling to engage in this fundamental element of economic life. Thus, as the city fused together two cultures, new hybrid designs for plazas and public spaces emerged.

## MEXICO CITY: PUBLIC SPACE AND URBAN DESIGN IN MESOAMERICA

Tenochtitlán—the capital city of the Aztec Empire—entered the landscape late in the history of indigenous culture in the Americas. The first ceremonial centers appeared as early as 1000 BC, but probably the most important Mexican ceremonial city emerged around 100 BC, flourishing until AD 300. This was the Toltec city of Teotihuacán, center of an empire on the central plateau of Mexico, north of present-day Mexico City. Teotihuacán was the ceremonial capital of a theocratic state, and it was probably the first planned town where religious rulers created an architecture that reflected the social hierarchy and religious belief system of the state.[2] The structure of Teotihuacán, with its vast pyramids, open spaces, and pathways, is part of an essentially artificial spatial system. The public plaza and axial processional spaces were used for ritual marches where members of conquered rival armies would be led to the sacrificial altar raised on the truncated pyramid.

The pyramids were designed to point toward the heavens and toward the realm of the gods. From the plaza below, the pyramid slope was so steep that observers would lose sight of persons being taken to the top, as if they had already disappeared into the heavens. The pyra-

mids represented the sun and the moon, heavenly bodies. The long sacrificial promenade has been called the Avenue of the Dead. Public space primarily existed to enhance the ritual, to remind citizens of the order of the universe of gods, and to elevate the status of a class of priests and nobles who could communicate with them. The sunken central square is thought to have been a market as well,[3] but its main function was artificial, to create a space that reinforced the hierarchies of power and religious beliefs.

*Public life in the pre-Columbian city of Teotihuacán unfolded on vast, axial processional spaces.*

Such planned urban designs show up in other regions of Meso-america, from the Yucatán cities of the Maya to the central Oaxa-can cities of the Zapotec.[4] The Maya planned their cities in concentric rings: the inner central complex, the intermediate center, and the surrounding agricultural countryside. The inner complex housed the high-density urban center, physically organized around a group of plazas, courtyards, and platforms surrounded by stepped pyramids and palaces.[5] In Tikal the "Great Square" was the true center; three causeways converged upon it, and the most important religious and civic functions were carried out here. In Tikal and other Mayan cities like Chichén Itzá or Palenque, the open spaces or plazas were vast in scale, which is not entirely surprising, given the gargantuan temples and pyramids arrayed around them.

These cities do not evoke a landscape of everyday living; they were meant to awe and intimidate, and to overshadow citizens. They represented the symbolic universe of gods and higher spiritual forces; they reminded indigenous inhabitants where the real powers supposedly lay. In Palenque, the spaces between the pyramids and palaces offered uplifting views into the dense, green foliage of the jungle. At Monte Alban, the Zapotec capital near present-day Oaxaca, the Great Square, which sits upon a mountain overlooking the valley of Oaxaca, has been described as "one of the most beautiful open spaces ever conceived by man."[6] The concept of the square was grounded in flexibility and monumental axiality. All of the surrounding buildings face the square and leave no openings toward the valley that surrounds the hill on three sides. The buildings provide a total sense of enclosure and detachment in relation to the surrounding topography, yet at the same time they are completely embedded in the setting.

The Aztecs were latecomers to the making of an indigenous Meso-american landscape. They arrived from the north in the eleventh and twelfth centuries. Aztec culture did not begin to flourish until the fourteenth century. In 1325 the new capital was established at Tenochtitlán, a complex of islands, canals, and causeways on the vast, but rapidly drying Lake Texcoco. At its peak, scholars believe the metropolis may have housed 300,000 people.[7] The city's morphology was complex: there were two primary landmasses in the lake—the main one at the center, and another, Tlatelolco, to the north. The city had a cruciform layout, with causeways running north–south and east–west. Although the lake was drying out by the fourteenth century, it remained a massive body of water and needed to be controlled. The Aztecs used a system of dikes, canals, aqueducts, and irrigation ditches. To the south, where there was more fresh water, they constructed *chinampas,* floating islands made of packed mud and stakes that, over time, would attach themselves to the bottom of the lake through marine vegetation. On the surface of the chinampas food crops were cultivated. There were few main streets in Tenochtitlán, apart from the land causeways, but boats could transport people through canals.[8]

The Aztecs founded the city in the place where an eagle had been seen perched on a cactus and eating a snake. According to Aztec beliefs, the eagle represented the sun, the snake embodied the night, while the cactus was the food of the sun (resembling a tree of human hearts). They built their city as a reflection of a universe where powerful gods—of the sun, rain, and earth—must be worshipped and appeased with human sacrifice. At the center of Tenochtitlán, on the main landmass in the middle of Lake Texcoco, where the eagle was seen eating the snake, the central urban complex was built. Around the grand plaza were the houses of nobility, the palace of the emperor, Moctezuma, as well as the monumental pyramid—the Great Temple. The temple was part of a vast sacred zone, some 2 million square feet in size, that was closed off from the rest of the city by a wall with serpentine figures on it.[9]

In all, Tenochtitlán was a well-planned 15-square-kilometer metropolis. It was a place of splendor, violence, human sacrifice, and worship of the sun,[10] with the high priests and nobility at the center, and clans organized in districts (*calpulli*) spread around the outskirts. The center claimed the highest status. Here lay the Great Temple and plaza and Moctezuma's palace. The lake was subject to the political organization of the Aztec state, with its human-made dikes, canals, and aqueducts. After a terrible flood in 1449, the leader Nezahualcoyotl set up an improved wall and dike system and built the main Chapultepec aqueduct. The lake also served as a form of defense. Since the center could be reached only by boat or by one of the causeways, the city could be well defended by Aztec soldiers.

The main plaza of Tenochtitlán was a vast open space sometimes used for commerce, although its main function was ceremonial. As the primary locale for worshipping the important Aztec gods, it was the site of religious festivals as well as the ritual sacrifices. It was the primary locale for worshipping the important gods. The main space for commerce, however, was to the north, in the market at Tlatelolco, which was a sprawling public space and the first great market plaza of the Americas.

Cortés and the Spanish conquistadores arrived in the Valley of Mexico in 1521. It was obvious that the Aztec Empire could not be displaced without controlling Tenochtitlán.[11] Having enlisted indigenous soldiers from among the satellite rival villages, Cortés approached the capital city, and soon lay siege to it. At the height of the attack, the main plaza of the Aztec city became a battleground. After the ensuing bloodbath, Cortés ordered his men to burn down houses and buildings around the great plaza. The invading army proceeded to destroy most of the city, leveling its great architecture and much of its infrastructure. Once the conquest of the city was complete, and the Aztecs thoroughly defeated, the conquerors waited for instructions from the king of Spain. The king decreed that a new capital city should be built on the same site as Tenochtitlán. Roads would be restored, the aqueduct renovated and made workable, and streams and irrigation ditches reestablished.[12]

One might wonder why the Spanish chose to build their first major colonial capital in Mesoamerica precisely on the site where the indigenous power they had just defeated had located its primary metropolis. Notwithstanding the disadvantages of the lake setting, and the immediate problems of cleaning out and disinfecting the post-battleground site, the location for the new Spanish imperial capital was strategic for a number of reasons. First, it was already the regional center of power over a network of settlements in surrounding territories.[13] The Spanish knew that control over the center also meant control over the periphery. Second, Tenochtitlán's morphology of lakes and surrounding mountains made it a highly defensible city; the Spaniards knew this very well, since they had invaded it only with great difficulty. It had not been easy for the conquerors to get into Moctezuma's inner zone on the main island. Third, and perhaps most importantly, the infrastructure—aqueducts, roads, causeways, canals, irrigation ditches—needed to manage a large city was already in place. A food supply system existed to serve the city, and dense populations of indigenous laborers lived nearby that could be marshaled to the immense city-building project the Spaniards envisioned. Cortés, it is reported, believed the two economic institutions of the Spanish conquest—the *encomienda* (collection of tribute on indigenous lands) and *repartimiento* (forced labor) would serve well in the Valley of Mexico.[14]

In the end, the Spanish royal court, heeding the advice of agents overseas, planned the construction of the great capital city of New Spain with some respect for the urban design and engineering feats of the Aztecs. Indeed, early in the sixteenth century, King Charles V gave only general guidelines to the colonists about how to design the towns of New Spain. This left room to utilize any advantages in the existing indigenous urban designs. More specific rules about city building would only come later, in the 1570s, when Phillip II took the throne. The first great urbanist of Mexico was Alonso García Bravo, the planner and chief architect of Mexico City. His plan retained the cruciform layout of the Aztec city, with its two great crossing causeways running perpendicular through Lake Texcoco. García Bravo's plan used the cruciform causeway configuration for the main roads, creating a gridded street system laid over the cruciform. The main streets thus resembled the Roman *cardo* and *decumanus,* crossing at the center, where a vast plaza would be built, more or less near where the main Aztec plaza had been located. Some of the original Aztec buildings—mainly the palaces of Moctezuma, Axayacatl (Moctezuma's son), and other important leaders—were left standing around the new plaza. The largest palace, Axayacatl's, would become the first home of the conqueror Cortés. The palace was a large, rectangular two-story structure, which initially served as both the living quarters for Cortés and seat of government, a New World version of the Spanish Royal Palace.[15]

A primary objective on the Spanish king's agenda was to eclipse indigenous culture by superimposing ornate and massive Spanish buildings and cities over the conquered territories. Some of the most systematic late-sixteenth-century planning documents ever written were drafted to impose strict guidelines for Spanish colonization of the Americas. Under the general body of codes known as the Laws of the Indies, 148 Royal Ordinances (*ordenanzas*) specified the selection of town sites, the layout of streets, the location and size of the plaza, the siting of buildings and the intra-urban location of social groups. While the laws were quite specific, they were not always followed to the letter. Spain was thousands of miles away, a difficult journey across the Atlantic under perilous conditions. While most of the early colonists, many of them conquistadores who fought with Cortés, respected the Spanish king, they also possessed a streak of adventurousness and independence.

There is, for example, some debate as to why Spanish colonial cities were all laid out in gridiron configurations. None of the 148 ordinances specifically required that such a plan be followed, yet the gridiron plan is one of the strongest and most consistent features of Spanish colonial urban design. Spain itself was discovering good urban design in the sixteenth century, following several centuries of medieval urbanism. Some have characterized Spain's town planning efforts in the 1500s as "unschooled, fumbling gestures."[16] It is probable that Spanish surveyors in Mexico City understood that the grid would work well there. Their boss, Alonso García Bravo, determined that the gridiron street plan would fit well into the existing Aztec morphology of canals, streets, and causeways. Also, the grid system followed the tradition of military town planning, derived from the Romans, and later utilized by the French in their *bastides*. This French urban design was familiar to the Spanish, since the *bastides* skirted the Pyrenees in the north of Spain and were found in the corridor of towns leading from southern France to the Christian pilgrimage town of Santiago de Compostela in northwestern Spain.[17] King Phillip II of Spain, who wrote the Royal Ordinances of 1573, was a great admirer of Roman town planning, and in particular of the works of the architect Vitruvius.[18]

However, by the time the ordinances were promulgated, Mexico City was already evolving, and one can imagine that the gridiron was employed alongside the new ordinances. City structure was a reflection of the imprint of Aztec city planning, as well as the work of surveyors working under the chief planner of Mexico City, García Bravo. Mexico City, importantly, became the blueprint for city planning and town design in other parts of Latin America.

The morphology of Latin American cities is distinctly centrifugal. The main square, or Plaza Mayor, is the nucleus, the "generative space" of the settlement.[19] The Latin American city would thus grow from the center, literally from the plaza outward, rather than from a larger, more dispersed design scheme. In Spain plazas were never the starting point of city evolution; they were usually created in the path of growth, often at the gates of the walls of the city in one era, and then as public spaces as the city leapfrogged over them and outward. In Latin America the public spaces typically were created first, and they became the nuclei from which urban growth would spread.

It is interesting to note, as alluded to above, that the sixteenth century, the time when Spain built the new cities of Spanish America, was a period when Spain itself was only beginning to improve its urban design strategies at home. So while the Spanish can take credit for designing colonial settlements across the Atlantic, in some ways the new settlements were more innovative and better examples of good urban design than the original cities in Spain, the latter still emerging out of the cramped medieval era. With the Laws of the Indies, Spanish colonial designers and city builders had the opportunity to start from the beginning, to design an ideal city generally without the constraints of history that had skewed the Spanish model. For example, one observer notes that the plazas of Latin America anticipated by as much as a century those of Spain.[20] This is not to deny, however, that the cultural

tradition of the plaza is fundamental to Spain's urbanism; as the great Spanish philosopher Ortega y Gassett wrote: "El Español es un hombre de plaza mayor" (The Spaniard is a man of the main plaza).[21]

As mentioned, the ordinances called for a town plan that divided the settlement site into streets, squares, and building lots beginning with the main plaza. Unlike the closed system of Renaissance ideal cities, the Spanish American plan called for an open system, where streets would emanate out from the main plaza, and growth could be continually projected outward. There were no walls around the Spanish American towns; emphasis was on expansion and colonization, rather than on enclosure and defense.[22]

The ordinances suggested that the size of the plaza be proportionate to the population of the settlement, taking into account the expected growth and the numbers of indigenous people in the region. The plaza was to be no less than 200 feet wide and 300 feet long, and no larger than 800 feet by 530 feet. An ideal plaza would be 600 feet by 400 feet (or 240,000 square feet).[23] In general, the plazas of the Americas were considerably larger than those of Spain. The ideal plaza of

*The Mexican plaza, from the beginning, was a "generative space," a core around which the city grew: plaza in Guanajuato, Mexico.*

240,000 square feet would not find an equal anywhere in Spain. The Plaza Mayor of Madrid, for example, was only about half that size.

The laws also set down a detailed routine for designing the street grid. The plaza would be the origin of four principal streets—from each of the sides of the square, two secondary streets would meet at each of the corners of the plaza.[24] In practice, this 12-street plaza plan was rarely used. The principal streets in most towns meet the plaza at its corners, rather than at the sides. Side streets, when they do exist, are minor ones. Most colonial town plans followed the 8-street model, rather than the 12-street one, and this means that the reality of most colonial Mexican plazas is different than the original plan intended.[25]

The Spanish ordinances stated that "the church shall not be placed on the plaza, but at a distance." The intention of the Spanish court was to create a visual presence for the church on the square, but also to set it away from government buildings situated directly on the plaza. By placing it back and on slightly elevated land, the Crown would be symbolically reminding the Church where the real power lay—with the king. The colonists, however, often chose to ignore this detail in the king's instructions. They built many churches directly on the colonial plaza.

The king had intended that the chief government building be the centerpiece of the main plaza. If the city were a major capital, the building would house the offices of the viceroy; if it were a smaller town, the building would simply host the municipal government (*cabildo*). While the laws did not specify architectural style for either government or religious buildings around the plaza, the styles then in vogue—mainly Renaissance and Baroque—came to dominate the urban landscape. In Spain church towers had usually been outlawed by royal decree, as they were considered extravagant. But in colonial Latin America it was not uncommon to find towers in buildings surrounding the plazas. They were used to hang the church bells, and more importantly, they were employed for the purpose of protection: towers served as lookouts from which to watch over the city. Since the colonial Mexican city did not have walls, it was necessary to engage in good surveillance. While most of these cities were not fortresses in the European medieval tradition, neither were they completely defenseless. In sixteenth-century Mexico City, most of the elite homes and palaces around the main plaza were like small fortresses, "with thick stone facades, massive wood doors, turreted roofs, and narrowly slit windows for archers and gunners."[26] Needless to say, these homes tended to be well armed. Church towers aided in creating defensible space for these young Mexican colonial cities.

We have seen that the building of colonial cities like Mexico City represents a fusion of two cultures—indigenous and Spanish. For Spain, the plaza was an incarnation of the ideal societal view of the Spanish royal family, which was financing the settlement of the Americas. The thinking of the royal family is crystallized in the design of the main plaza in Mexico City. The vast scale of the plaza reflected the Crown's ambition and grandiose plans for the Americas. The elegant Palace of the Viceroy to the east displays the power of the king. The importance of the Spanish church is established with the giant cathedral, although disagreements about its design left it unfinished for centuries.

The vitality of the Spanish plaza as the central urban place was firmly established in the Plaza Mayor of Mexico City. In parts of Europe as well as in Spain, the plaza was regarded as the essence of urban life, an essential node. If the city is viewed as a home, the streets are seen as hallways, while the plaza is the living room, *el salón,* the center around which human life evolves. No city in Spain can function without its plazas. It has even been suggested that the plaza is an expression of the Spanish-Portuguese religious view of the world: a place where humans act by divine faith, but with free will.[27] Yet the plaza's vitality as an indigenous space grew from a different worldview: the objective of the plaza was not to be a place for acting out of free will, but for fulfilling a series of rituals that preserve harmony in the universe, and must be achieved through community participation.

Some believe that the Plaza Mayor represented an architectural strategy for imposing brutal Spanish colonialism on indigenous Mesoamerican cultures. This view argues that the Spanish colonial legacy was one of violent conquest, destruction of the indigenous lifeways, and their replacement with the dominant European culture. In this perspective the plaza—with its rectangular streets, its Baroque churches, and its sumptuous palaces—is simply an artifact of Spain in the act of colonizing the Americas.[28]

There is evidence to support such a contention, harsh as it may seem. In Spain the plaza mayor was a functional space that evolved organically out of the medieval urban fabric. It was a marketplace first and a place of royal celebration second. There were never churches or cathedrals on the plazas mayores of Spain, and the government buildings emphasized local rule, not that of the royal court, or the national government. The emphasis in the Spanish plaza mayor was on civil life and local solidarity.

The Latin American plaza did not grow spontaneously. It was called the "plaza of the state," created by the Spanish king as a centerpiece of royal control of New Spain and her towns.[29] Here stands the cathedral or church, powerful and weighty. State buildings, such as the Palace of the Viceroy, dominated the plaza and reminded the citizens at all times who was in control.

Sixteenth-century colonial Mexico City was not lacking in plazas. There were five main ones and 23 smaller ones.[30] Around the plaza mayor were the most prestigious lots, deeded only to the conquerors, their families, and officials of the Spanish royal family. Lots were given by rank: foot soldiers received smaller parcels of land than cavalrymen.[31] In order to ensure that the cities would keep their populations, soldiers who built houses were required to stay for a minimum period of one year. Realizing that the conquerors might have wanderlust and want to move on, the court created incentives and rules to make them stay. Any attempt to build great cities without the people to nurture them was a guarantee of failure.

### COLONIAL QUERÉTARO, MEXICO

In 1994 a publication in the form of a comic book entitled "Return to Our Streets" began circulating in Querétaro, a medium-sized city that anchors the region called the Bajío a two-hour drive north from Mexico City. Sponsored by the Governor's office of the State of Querétaro, the publication told the story of three strangers who meet on the streets of the historic center of old Querétaro. The three main characters include a conservative storeowner, his neighbor—a local resident—and a visitor from the suburbs. The storeowner is passionately opposed to downtown revitalization, and he speaks with hostility and cynicism about the role of local government. Further, he argues that any attempt to pedestrianize downtown, including the exclusion of automobiles from certain streets, will severely hurt local businesses.[32]

The publication then employs the more liberal voice of the storeowner's neighbor as well as that of a young, open-minded visitor from the suburbs to explain the virtues of revitalization of the historic center. Through fantasy-like drawings and clever dialogue, the text demonstrates how fewer cars and more pedestrians can lead to a completely different kind of historic center—one where restaurants, cafés, galleries, nightclubs, boutiques, bookstores, and other commercial spaces create a critical mass of activities that make downtown attractive to residents, shoppers, and tourists. This, in turn, draws more business and economic development, while improving the quality of life for residents, by removing the noxious presence of automobiles in the historic center. Over time the historic downtown becomes a walkable, vibrant urban space, and a highly visible tourism district, allowing for a greater number of outside visitors, and even more business for inner-city merchants.

In 1996, two years after this publication appeared, Querétaro's central historic quarter was declared a World Heritage Site by UNESCO, placing it among the prestigious list of Mexican downtowns recognized globally for their colonial historic heritage. The story of Querétaro's evolution, and of the preservation and reinvention of its historic plazas and urban spaces, offers an important companion narrative to the case of Mexico City. For those who might argue that Mexico City is a special case, due to its status as the colonial then national capital, and due to its special circumstances as a megacity with some 20 million inhabitants, Querétaro offers a case more typical of dozens of other medium-sized Mexican cities, with populations ranging from 500,000 to 3 million.

Querétaro was among a number of colonial settlements created by Spain in the sixteenth century as outposts for expansion into unsettled frontier zones. Querétaro was, in fact, the fortress town and administrative center for the expansion north of Mexico City into a region of great mineral wealth. It was founded in 1531 as a port of entry for goods and colonists heading north along the Camino Real (royal highway).

The settlement actually formed as a result of a pact between local Otomí Indians and Spanish colonists, described as "an uncertain, troubling and imprecise union."[33] The Otomí people helped the Spaniards defeat regional indigenous armies, and thus were granted an

*The aqueduct of colonial Querétaro is a reminder of the city's legacy of centuries-old stone buildings.*

unusually important role in the city, a role that would ultimately be manifest in the urban morphology of the city. When serious mining ventures began in the nearby cities of Zacatecas (1548) and Guanajuato (1554), Querétaro's function as an urban center quickly expanded. It now housed military operations responsible for enforcing security over trade and mining caravans traveling north and south through the region. It also was charged with the protection of the mining cities from raids by the Chichimeca tribes.

Querétaro's early physical form reflected its cultural origins, which were arrayed over the built landscape in two contrasting social ecologies: a zone of churches and rectangular, gridiron streets, on the one hand; and a district of irregular, spontaneous street patterns and secular land uses, on the other. The religious zone was designed by Juan Sánchez de Alanís, according to the Spanish colonial plan, and it consisted of a main plaza and principal church, the Church of San Francisco, as well as numerous convents, monasteries, temples, and cloisters, all laid out within the gridiron pattern between 1550 and 1600.[34]

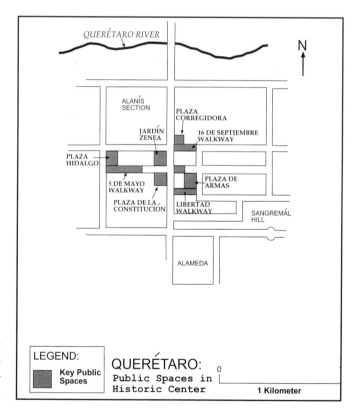

*Querétaro: public spaces in the historic center.*

To the east of this district lies Sangremal Hill, the oldest portion of the city, and its secular quality, irregular street layout, and hilly, windy topography stand in stark contrast to the Alanís zone. Many of the streets in fact follow the original morphology of the ancient Otomí town that covered Sangremal Hill before the Spanish arrived. Once again, as in Mexico City, we note that the Spanish colonial urbanization pattern often built on the existing ecology of indigenous city builders. Indeed, the early urban social ecology of Querétaro is a fitting metaphor for Mexican society: an indigenous, spontaneous, secular district and a Spanish Catholic, logical, rectangular zone. Sangremal possessed not only the secular spirit but also the land uses of civil society—private homes, public squares, markets—to go with it. Of course, as in Mexico City, over time the lines between the secular and the religious spaces, between indigenous ecology and Spanish colonial ecology, began to blur, and soon they disappeared into the larger morphology of Spanish colonial urbanism.

### REVISITING MEXICAN PUBLIC SPACES

Colonial plazas have survived in Mexico City and in other Latin American megacities, but they are threatened by a magnitude of urban growth that, absent good planning and urban design, could leave traditional plazas unable to function. Like elsewhere on the planet, they are increasingly compromised by new technologies in transport, which move citizens faster through urban space, and in communications, which shift their orientations into nonspatial realms such as private automobiles and video media. Where plazas in Mexico have survived, they have done so in cities that have successfully retained graceful, functional downtowns, spaces that are celebrated by citizens. One scholar has posed the question: "Why do Mexican social, political and family life continue to unfold gracefully under stone arcades, at sidewalk cafés and within earshot of fountains in plazas, while the civic areas of so many U.S. cities continue to decline in a swirl of graffiti and litter along sidewalks emptied of people?"[35]

From the late colonial period on, most Mexican plazas were, in fact, barren and used mainly as parade grounds, or in some cases markets.[36] Things began to change in the middle of the nineteenth century. Ironically, it was a foreigner—the Austrian Duke Maximilian, appointed Emperor of Mexico by Napoléon III in 1864—who was responsible for changing the design of Mexican plazas. Maximilian's ideas permanently restructured the connection between plazas and urban life in the period of industrialization and urbanization that followed his brief mid-nineteenth-century stay in Mexico. When he arrived in Mexico City, Maximilian quickly convinced Mexicans to plant trees and flowers and otherwise beautify the Zócalo (main square) of Mexico City. This strategy mirrored developments in France at the time, where the landscape architecture profession was turning out new plaza-garden designs in the heart of the city. It has been said that this symbolized the management of nature and the triumph of rationality over barbarism.[37] It also fit with the late-nineteenth-century romantic age in urban design. The new plaza-garden idea so appealed to Mexicans that squares in other cities were targeted for similar design modifications.

By the twentieth century most Mexican plazas were covered with fine manicured bushes and trees, flowers, cast-iron benches, and kiosks. The kiosks, or pavilions, were considered a symbol of opulence and urbanity.[38] Many plazas were soon bordered by arcades with sidewalks (*portales*), vendor stands, cafés, hotels, restaurants, and stores.

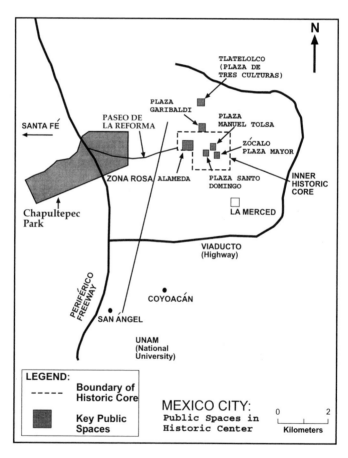

*Mexico City: public spaces in the historic center.*

The beautification of the plaza brought with it a surge in economic activity, as the plaza became a vital commercial space within the city. By the twentieth century the *plaza-jardín* (plaza-garden) became a comfortable break in the urban fabric, a place to escape from the noise and fast pace of the bustling city. Yet, it also evolved into a place with a life of its own, a dynamic social and economic niche within a rapidly changing urban landscape.

While various political forces negotiate their future, the fact is that historic public spaces remain as valuable treasures in urban Mexico. They tend to appear in distinct categories throughout Mexico: the main square (*zócalo*), organic or neighborhood squares, promenades and parks, and church plazas. As one reviews the rich histories of these spaces, beginning with an outline of Mexico City's below, one can begin to appreciate how these plazas have become anchors in defining place identity and thus adding value to the historic centers of Mexican cities.

### THE PLAZA MAYOR AND THE STATE: MEXICO CITY'S ZÓCALO

The main plaza of the Aztec city of Tenochtitlán became the Plaza Mayor of colonial Mexico City. When the Spanish conquerors invaded Tenochtitlán, they destroyed most of the temples and other buildings. Cortés and his soldiers are said to have commented on the beauty of this vast canal city, and with their entrance, Cortés instructed his men to spare several of the more grandiose palaces around the main plaza, even while the rest of the city was being sacked and destroyed. The Spanish urban plan employed the model of the Roman *castrum*, or fortified town, in which a 16-block rectangular cantonment would be built around the central parade grounds of Plaza de Armas.

Although the Spanish conquistadores, acting on the orders of the royal court in Spain, intended to create a hierarchy of towns that erased the memory of indigenous culture in Mexico, they were not always able to do so. In designing Mexico City they sought to impose the imprint of imperial Spain on the site, yet the scale of the new plaza they created—the main plaza of Mexico City—was far more Meso-american than Spanish. It was a vast open plaza, whose monumentality, even today, evokes memory of Aztec cosmology and architecture, rather than the enclosed squares of medieval and Renaissance Europe. One writer has described the Plaza Mayor of Mexico City as a square that lies at the center of a great mystery.[39] The sense of mystery remains today.

The colonial Plaza de Armas was part of the larger design plan of

García Bravo. The plaza was designed to be 1,000 feet by 720 feet in size (about 720,000 square feet). This was somewhat reduced as new projects like the Cathedral or the Palace of the Viceroy (later the National Palace) were located here. At its inception, the Plaza de Armas was mainly used as a military parade ground, principally in the period 1525–1550. It was also utilized as a place for the celebration of events related to the royal court in Spain. In 1538, to celebrate the visit of King Charles V to Mexico, an elaborate festival of several days was planned in advance. The Plaza de Armas was transformed into a forest—groves of trees were planted, birds were installed in cages, tigers were put in other pens. Deer, foxes, rabbits, and other animals were set loose. A royal hunt would be held on the converted plaza space; this would be part of a larger sumptuous celebration with music, horse racing, bullfights, and elaborate meals. While the pageant unfolded the aristocrats watched the events on the plaza from the roofs of their palaces, while "sipping their long cool drinks, and stuffing themselves with marzipan and coated almonds."[40] The great feast was highlighted by the reenactment of a historic battle in the forest between Christians and Moors. The reenactors were the same conquistadores who had secured Mexico for the Spanish Crown.[41]

In the middle of the sixteenth century, a built environment reflecting the main institutions of colonial Mexico appeared around the edges of the main plaza. It consisted of the two main buildings representing church and state—the Cathedral and the Palace of the Viceroy. Until then most of the land around the Plaza Mayor had been allocated to provide housing for the most privileged conquerors, including Cortés, who took over the former Palace of Moctezuma, among other buildings.[42] In 1562 the Palace of the Viceroy was completed on the east side of the plaza, the former site of the houses of Cortés. The Cathedral was begun in 1573, inspired by the Gothic design of the cathedral of Salamanca, Spain, which had been completed in 1560. The Cathedral in Mexico City was built slowly, and took more than two centuries to complete, during which time its style changed from Gothic to Baroque.

In 1573 the Laws of the Indies institutionalized the concept of the Plaza Mayor as the anchor of colonial towns, around which the standard buildings would be the church and town hall (*cabildo*) or government palace (the latter in the larger cities). Mexico City also set the tone in creating an urban design model that favored the main square as the magnet for elite residential location. In 1573, when King Phillip II was writing his Royal Ordinances for the Laying Out of New Towns as part of the Laws of the Indies, much of the infrastructure and spatial form of Mexico City was already in place. Its main plaza was already the fulcrum of city life that Phillip wanted it to be; it was as vital a space as any Renaissance plaza in sixteenth-century Spain. Yet, it reflected the peculiarly colonial heritage of singling out the two great buildings (town hall and cathedral) to demand the colonists' loyalty to Crown and Church. For example, the use of the plaza for military parades nourished the image of the Spanish Crown (which paid for the army) in the minds of the colonists.

The plaza also reinforced the highly centralized nature of Spain's imperial command over the colonial empire. In one central space all of the major activities of the city and society unfolded—religious cel-

ebrations, solemn events (funerals, etc.), the administration of justice, even weddings. On the northeast corner of the plaza on Tuesday, Thursday, and Saturday afternoons, the Mayors of the Tribunal of Crime would meet to hear civil complaints in the manner of similar institutions that had been set up in Spain in the cities of Valladolid and Granada. Criminals found guilty would be bound and mounted on a mule, taken to the plaza where a list of their crimes, as well as their sentence, would be read. Then the criminal would be marched through the streets around the plaza, and a crowd would begin to follow. The procession would arrive back at the plaza, where the punishment—a beheading or a public whipping—would take place. This permitted the Crown to impress the public with its authority,[43] and symbolically, it did so on its most powerful space—the main plaza. The administration of justice during the seventeenth-century Inquisition was car-

*Mexico City's Zócalo is an enclosed plaza anchored by the National Palace (in background), which symbolizes the preeminent role government plays in shaping Mexican cities.*

ried out on the main plaza in the form of swift and brutal autos-da-fé. Those found to be heretics by Inquisition officials were tortured and executed. Many were burned alive. Mass executions began to take place on Mexico City's main plaza between 1649 and 1659.

With time the plaza's main purpose became commercial, rather than military. By the seventeenth century an open-air market, the *tianguis,* had located on the plaza in the Mesoamerican tradition. The difficulties of colonial life in Mexico City were many, however, and these were often manifest on the main plaza, despite the best efforts of the government. The streets around the colonial plaza, according to one chronicle, were full of sewage and pestilence, dead animals, and old rags.[44] Avenues were unlit and lacked curbs or drains, and people threw garbage out of windows directly onto the streets. The Plaza Mayor served as a public market, where live animals were brought in, and at times slaughtered on site. There were puddles of water around the main fountain, flies hovering in the market around food, and people sleeping in doorways of buildings facing the plaza. All told, it was not a very healthy ambience, having, as one author stated, "un aspecto asqueroso y poco culto" (a repugnant and uncultured character).[45] The Plaza Mayor in the eighteenth century continued to be a vital center of the city, but as Spain's riches diminished, Mexico developed a growing class of homeless and poor. The Plaza Mayor became the home of wandering vendors, beggars, the blind, crippled, and sick (the city had few hospitals in the 1700s), while the priests, nobles, and landed gentry traveled through the plaza in or on chairs carried by servants. The social polarity that would bring Mexico to a revolution by the early 1900s had already been cast.

In the early nineteenth century Mexico achieved its independence, and the plaza became known as the Plaza de la Constitución. Fountains and a kiosk were installed. From 1864 to 1867 Napoléon III's appointed Emperor of Mexico, Maximilian, transformed the main plaza of Mexico City into a park with palm trees and fountains, consistent with his French and Austrian landscape experiences, as well as those of his Italian wife, Carlota.

During the administration of Porfirio Díaz, in the late nineteenth century, further improvements were added: a flower market, a book market, and electric trolley station. The Plaza Mayor had become a green space with trees and flowers. The Cathedral, which had been completed in 1813, dominated the plaza with its Baroque heaviness. The adjacent National Palace was a more graceful building of classical proportions. During this period the term *zócalo* was coined in Mexico. The *zócalo* referred to a pedestal that stood on the main plaza awaiting a monument to independence that was to be erected upon it. The monument was never actually built here, but the term became synonymous with the Plaza Mayor, and was soon adopted to refer to the main plazas of cities and towns all over Mexico.[46]

## ORGANIC PUBLIC SPACE: PLAZA SANTO DOMINGO

The Plaza Santo Domingo has been called the second most important plaza in Mexico. In the city of Tenochtitlán the space was a prestigious site occupied by the Palace of Cuahtémoc, one of the great Aztec leaders. It is thought that the actual site was, in Aztec times, an open space with gardens and pools adjacent to Cuahtémoc's palatial home.[47] The plaza lies today just north of the center of the city. In 1538 a Dominican convent was established on the site, a more permanent complex of buildings around the original pre-Hispanic plaza. Some of the important conquistadors, including Cristobal de Oñate, moved to houses around the plaza. The plaza's first arched enclosures, called the Portales de Oñate, were built. The Church of Santo Domingo, rebuilt in 1575, anchored the plaza, but it was already sinking in the muddy clay subsoil that was Lake Texcoco in the late sixteenth century.

The architecture around the Plaza Santo Domingo during the 1500s has been described as "medieval."[48] The difference, in Mexico City, as mentioned earlier, was that no walls bounded the city; its fortifications consisted of individual houses solidly built like forts, some with towers, all with good supplies of guns and horses. The plaza managed to endure through the efforts of the Dominican monks, who were convinced that it would provide a splendid view for their church.

An important building on the plaza, apart from the Baroque Church of Santo Domingo, was the Tribunal of the Holy Inquisition, founded in 1570 by the great Inquisitor Bishop Pedro de Moya. The Tribunal was a somber Renaissance building, in front of which executions and autos-da-fé were announced in the sixteenth, seventeenth, and eighteenth centuries, at 10 o'clock each morning. In 1574, at the first tribunal, 73 people were sentenced, including 5 who were burned alive.[49] The Tribunal was subsequently occupied by Congress, the Government of the State of Mexico, the Tribunal of War and Navy, and finally, the School of Medicine. In 1933 it was made into the National Academy of Medicine and the Museum of Medicine of Mexico; it continues to house these functions today.

Another key edifice bordering the plaza is the Customs building, completed from 1770 to 1780. The Customs House had two grand entrances with two-story-high doors to let carts and wagons in for inspection. The building of the Customs House brought to the plaza an active flow of daily traffic of vehicles, mules, donkeys and a bustle of offices of registration and inspection. By the early nineteenth century the plaza had become a place to hire a carriage.

During the mid-nineteenth century the portals around the plaza were filled with an emerging class of "evangelistas," or letter writers. The writers offered their services to illiterate clients during the period following Mexico's independence from Spain. At that time Mexico was an agrarian nation with a large population of illiterate people. Such people, in Mexico City, hired the letter writers to fill out income tax forms or write love letters under the shady and rainproof portals that ran the length of the plaza. In the words of one observer: "[T]hey work in a beautiful

place, among stupendous columns supporting the wooden rafters, that, together with the arches, give a splendid perspective."[50]

*Classical Greek columns line the portals on one of Mexico City's organic neighborhood-oriented squares: Plaza Santo Domingo.*

The evolution of the scribe into an institution on the Plaza Santo Domingo is a reflection of how Mexican people have given life to their plazas. In a larger sense, it demonstrates how public spaces, through a series of overlapping events, become organic spaces—empowered with unique qualities in certain locales. History conspired to bring the Dominicans to create this plaza. It then attracted two important colonial land uses: inquisitional justice and customs collection. This created a magnetic attraction of people to the site, which in turn brought in a class of permanent workers—scribes—to service the demand for writing. The scribes chose their plaza because of its proximity to government sites, mainly the Customs House. Over time they became as important to the plaza as the buildings around it. Speaking about the scribes, one observer stated: "[A]ll he needed to accomplish his work was the following—spiritually, a fairly clear mind; materially, an old desk with inclined top, two chairs with *tule* [reed] seats for himself and his client, several parcels of paper in various sizes, shapes, forms and colors, one ink pot with two or three feather pens, and a knife to sharpen them."[51]

## PUBLIC SPACE AT THE ALAMEDA

After the Plaza Mayor and the Plaza Santo Domingo, the Alameda may be the most well known public space in the historic core of Mexico City. It is also the oldest promenade in the city. In 1592 the Viceroy, Luís de Velasco, proposed to the municipal government that a "paseo" (walking space) be created. The proposal was approved. The new promenade was sited in a rectangular space that had once been the bed of a wide stream, one of the many *acequias* (streams) that cut through the sixteenth-century colonial city. The corridor was called Water Street; nearby, on the higher land, one of the early city markets—the Tianguís de San Hipolito—was located. Following the draining of the marshland, the new paseo was dedicated. Because the site was abundant with *álamos,* or poplar trees, the space became known as the Alameda, the walk of the poplars.

In its early incarnation in the seventeenth century, the Alameda was fenced, with a fountain at its center. In 1730 there were some 4,000 poplars growing there.[52] Throughout the colonial period the Alameda was a protected space primarily for the affluent citizens of downtown Mexico City. The eighteenth-century viceroy, the Count of Revilla Gigedo, authorized a prohibition from the Alameda of "any person broken down, dirty, dressed in a shawl, blanket or shoeless."[53] So, although the Alameda was an exclusive site from its origins, it also evolved into a popular public meeting place in the late colonial period, and even a place where duels were fought. After 1820 the wrought iron fence was taken down, and it became an even more popular space for all city residents.

The two main church plazas of the historic center lie just north of the Alameda. The Plaza de Santa Veracruz is a sunken public square wedged between two churches across the street from the Alameda. On one end is the Church of Santa Veracruz, a Baroque church built in 1736, and on the other end sits the Church of San Juan de Dios, built in 1730. The parish was originally part of a larger complex that included a hospital, which provided medical help to the underrepresented (blacks, mulattoes, mestizos, etc.).

The Plaza de San Fernando sits in front of the Church of San Fernando, built in 1755 adjacent to a school. This was an important church-convent-school complex in the eighteenth century, and many priests lived around the plaza. In 1858 an earthquake destroyed most of the priests' homes, and subsequently part of the convent complex was demolished. Late in the nineteenth century the surrounding neighborhood, Colonia Guerrero, began to become more densely populated. The former dominance of the clergy in the surrounding space diminished. Around this time, in 1872, the city's only cemetery of the "romantic age" was built just off the plaza. The Panteón de Hombres Ilustres (Pantheon of Famous Men) was originally built to bury former president Benito Juárez.

## SUMMARY

Mexican public space can trace its roots to indigenous town construction and to Spanish town planning. In both cases the public squares, parks, and plazas had both symbolic and functional importance. One must also acknowledge, however, that from their inception plazas in Mexico were highly politicized spaces. In indigenous Mexico the priests and nobility used the plazas to dramatize the powers of the gods, instilling fear in uneducated peasants, and therefore making them more dependent upon the ministrations of the higher classes. In colonial Mexico plazas were part of the royal family's strategy of using design to advertise the power of the king and his royal consorts.

Politics continues to mold urban form, and its public and open spaces in modern Mexico, as we shall see in the next chapter. After the Mexican Revolution of 1910, the new government of Mexico sought to use public spaces, especially plazas, to promote a sense of nationalism, and thus keep citizens in line. Plazas effectively served the nationalist agenda of the main political party of twentieth-century Mexico, the PRI (Revolutionary Institutional Party). By co-opting downtown Mexico City's historic urban spaces, the PRI strategically used the city to foment its political agenda. However, as Mexican cities boomed in the late twentieth century, the competition among interest groups accelerated. The state has been only partially successful in exploiting plazas and public spaces for its nationalist propaganda objectives. The stakes have grown in historic centers and in inner cities. Many elements now impact the old colonial downtown, including globalization, trade, political modernization, and economic expansion. Public spaces frequently become the focal points of strategic political battles over the future of Mexican urbanism.

## Revitalizing Historic Centers in Urban Mexico  6
### POLITICS AND PUBLIC SPACE

During the twentieth century traditional Mexican public spaces were bombarded by the political and economic forces of modernization. Yet plazas, gardens, parks, and promenades were still capable of becoming powerful cultural anchors. Mexicans embrace their past; the modern Mexican political system built its power base in part around nationalism and the celebration of history and culture. Public spaces served well as symbolic places to implement the national government agenda.

In Mexico, as well as in the Mediterranean region (and most of Latin America), traditional public space forms survive, although they continue to face challenges to their existence. The public plaza has always been an adaptable space, taking different forms based on who its principal users were. In rural indigenous towns, plazas tend to be highly functional—usually serving as markets. In the middle- and upper-class neighborhoods of modern metropolitan areas, plazas appear in the form of the plaza-garden, a design prototype derived from European landscape architecture, and then adapted to Mexican urbanism.[1] Two essential kinds of public spaces have been observed in Latin American central city districts: the market and the plaza. The market is a place where nature becomes a commodity; it is a business space—of focused, engaged interaction. In the market, space has a premium, and is subject to competitive bidding, much like the rest of the city. The plaza, however, is a more tranquil, unfocused sphere, a plaza-garden where people can be spectators, and remain dispersed and distant from others. Unlike in the market, competition for space in the plaza is less intense. Rather, people in Latino town squares report a sense of being on stage, in a highly decorated, ornate place.[2]

Given the increasing pace of competition for urban space in the modern city, it is difficult to imagine how Mexico's public plazas can continue to survive. In one study of the plazas of Guadalajara, Mexico, it was found that if middle-class users could not be enticed into staying in the downtown, and using the plazas, the squares would fall into decline.[3] The study described an increasing disdain toward downtown squares among middle-class users, creating an emerging pattern of exclusive use of plazas by lower classes, and the general perception that plazas were becoming marginal spaces.[4] To a great extent, these observations, made in the late 1970s, continue to apply to Mexico's downtown spaces today, particularly in large cities like Mexico City and Guadalajara. The findings also resonate for the case of urban Spain, and in particular Madrid,[5] although there are exceptions.

Yet, studies of Mexican plazas have also found much to celebrate. Plazas are viewed as "immaculate and finely sculptured physical symbols of the city."[6] In Guadalajara the use of the main plazas in downtown has been estimated at as high as 8,000 people in a single day (usually Sunday), with overall averages of some 500 people per plaza per day. People who frequent the plazas range from "leisured occupants" (retirees, lovers, women with children, students) to "workers" (street vendors, beggars, shoe shiners, sweepers, etc.) and "passersby" (sightseers, sexual cruisers, people chatting, those waiting for the bus). If such a diversity of users could be maintained, it was found, the plazas would have a better chance to survive.

This raises the larger question of the future of downtown space in Mexican and Latin American cities. While most of the historic cores of urban Mexico were formed in the colonial era, and are architectural treasures, they have also been vital urban economic spaces for most of this century. This represents a significant departure from the case of most American cities, which, decades ago, discarded their central business districts as primary business nodes, allowing the suburban areas to dominate the urban economic landscape.

In this chapter I review the cases of Querétaro and Mexico City. Both are examples of large cities whose historic centers have survived. Both face political pressures in determining the future of their public spaces. Querétaro's downtown was fortunate to benefit from a set of elite property owners who were convinced their wealth could be increased by preserving history. Mexico City's case is more complicated, due to its size and the rapidity of growth in the twentieth century.

Mexico City's colonial downtown remained important throughout the 1800s, bolstered in mid-century by the efforts of Emperor Maximilian and his wife, Carlota. Arriving from Europe, the ruling family worked to dignify Mexico City's public life by beautifying the Zócalo, as well as creating the Paseo de la Reforma, a promenade that ran from the Plaza Mayor to Chapultepec Park, the largest green space in the downtown. In the middle of the nineteenth century, the entire metropolis covered only about 4 square miles.

During the "Porfiriato" (the regime of turn-of-the-century president Porfirio Díaz), a period of growth and heavy foreign investment, particularly from the United States, Mexico City began to expand spatially. Through the two and a half decades of the Díaz regime, the city extended its boundaries to the edges of the now dried-up former Lake Texcoco.[7] Still, before 1920 most of the elite remained in large palaces and prestigious homes around the Zócalo, and the historic core became elegantly European with neoclassic buildings, promenades, and public gardens such as the Alameda. Downtown Mexico City became the showpiece of the Porfiriato, a Mexican version of Belle Epoque Paris, replete with electric lighting, streetcars, neo-Baroque statues, department stores, and elegant restaurants.[8]

After 1920, as mass transport improved, and as automobiles became available, wealthy residents moved out of the urban core to the south and west, while the poor moved north and east, often illegally occupying land converted to residential use. Growth rates, mainly driven by rural-to-urban migration, were staggeringly high in the five decade period 1940–1990. By 1990 the population of Mexico City was approaching 20 million, and people were spread over some 480 square miles.[9] The city had grown so swiftly that land-use planning and transport infrastructure could not be adequately matched to the growth. Gargantuan problems of traffic congestion, serious air pollution, and housing shortages gripped the city in the 1970s and 1980s. The devastating earthquake of 1985 only added to the infrastructure and planning problems of one of the fastest-growing and largest cities in the world.

Anarchic growth and oversaturated transport arteries are major contributors to the urban quality-of-life crisis and to the declining quality and functional relevance of public space. Mass transit systems are heavily used during rush hours, making intra-urban travel extremely difficult and time-consuming. Automobile usage has rocketed upward despite the traffic jams and lack of parking space. It is estimated that in 1950 there were 41 inhabitants per vehicle in Mexico City, while in 1990 there were 2.7 inhabitants per vehicle.[10] Today there are some 3 million vehicles operating in the city, and 22.5 million person-trips made each day. With more people in cars, and with the gridlock, pollution, and a deteriorating quality of life, the use of public space is declining. A recent survey of Mexico City residents showed that people prefer to spend their leisure time at home, rather than venturing out to use public facilities.[11] On weekends a majority of residents either stay home or leave the city entirely. They speak of a hostile Mexico City in which it is hard to get around, and where the environment is polluted and unsafe. Surveyed respondents showed a preference for staying out of public space during their leisure hours. People who are on the

*Streets and other public spaces in and around the historic district's Zócalo in Mexico City are saturated with people and markets.*

streets are increasingly there for functional reasons—for shopping, getting to work, or meeting business colleagues. Meanwhile, Mexico City leaders are pushing to move their city into the era of global culture with electronic and telecommunications linkages. This will only serve to further widen the gap between residents and public space, creating what has been called a "city without a map."[12]

The problem of Mexican historic urban cores is neither unique to Latin America nor to cities in general. Much has been written about the general problem of inner-city decline in western cities of Europe and North America (United States and Canada), the clearing of slums, suburbanization, and the general decentralization of the metropolis.[13] In North America attention has been devoted to the gentrification and revitalization of the inner city over the last three decades.[14] This return to the inner city has been driven by profit-seeking actors (developers, realtors, banks, etc.) and by the shifting cultural tastes of certain urban social classes, who suddenly rediscovered the use value of living near the city center.

It has been argued that in Latin America the experience of downtown as in Europe and the United States has not been replicated.[15] There are a number of reasons for this. First, Latin American cities did not experience the same massive scale of upper-income suburban decentralization. In fact, the periphery of Latin American cities has been dominated by poor squatter communities. Second, while population loss has occurred in Latin American inner cities, it has not been as dramatic as in the United States. And also, Latin American cities have not experienced the large-scale gentrification that emerged in Europe and North America. In Latin America cities have been weakened financially by national economic crises, while local governments have been hard-pressed to find sources of revenue to revitalize the inner city. This "stalled gentrification" is seen as being driven by three factors: the weakness of urban planning in political cultures that tend to be very centralized, the failure of the private sector to be a leading actor, and the loss of confidence in the downtown among the elite social classes.[16] Part of the problem may also lie in the increasingly complex political competition being waged over the future of Latin American downtowns. In another city recognized by UNESCO, Puebla, there has been an intense and well-documented battle between street vendors, merchants, and the government over the future of downtown. This fight shows the lengths to which all of these groups will go to manipulate the use and regulation of public space in the city center.[17]

### MODERNIZATION, PUBLIC SPACE, AND HISTORIC QUERÉTARO

Public space has played a critical role in the evolution of contemporary Querétaro's historic downtown, particularly in anchoring the revitalization of a district that was economically distressed only two decades ago. Historically, the downtown suffered its most severe setback when many buildings and spaces were destroyed or severely damaged in the mid-nineteenth-century War of the Reformation, and during periods of instability associated with the foreign governance by Austrian Duke Maximilian. Following this unstable era, the new independent Mexican government decided to confiscate church properties in cities and either demolish or recycle them to secular use. In Querétaro dozens of cloisters, convents, monasteries, gardens, and even churches were demolished or transformed for other uses in the late nineteenth century. This led to the overall densification of the downtown, as more activities filled in the previously undeveloped church gardens, patios, or cloister spaces. At the same time, many of these spaces were converted back into "modern" public spaces—gardens, squares, and promenades.

From 1900 to 1950 Querétaro retained its colonial scale, and the historic center did not change dramatically. However, in the 1950s and 1960s the industrial boom in Querétaro led to a period of dramatic urban growth; the city's population expanded from 60,000 to nearly 1 million in the next four decades. This massive growth triggered a period of spatial decentralization, with industry relocating to the north of the city and residential suburbs spreading out in all directions across the surrounding rough topography of canyons and hills.

This massive growth, the exodus of capital and people to the suburbs, and the emergence of automobiles posed challenging questions about the future of downtown Querétaro. Mexico did not have a national planning law until the 1983 Law of Human Settlements was passed. Thus, no single system of laws and rules governed the planning and preservation of historic colonial districts, and in other cities in Mexico valuable cultural heritage was destroyed. But Querétaro had the advantage of a strong regional tradition of pride in local history and respect for the past. Some date this cultural attribute to the late-nineteenth-century resentment by Querétaro citizens of the destruction wrought upon their city by the War of Reformation and the subsequent War of Intervention. The failure of the Federal government to offer reparations to the city following these events led to a determination among Querétaro residents to protect their historic patrimony in the future.[18]

Following this logic, local officials organized a revitalization effort in Querétaro's historic center as early as the 1970s. One project focused on removing traffic and creating pedestrian *andadores* (walkways) downtown. During the administration of Governor Camacho Guzman (1979–1985), formal programs for downtown redevelopment were initiated. These efforts set the pattern for subsequent governors of the state. The revitalization programs brought the following diverse interest groups together: the governor; the municipality; the federal agency in charge of historic monuments—INAH (Instituto Nacional de Antropología y Historia); and elite families who owned land, houses, and businesses in downtown. A limited opposition of land speculators or poor people afraid of losing their homes stood against the forces of change, and clearly did not have the power to successfully block revitalization.[19]

Pedestrianization and downtown redevelopment gained considerable momentum during the administration of Mexican president Carlos Salinas (1989–1995). Salinas sought to create national development programs like "Solidaridad" and "100 Cities." Querétaro successfully became a member of the 100 Cities program and was able to procure financial support for a number of development projects, including a traffic recirculation plan to detour heavy vehicles out of the city center, a modern bus terminal, remodeled historic streets, and new mass transit.

Central to the downtown redevelopment model employed in Querétaro was an emphasis on protecting the center city from automobile traffic by reintroducing pedestrian space. To do this, a system of interconnected plazas linked by walkable spaces was created. The two anchoring plazas in this system are the Plaza de Armas and the Jardín Zenea. The Plaza de Armas is a rectangular, Renaissance-style space first laid out in the sixteenth century. It continues to pre-

serve its original form today—two-story colonial buildings, with covered portals on two sides. A three-sided "U-shaped" hedge of laurel trees runs along the interior edge of the plaza, creating a parallel edge to the buildings. This edge is further accentuated by the cutting of arches into the laurel hedge that match the arclike pattern of the portals. To the west the plaza is anchored by the Government Palace; in the center of the plaza are a fountain and statue of Querétaro's historic

*Querétaro's historic core has successfully revived pedestrian-scale public spaces.*

Marquis de Villar, a wealthy city father who aided in the urban development of eighteenth-century Querétaro, including the construction of the aqueduct, a structure that remains today. The most impressive feature of the Plaza de Armas is its aliveness—pedestrian streets flow in at two corners, and it is surrounded by cafés and restaurants. The combination of these two simple urban design features assures that this plaza will remain a vital pedestrian space.

Jardín Zenea sits upon the former atrium of the San Francisco convent; it was created when church properties were liberated in the late nineteenth century. The name "Zenea" is, in fact, the name of the governor—Benito Zenea—whose administration dismantled the atrium, demolished the San Francisco convent gardens, and replaced them with the lush public garden that is loved by Querétaro's citizens. Today it is a colorful plaza, due not only to its flower gardens and trees but to the numerous balloon or toy vendors permitted here by city officials. In the center of the garden is a landmark of nineteenth-century landscape design—the Fountain of Hebe, the Greek goddess of youth, who continually pours water from ancient Greek jugs down into the fountain.

Running directly west, following a one-block interruption, is a continuation of pedestrian promenades arriving at the third major anchor in the downtown system of public space: Plaza Hidalgo. This public plaza also lies on a former religious space—the Santa Clara convent. Plaza Hidalgo is another rectangular space in the French romantic landscape tradition. It is also surrounded by a wall of green, one-story-high laurel bushes, impeccably pruned to proportionately match the buildings. It is further decorated with Baroque lampposts with white globes and a balustrade that cuts the space in two. One of the most traditional cafés in the city, the Café de Los Naranjos (Café of the Oranges), is on one corner; its name refers to the orange trees that previously grew in the gardens of the convent.

As we shall see in the case of Mexico City, Querétaro's downtown redevelopment faces a number of political conflicts: how to plan for tourism development, how to accommodate the demand for space by street vendors, and how to modernize the planning process. Recent gubernatorial administrations in the 1980s and 1990s recognized that Querétaro's downtown, with its rich colonial heritage and human scale, holds enormous economic potential. Nearby cities, especially San Miguel de Allende, have profited dramatically from the globalization of their tourism economy. Up to now Querétaro has kept a low profile in tourism—indeed, it is the 14th-largest metropolis in Mexico, but ranks 32nd in tourism revenue nationally. Downtown Querétaro has very high potential for sustainable economic growth—using historic preservation, properly scaled commercial development, traffic management, and urban design programs that emphasize pedestrianized streets and public plazas. In such an economy, the number of residents living downtown can increase, while the number of local businesses (boutiques, restaurants, hotels, cafés, bookstores, art galleries) could double or triple in number and revenue.[20]

The street vendor problem is national in scope; it has received considerable attention in Mexico City, as I will discuss further on. Every large Mexican city has thousands of street vendors who demand the right to locate in the historic center, the place where the largest number of pedestrian clients circulate. The government must weigh the rights of citizens to engage in informal marketing against the larger public interest in preserving the public safety and accessibility of public spaces for all users. In Querétaro, state and local governments have traditionally been quick to impose restrictions on street vendors and not allow them to build a political power base in the historic center. During the 1980s and 1990s, state government used police and other officials to clear vendors out of the historic center's parks, gardens, plazas and promenades. Formal policies and regulations regarding street vendors were put in place; these included a photo-credential program, identification cards, a negotiating commission, a public fund to finance vendor management projects, and a plan to create alternate sites for vendors—in public markets, for example. This dual approach—enforcement and planning—allowed Querétaro to avoid the confrontational politics that occurred between local officials and street vendors in places like Mexico City and Morelia, cities where it has been much more difficult to remove vendors from the historic center.[21]

The politics of public space tend to reflect the character of national politics—where party affiliation and connections with powerful leaders often overshadow serious consideration of planning and urban design. The recent remodeling of another of Querétaro's important downtown squares, the Plaza de la Constitución, offers a vivid illustration of the new politics of urban Mexico. Plaza de la Constitución was originally built in the 1960s, a typical early-modern design—one story of underground parking, and a treeless, formal public square above. The plaza's lack of shade caused it to fall into disfavor—one resident described its microclimate as "un calor infernal" (an infernal heat).[22] It was dramatically underutilized between 1970 and 1990, leading the city to decide to demolish it. In 1990 a new competition was held for engineering the multistory underground parking structure. In 1995 a second competition was initiated for the design of the plaza above. Plaza design competitions in Mexico are notoriously political—every famous architect wants to put his or her stamp upon a major public plaza. Querétaro was no exception; a number of prominent national figures, including Pedro Ramirez Vasquez,[23] lobbied to be awarded the prized commission. On top of this, local architects who were aligned with the governor of the state lobbied the government to be awarded the design. A lot of pressure was being brought to bear, and the governor felt the heat.

Not until a new administration came to power in the late 1990s did the design competition reach a conclusion. The new Partido de Acción Nacional (or PAN) governor's office suggested a radical solution that shocked many designers: that all of the candidates pool their ideas to create a joint solution as a public service. This meant that no one architect would win the competition; rather, it would be designed by committee. Most of the top designers and other locals quickly began to drop out of the competition. The best two remaining candidates were given the project.[24] This outcome suggests that in a more democratic, open political system, which Mexican politicians publicly aspire to, decisions about inner-city design and public space may begin to be made on the basis of merit, rather than on the basis of a traditional spoils system. This would represent a dramatic change for Mexico.

## GLOBALIZATION AND THE POLITICS OF REDEVELOPMENT IN MEXICO CITY

At the beginning of a new century, Mexico City, the largest metropolis in the Western Hemisphere,[25] faces a historic watershed. Mexico

*Northeast corner of the renovated Plaza de la Constitución, in the heart of Querétaro's historic center.*

City's future hinges upon two intersecting sets of conditions: first, the increasing globalization of the Mexican economy, accelerated by the North American Free Trade Agreement, with Mexico City evolving into the administrative headquarters; and second, the changing political landscape in Mexico, highlighted by democratization and decentralization of political power, the latter forcefully illustrated by the first elected mayor of Mexico City taking office in the fall of 1997, and by the election of Vicente Fox, as president of Mexico in December 2000, the first-ever successful candidate of an alternate party (PAN).

The long-awaited revitalization of Mexico City's historic center is now subject to this same set of new conditions. This section examines the politics of redevelopment and the role of public space in the historic center of Mexico City. Ten years ago, UNESCO designated Mexico's centro histórico as a "Patrimony of the Humanities," based on the fact that it has the largest collection of Spanish colonial era buildings and public spaces in the Americas. Despite this prestigious designation, until recently relatively little has in fact been done to address the future of Mexico City's historic core.

Various development scenarios for the historic center have been proposed. These include 1) its complete preservation as a historic site, with limited access; 2) its redevelopment as a tourism and high-tech commercial center; or 3) its regeneration as a residential zone with supporting services. Obviously, what is needed is a comprehensive economic development and land-use strategy that lays out exactly what mix of these various scenarios will work best. Each scenario implies different outcomes for the various interest groups concerned about changing land uses in the city center. Each also will imply different scenarios for the preservation and use of valuable public spaces in the historic zone.

This discussion must be framed by the recognition that, in every sense, downtown Mexico City is a contested space. The traditional business core encapsulates competing interest groups: residents, street vendors, taxi unions, merchants, the federal government, the Mexico City municipal government, political parties, investors, property owners, politicians, planners, and realtors. The politics of Mexico City's downtown must account for a number of local factors: first, the historic center's utilization by the Mexican state as a symbolic space to legitimize the government; second, transformations implied by foreign investment and NAFTA; and third, the increasing importance of popular political interest groups in determining the outcome of location conflicts in the historic core. These factors set in motion scenarios that are in conflict with each other. For example, if downtown is to

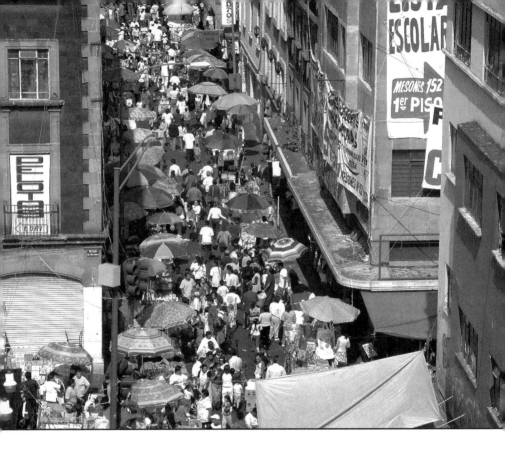

be preserved as a monument to Mexican identity, then transformations in the interests of NAFTA may be compromised. Equally, alterations in the use of land for foreign investment directly conflict with the needs of the popular masses—that is, poor residents, workers, and street vendors.

Mexico City is an ideal laboratory for examining the politics of inner-city land use. As the national capital, the economic and political heartland of the nation, the command center for NAFTA, and the largest metropolis in the Americas, the stakes are indeed high with regard to the future of downtown. NAFTA encapsulates a trend that was at work throughout the 1900s, but that has now reached its greatest magnitude ever: the increasing importance of foreign capital in the transformation of the metropolitan area. Mexico City's destiny, like that of many other "global cities," is firmly tied to the world economy, but especially to the economy of its major trade partners, the United States and Canada. Thus, even the politics of inner-city land use, as we shall see in the discussion below, must contend with both national

*Contested space in Mexico City: street vendors compete for survival in the increasingly congested streets around the inner city.*

and international interests. The future of downtown Mexico City may no longer be solely dependent on the vision of state and/or national actors, but on transnational real estate investment firms contemplating everything from tourism and commercial development ventures to high-tech office development.

Mexico City's downtown must also be understood within the context of the larger issue of metropolitan decentralization, and specifically, the shift of the centers of economic activity and the zones of commercial concentration toward the west and south. The gradual southward and westward exodus of high-income residents (and investment) has slowly moved the "center of gravity" in Mexico City in those directions. There is an ongoing major buildup of commercial, office, and high-tech manufacturing activities along the corridor that runs from the Zona Rosa and Polanco to the new development at Santa Fe. In many ways the "new downtown" can be said to be located somewhere around Polanco. Santa Fe, a high-density commercial, office, manufacturing, and elite residential zone has further exacerbated this shift toward the west. There are also important commercial agglomerations to the south, including those along busy Avenida Insurgentes, heading toward Coyoacán, San Angel, and Universidad Nacional Autónoma de Mexico (UNAM, the National Autonomous University of Mexico).

Where does the above leave the historic center? First, one must recognize that Mexico City's historic district is defined as a space enclosing both "inner" and "outer" cores. These cores are referred to in government plans as "Perimeters A and B," as defined by the Mexican government's 1980 act that identified the historic district.[26] Within these two zones lies a rich complement of historic buildings, plazas, and monuments. The 1980 study by the Special Commission on the Historic Center found 743 landmark buildings, 542 monuments, 67 religious buildings, 78 plazas and gardens, 26 fountains, and 19 cloisters.[27] Cultural patrimony is a driving force in defining the historic center's function and role in the metropolis. Downtown no longer is the primary node of commercial and office activity in the metropolitan region (having been displaced by emerging centers in the south and west, as mentioned), although its symbolic value continues to attract government and private sector office and tertiary activities.

In fact, the symbolic role of downtown is its greatest asset. Symbolism and history have been exploited by the Mexican government since the 1930s and 1940s.[28] The Mexican ruling party (PRI) and its leaders sought to construct a myth of collective memory, whereby the historic center is transformed into a sacred space and symbol of national identity. The most obvious example is the Zócalo, where all of the land-scaping, benches, and other furniture and adornments were removed decades ago to create a ceremonial plaza of the state. The plaza was transformed into a "museumized" space of national identity, used to reinforce the importance of the Mexican government and its political system. The government encouraged the gradual "museumization" of much of the historic center in a similar way: a nearby civic square, the Plaza de Manuel Tolsa, adjacent to the Palacio Nacional de Arte and the Palacio de Minería, has also been "hardened"—cleared of all ven-dors and decoration, save one equestrian statue, thus transforming it into a kind of monument to the state. Nearby is the great Plaza Tlate-lolco, or Plaza de Tres Culturas, managed by the Instituto Nacional de Antropología y Historia (INAH). Tlatelolco is an important icon for the government, since its heritage cuts across the two most impor-tant historic influences: the Aztec, whose ruins underlie the site, and the colonial Spanish, strongly represented by the colonial era church building.

Further complicating the situation facing the historic center are the emerging quality-of-life problems. Mexico City, like many megaci-ties, has experienced a significant decline in quality of life over the last decades.[29] Because the historic center continues to house important government and other office activities, as well as tourism and com-merce, a great deal of traffic passes through and around the center. Furthermore, millions of city dwellers come to the center by taxi, bus, or the underground subway (Metro). The center is increasingly crowded, noisy, and chaotic, not to mention polluted. Older buildings continue to deteriorate, a problem that is obvious when one observes the amount of structural building repairs going on in and around the downtown.

Neighborhoods are badly congested and infrastructure is worn down. There is an emerging pattern of abandonment. Unemployment, underemployment, and subsistence living leave a population of mar-ginal street dwellers, including some 30,000 vendors in Perimeter A, as well as homeless people and criminals. Many buildings are badly main-tained, physically falling apart, or abandoned. There are numerous site planning violations, such as noisy, polluting workshops lodged illegally into the historic zone.[30] A Special Commission produced a diagnostic study that classified the problems of the zone in several categories: 1) housing/commerce, including lack of housing; 2) patrimony/ architec-ture, most notably the deterioration of privately owned historic build-ings; 3) transport, especially increased automobile traffic, lack of park-ing, noise, and poor circulation; 4) urban image, the need to control traffic, pollution, noise, and street vendors, so as to beautify the streets, plazas, gardens, monuments, and so forth.[31] Without steps to improve these elements of downtown, the commercial and economic decline will continue. It will be increasingly difficult to attract investors, particularly if the national economic picture worsens.

## POLITICS AND CONTESTED PUBLIC SPACE

Urban space is rarely neutral or apolitical. In most cities almost any change in the use of existing urban space, or any proposed new use of space, is likely to engender competition among different actors. The term *location conflict,* coined nearly two decades ago in urban geography, captures the essence of negotiation and conflict that often occur among competing interest groups. Most location conflicts involve different actors competing to optimize their advantages and minimize their disadvantages.[32]

Inner-city redevelopment politics do not always adequately represent the interests of workers and lower-income residents. This "popular sector" has recently started to reassert its voice in downtown. For example, in Mexico City, following the devastating earthquake of 1985, some 30,000 people died, 30,000 homes were destroyed, and 60,000 homes were damaged. An estimated 200,000 workers were displaced, and several hundred thousand people were left homeless. The government organized a reconstruction program called the Renovación Habitacional Popular and built some 42,000 new homes. But this still left a wide housing deficit. A tremendous urban solidarity movement was brewing, and it soon took shape in Mexico City, as hundreds of thousands of residents were mobilized. That movement helped create a popular political voice that grew louder as its leaders began to lobby for more housing construction and better representation in government redevelopment plans for the downtown.

Public spaces have been increasingly utilized by the popular sector as a forum for political protest. This was true in Mexico City during the student movements of the 1960s, culminating with the marches to the Zócalo, and with the terrible massacre at Plaza Tlatelolco, a public space in the center of one of the largest public housing complexes in the city. Public space became politicized again in the 1980s, particularly as a national urban social movement began to take hold.[33] In Mexico City popular protest inundated the major plazas and public spaces. For example, in the Zócalo, in the first seven months of 1992, there were 2,412 marches and demonstrations ending up there, an average of 11 per day![34]

The popular sector has become one of the two distinct voices in the politics of Mexico City's downtown. It represents members of the lower- and working-class residential sectors who believe that the downtown space should be liberated for the construction of more housing for the lower and working classes. It opposes government-sponsored efforts to revitalize the downtown solely as a historic core

zone for tourists, where public spaces would be for outsiders rather than residents. The popular sector also opposes "tertiarization" of the downtown—that is, its conversion to a service zone, dominated by commerce, banks, and offices.[35] The Left, which has often aligned itself with the popular sector, has not really crafted a strategy for the downtown zone. As critic and writer Carlos Monsiváis has said, "[T]he left gave the gift of the past (the historic zone) to the right."[36]

On the other side, the private sector offers a different form of opposition to government revitalization. The private sector wants to convert the historic downtown into a privatized international tourism zone.[37] One example of this kind of private-sector ambition is the Plan Alameda, a project that proposes to remove buildings around the Alameda, one of the treasured public spaces in the downtown. The new development would displace residents and install a giant hotel/luxury housing/office and commercial complex. The architecture would all be postmodern, some designed by American architects. Despite protests among residents, designers, historians, and small businesses, the project continues to move forward. It won government support,

*Public space and protest in downtown Mexico City.*

particularly during the Salinas administration, which strongly backed the private sector in these kinds of ventures. The Alameda development continued to evolve during the Ernesto Zedillo administration, although it was slowed by fiscal delays due to a struggling economy. Later, during the Fox administration, development picked up again, with the first major hotel/convention complex completed early in the 2000s.

The popular sector stood in strident opposition to that project. It insists on a plan that would democratize the urban development process and generate a balance between job creation, housing, and environmental protection, while preserving the historic monuments, revitalizing spaces, and creating good land-use plans. The popular sector wants the tenancy of residents to be protected while redevelopment is undertaken. Many residents who already live in public housing tend to take a dim view of historic buildings and public spaces. Their concerns are more immediate—the well-being of their families. Thus, it is not always clear who will defend the patrimony and who will want to modernize it.

The main reason the "quality of life" problem is relevant to the historic center is that a sizable population lives in and around the historic center in such areas as Alameda, Merced, and Tepito. The population of the central city and vicinity was estimated to be around 2.7 million.[38] Recent population data suggest that the innermost *delegaciónes* (districts) around the historic center have a total of 1.02 million inhabitants.[39] Most of these residents tend to be working-class and lower-income city dwellers. As a group they represent a major voice in the contest over downtown spaces. Their objective is to protect the quality of life for residents in the central city, while lobbying for the government to build more affordable housing. As mentioned, residential political power has become an important element in Mexican politics, owing to the rise of urban social movements and popular protest throughout Mexico. Unfortunately, the interests of the popular sector collide with a different vision of the historic center that has been termed "refunctionalization," where the historic center is transformed in the interests of tourism and business, and where the poor are largely excluded.[40]

Meanwhile, other groups also compete for access to the best possible outcome in this arrangement. For example, *ambulantes* (street vendors) have been a volatile political force in the politics of downtown Mexico City. In a society that is unable fully to employ its working-age population, a vast array of informal economies emerge to allow these city dwellers to survive. One important activity, is, of course, street vending. The problem of street vendors in Mexico City dates back to the 1930s when laws were created giving the government the right to regulate street vendors so that they would not interfere with public spaces. In 1967 the government published in the *Diario Oficial* a set of regulations prohibiting and controlling vendors in public streets, where they might obstruct traffic, or interfere with residents' use of the streets, get in the way of ongoing construction, block vehicular circulation, or otherwise disturb the downtown.[41]

Three factors have served to limit the ability of the government in cracking down on the street vendors. First, the traditional political system of "clientelism" often co-opted the vendors and rewarded them for working within the dominant political party, the PRI. Second, the government never officially wanted to take a stance against an obviously popular sector. And finally, the sheer size of this sector—some 25,000 vendors in Mexico City alone—has made it difficult for the government to challenge them.[42] During the late 1990s analysts claimed that some of these 25,000 vendors had become a kind of mafia, which first stole the legitimate goods then resold them on the streets of downtown Mexico City.[43]

Street vendors are not a monolithic group in Mexico City. They comprise three kinds of actors: movable vendors (*ambulantes*), semi-movable sellers (*semiambulantes*), and fixed vendors (such as newspaper stands). Each subgroup takes slightly different positions on the politics of vendors and space. The big challenge for the city planners is where to locate vendors. Logically, the *ambulantes* want to be in the places where the largest flow of pedestrians occurs. And that is precisely where the government planners *don't* want the vendors to be, as the downtown streets are already severely congested, and store owners and businesses are strongly opposed to having competing sellers on the public streets and plazas.[44]

As Mexico City's downtown space becomes more valuable, as I discuss further on, there will be even more pressure from landowners and global businesses to keep the streets free of clutter, and especially, to keep *ambulantes* out. Planners are now looking to downtown public spaces—plazas, gardens, and so forth—as anchors for redevelopment.[45] In this scenario the government would recuperate some 63 civic squares, plazas, and gardens in and around the historic center, physically rehabilitate them, install new facilities (like bathrooms), expand police presence, and promote cultural programs like "Sunday plazas in the historic center," which will bring antique dealers, artists, book fairs, and entertainers to downtown squares.[46] Clearly *ambulantes* in large numbers would not fit into this vision. Instead, planners want to restudy new locations for vendors, to determine what kind of substitute markets can be designed and how product sales can be controlled. But vendors resist this whole notion of their reinvention. Moving takes them away from their main profit locales, and having their merchandise sales controlled means many will not be able to sell illegal or stolen items, a major source of revenue. Thus, there is a serious conflict brewing, and as one senior planning official noted, "We're at an impasse. It's going to end up as a political decision."[47]

Further complicating the street vendor debate is the growing importance of the informal marketing of pirated CDs, DVDs, and computer software on the streets of Mexico City. Globalization means that new technologies are penetrating Third World countries like Mexico. Global media glamorize movies, music, and other forms of entertainment. The high cost of entertainment consumer goods (DVDs, CDs, video games, software) makes these products inaccessible to working-class and poor Mexicans unless they purchase copies sold on the street. The easy availability of computer software copying has made pirating a globally profitable industry.

## PUBLIC SPACE AND REDEVELOPMENT POLITICS: THE ALAMEDA DISTRICT

The Alameda district offers one of the most timely case studies of the politics of public space and processes of location conflict in Mexico City's historic center. The Alameda district is a 64-block neighborhood that lies on the edge of the core of the historic district, directly adjacent to the Palacio de Bellas Artes (Palace of Fine Arts) and the Alameda, one of Mexico City's most treasured public spaces. The district encloses a residential community of about 12,000 population.[48] Within this community lies a mosaic of diverse land uses and subzones, including wholesale and retail marketing, mixed-use medium-density residential with commercial and office space, green spaces and public plazas, and several monuments and historic sites.

At the turn of the century the Alameda district was a fairly prosperous community and attracted Art Nouveau and Art Deco buildings, particularly in and around its most important edge, the Avenida Juárez. By the 1950s and 1960s, this section of Avenida Juárez and surrounding blocks were developed into a commercial/entertainment district with elegant hotels, restaurants, tourism, conventions, and nightlife. Over time wealthy residents moved to more desirable locations in the hills of Chapultepec and Polanco, or in the south. Many properties were rented to tenants with limited incomes. Landlords gradually began to disinvest in the neighborhood, especially when the government imposed a rent freeze in 1946.[49] Things quickly slid downhill through the 1960s and 1970s, a decline that was accelerated by the aforementioned decentralization that continued to move high-status activities away from the center. The 1985 earthquake added momentum to the serious decline of the Alameda district. The earthquake damage was especially heavy here, because the district sits in a low-lying part of the city, where there is a considerable quantity of water in the subsurface, making the land highly unstable.[50] Important buildings were destroyed, residents displaced, and businesses shut down.

As mentioned, the earthquake created an opening for a new spirit of revitalization among residents, community leaders and the government of Mexico City. Between 1989 and 1991 a fideicomiso (trust) was set up by the city government to coordinate various efforts to revitalize the district. As one traces the evolution of the redevelopment controversy associated with the Alameda, the nature of Mexican urban politics clearly emerges—with its various actors, objectives, and competing interests. A useful lesson in the politics of public space and redevelopment thus unfolds.

### 1. Rise of a neighborhood protest movement, 1985–1992

Three years after the earthquake, Carlos Salinas was elected president of Mexico; his administration encouraged a climate of "NAFTA optimism." Some of that optimism would later contribute to the coalition of Mexican and U.S. interest groups focused on redeveloping the Alameda district. The neighborhood clearly suffered a number of problems, apart from the earthquake damage. Long years of neglect by absentee landowners had taken their toll on buildings, many of which were in need of structural repair or overall rehabilitation. There were too many chaotic land-use arrangements and inefficient uses of space. The produce and chicken markets were badly regulated and represented a public health problem. Public gardens were badly maintained. A high percentage of the rental housing units were substandard, and in various stages of deterioration. There was an abundance of street vendors and black market buying and selling, which contributed to the chaos and disorganization of the zone. Vacant spaces with potentially high land values were abandoned or underutilized.[51]

Government officials, along with some urbanists, architects, and other observers were convinced that many of the buildings and sites damaged by the earthquake, particularly those along Avenida Juárez and near the Alameda garden, could be cleared and upgraded for commercial development and tertiary activities. The government also recognized that it needed to do something to revitalize a zone that was so severely damaged by the earthquake. During 1989–1990, the fideicomiso was set up. Vacant land sites along Avenida Juárez were purchased to create a larger development plan, rather than allow the land to be developed lot by lot.[52]

At first the question of the Alameda district's development was limited to closed circles within the government of the Federal District and those architects, developers, and investors interested in the project. Sometime in 1990–1991, a Dallas-based real estate firm called RTKL Consortium, along with a Mexican company, Danhos, proposed to redevelop 11 blocks for office use. The plan was very high-tech and vir-

tually ignored the community's residents. A strong protest was raised by a neighborhood coalition calling itself Asociación de Residentes, Comerciantes y Trabajadores de la Zona Alameda. The organization's main goals were creating more housing in the community, protecting the quality of life in the area, and preventing the destruction of neighborhood historic buildings and monuments.[53]

*Neighborhood activism finds an expression on the walls lining vacant properties in the Alameda district of Mexico City during the 1990s.*

### 2. Neighborhood activism, 1992–1994

The last two years of the Salinas administration marked a period of intense activism within the neighborhood coalition. Detailed studies were carried out by researchers hired by the community and the Federal District government. The community political organization lobbied for recognition by the government. Some observers view this as the peak period of neighborhood power.[54] The movement received a great deal of attention in the press, and it was able to get various government entities to agree on a redevelopment plan that recognized the needs of residents. A number of workshops were set up among consulting planners, designers and government officials. Various urban design guidelines were agreed upon, and the general feeling was that the community's needs were getting greater attention.

But at the same time the Salinas administration was apparently secretly granting permission to some insider developers to go ahead and redevelop lots ahead of the plan's timetable, even if their projects didn't comply with the plan's objectives.[55] Worse still, some of the buildings the Salinas administration apparently allowed to be remodeled, including a Banco de Mexico project, were not in conformance with the new design plan being developed by the Departamento de Distrito Federal's own planning department, through the Alameda trust. There were rumors afloat suggesting that the Salinas family may have had direct interest in real estate in the district.

### 3. Globalization, 1994–1997

This period was ushered in by the entry of a major new global actor onto the scene: Reichmann International. Reichmann, a Canadian-based real estate conglomerate, was, in 1994, one of the wealthiest and most successful transnational urban development operations in the world,[56] whose marquee projects included Canary Wharf (London), the World Financial Center (New York City), and First Canadian Place (Toronto). Reichmann proposed a high-tech, mixed-use development that would concentrate around medium- to high-density corporate and financial office buildings, a luxury hotel, a commercial complex, and tourism/entertainment activities. By the time Reichmann entered the scene, community activists had become much more powerful. When Reichmann and the Alameda trust began to meet with the community, the Reichmann project was forced to scale back some of its plans. Furthermore, it had to make the 11-block development part of a comprehensive community design plan that would include more new housing for moderate-income families; improvement of local parks, streets, and other public spaces; new commercial, health, and education facilities; and rehabilitated historic buildings. Later, other plans were added to the project, including the revitalization of the San Juan market zone and the small Chinatown district.[57]

Ironically, while a great deal of competent design work, planning research, and community participation was taking place, the Mexican government dropped a bomb on all this goodwill. Exactly one day before the end of President Salinas' tenure, a federal decree was issued calling for the immediate implementation in the Alameda district of an urban design plan that dated back to 1991 that favored converting the district into high-tech office buildings and commerce, with no public investment in social-interest housing or neighborhood improvement. In the words of one observer, the Salinas decree essentially "turned back the clock to 1991, ignoring everything that had been done since."[58]

A second irony was, of course, that the moment the Zedillo administration took power, the nation was greeted with an economic crisis, and this essentially shut down any development plans for the Alameda district. Actually, the government crisis ran parallel to a crisis of real estate investment losses at Reichmann International. Meanwhile, some of the community leaders from the original Alameda Asociación had themselves become more powerful in the community, and in the new government. Some leaders were no longer merely members of popular social movements, but had become elected to the Assembly of the Federal District (Diputado del Distrito Federal, or DDF) government. Most prominent in the Alameda was one of the Asociación's original leaders, Susana Quintana, who was now in the DDF Legislative Assembly.

### 4. Shifting political actors, courting international capital, 1997–early 2000s

In August 1997 Cuahtémoc Cardenas became the first elected mayor of Mexico City, representing the left-of-center Partido Revolucionario Democratico (PRD). Prior to the election of Cardenas, Mexico City was referred to as "the President's city," since the president of Mexico appointed the mayor, and thus controlled the entire apparatus that governed and managed the city.[59] With Cardenas' arrival, this would all begin to unravel. As he and his advisers made clear in their campaign publication on Mexico City, the region would become a "city for everyone," a more democratic, sustainable city where government facilitates an equitable distribution of resources.[60] In his campaign literature Cardenas committed the government to the task of revitalizing the historic center, with an emphasis on building more housing for the working class, and improving their quality of life. Just after his election this point was further emphasized by the first major diagnostic study of the historic center.[61]

For the Alameda district the election of Cardenas brought mixed results. On the one hand, a period of uncertainty ended, and a clear signal was given to investors that they could proceed. On the other hand, the old Mexican pattern of "build first, plan later"[62] remained. This was most clearly illustrated by the prospect of two big development projects moving forward: the mixed-use, office/commercial/entertainment complex by Reichmann and a hotel/convention center promoted by the Mexico City–based international development firm Danhos. Further, the appointment by Cardenas of an international trade expert, Lic. Alfredo Gutierrez Kirchener, formerly with PEMEX and the Brookings Institution, seemed to suggest that the Alameda was making an aggressive move toward courting international capital. Kirchener openly admitted he was courting both Reichmann and Danhos, and he even suggested that the Walt Disney Company might be invited in, since, as he put it, "the Disney model for redeveloping 42nd Street in New York City may be the best example for Avenida Juárez in the Alameda. Both are major commercial arteries anchoring theater, hotel and restaurant districts."[63] Signs of change began to adorn Avenida Juárez: the pedestrian space was repaved and widened, new benches were added, and an array of new trees were planted along the popular walkway.

Despite these changes some believe the Cardenas administration did not adequately address the major design problems facing this neighborhood. Given its short, three-year term, the feeling was that Cardenas' group should have started a whole series of catalyst projects that would move toward the goal of improving the neighborhood for the working residents. There was anger over the contention that the design competition for the nearby Zócalo (main square) was a largely cosmetic and symbolic event that, while attracting a great deal of publicity, diverted attention away from the more concrete planning challenges. One observer stated, "We don't need fascist spaces like the Zócalo. A city that is democratic shouldn't have these spaces."[64]

With the election of PAN candidate Vicente Fox to the presidency in December 2000, and the appointment of a new mayor, the Alameda projects passed through yet another stage. The Fox administration's positive signals on promoting development gave most of the investors a green light to proceed with plans. But now a new design and planning team would have to be formed. In the spring of 2001, the Zócalo was in the international spotlight as the Zapatista movement's march across Mexico headed toward its conclusion in the national capital's historic town square. Issues of design and planning were overshadowed by larger concerns about human rights. A year later, the downward spiral of the economy and post–9/11 terrorism and security concerns once again interrupted momentum. Even though a major high-rise hotel/convention center complex was finally completed shortly thereafter, the future of the downtown historic center and its public spaces is still up for grabs.

## GLOBALIZATION OF THE HISTORIC CORE

In the new millennium globalization became one of the major areas of conceptual discourse in urban planning.[65] Yet, studies of globalization's impact on historic downtown zones are scarce. Clearly, Mexico, which once prided itself on defense of its national cultural patrimony through exclusion of foreign capital ventures, has now rocketed into the global age. Mexico City lies at the forefront of this shift. In Mexico City's urbanized region, the thinking has been that global capital tends to invest in the periphery.[66] This is clearly illustrated in the megacomplex of Santa Fe, a satellite large-scale, mixed-use new town on the eastern edge of the urban area. Santa Fe represents the largest concentration of global capital, as well as global technology and design. Many foreign (U.S., Canadian, European) architects and engineers are involved in the construction of Santa Fe. In one of the biggest foreign ventures, a new mixed-use development will be designed by the Los Angeles architect team of Jerde Partnership.

But globalization has also come to the historic core of Mexico City. UNESCO's designation of the historic center as a World Heritage Site provided a crucial form of international legitimation of the historic infrastructure of downtown, and a catalyst for schemes to promote new investment. This began a process of overcoming the negative stereotypes of Mexico City spread by global media. The globalized media coverage in Mexico City focused on negative events: the devastation of the 1985 earthquake; the problems of air pollution in the early 1990s, prior to the signing of NAFTA; and 1990s reports of crime against foreign visitors, particularly in the form of taxicab kidnappings. Mexico City's glamour as a tourism destination had never been particularly high; it was offset by beach destinations or more famous historic sites. UNESCO's designation reminded the world design community that the central core of Mexico City is a treasure trove of historic buildings, streets, patios, and plazas.

Globalization typically involves the movement of international capital toward newly discovered profitable locations. In post-NAFTA North America, Mexico realizes it needs foreign capital to transform the downtown.[67] Foreign capital recognizes the market potential of Mexico City's giant population concentration, as well as its symbolic importance as the trend-setting location for the entire nation. If an international firm wants to market its product, success in Mexico City will provide important leverage for opening markets elsewhere in Mexico. Therefore global capital has been very interested in Mexico City since the early 1990s.

NAFTA opened the way for global hotel chains to fill a huge gap in the city center: the lack of high-end (four- and five-star) hotels. A number of international hotel chains have arrived in Mexico City's historic center. Also arriving have been global restaurants, food vendors, houseware stores, media companies, and other consumer goods outlets. This has unleashed an explosion of globalizing entrepreneurship in the city, with the opening of Internet cafés, advertising companies, real estate operations, marketing, and other global enterprises.

Foremost in the minds of many planners in Mexico City is the need to reconstruct the downtown to facilitate its connection to the world economy. One of the icons of downtown modernization—the Latin American Tower—joined the globalization campaign by planning a *Globalization* major structural rehabilitation. This building is a kind of symbol of *has become* 1960s modernist architecture at its best, and its redesign would make *a ubiquitous* it available to global service industries seeking office space downtown. *force, reaching* It is also a testimony to a form of earthquake-prevention technology *even the* that Mexicans can point to as successful—the tower was undamaged *historic core* by the 1985 disaster. *of Mexico's*

*of Mexico's* Perhaps the most glaring example of the penetration of global capi-
*national* tal itself in the historic center lies in the Alameda district. The attraction
*capital.* of the Alameda was that it was adjacent to the historic quarter, but not

inside the boundaries of the landmark district, where severe restrictions on building height and development would impede large-scale investment. Historic preservation at the core led global capital to the Alameda, where opportunities existed to take advantage of the attractions of the historic center, without paying the huge regulatory costs.

As mentioned, Mayor Cuahtémoc Cárdenas' late-1990s appointment of an international trade expert, with no previous experience in urban development, to head up the major promotional and development agency for the Alameda district suggests the government was committed to using global capital to finance the revitalization of downtown Mexico City. By the early 2000s President Vicente Fox gave no evidence to suggest that this trend would not continue.

Mexico's NAFTA-era embrace of transnational consumer products, especially from the United States, has clear impacts on the quality of downtown. For example, many global corporate consumer chains have arrived in the historic core in the form of "commodified" spaces—from global corporate retail outlets and chain stores (7-11, McDonald's, Wal-Mart, etc.) to shopping malls. One of the most striking forms of commodified space growing throughout Mexico is the tourism enclave. Tourism brings in some $10 billion in foreign revenue a year, making it Mexico's second or third most important "export" activity. The question is: To what extent is Mexico altering its built environment and public spaces to create "other-directed landscapes," places designed for tourists, and not locals?

Examples of commodified tourism spaces abound. In Mexico City the Zona Rosa neighborhood typifies this trend; it has been around for much of the second half of the twentieth century, but the alterations have become more severe since the 1993 signing of the North American Free Trade Agreement. This globalization of Mexico City's built environment should be a red flag for the government to rethink its urban future. The juxtaposition of new technology, global media, transnational investment, and free trade imply a new kind of city building that could disrupt or even destroy the strong neighborhood identity, the dynamic street life and pedestrian scale of much of the central urban core, and the active and convivial public spaces that survived modernization in the 1900s.

### PUBLIC SPACES IN TRANSITION IN THE HISTORIC CENTER

Global investment and redevelopment could bring fast-paced changes to the historic center of Mexico City. Under the pressure of economic expansion, some of the traditional public spaces could either significantly change or even disappear in the early decades of the twenty-first century. This leads to the question: What is the current state of public spaces in Mexico City's historic core? It seems appropriate, on the eve of the inner city's transformation, to revisit some of these spaces, focusing on the history of recent changes and the condition of these public spaces today.

### The Zócalo

The transformation of the Zócalo began with a wave of modernization projects initiated by the Mexican government in the 1950s. These changes would permanently alter the Plaza Mayor. From 1953 to 1958 the government removed all trees, flowers, benches, and other amenities on the plaza, leaving only a vast expanse of unshaded pavement, a gargantuan open space some 415,000 square feet in size. This constitutes the visual form of the plaza today—a giant, monumentally scaled public space, indigenous in its proportions, modernist in its materials. One study terms the plaza "an esplanade denuded of monuments."[68] Not only were trees removed, but so were the trolley line and supporting infrastructure. A Metro station entrance was added on one side in 1969–1970.

Virtually everything on the Zócalo was paved over—as if this might return the plaza to its earliest colonial condition—a military parade ground and arena for large public gatherings. The plaza, returned in a sense to its original royal form, has become a place where the Mexican government can celebrate and promote itself, under the guise of nationalism.[69] National holidays are celebrated here. Each September 16, a half million people gather to hear the President declare Mexico's independence. Such gatherings were vital for most of the twentieth century to a nation where one political party held power, and where such power depended on promotion through nationalist displays.

One would imagine that the new democratic government of Mexico might want to transform the Zócalo as a way of symbolically demonstrating that the political landscape is changing. Indeed, during the late 1990s the Zedillo administration held a design competition to begin such a process. After a great deal of maneuvering, a design team was selected. However, the election of a new president in December 2000 meant a new administration, and by early 2001 the Fox administration had canceled the design commission, and once again the status of the Zócalo was uncertain.

During the 1990s the Mexican government seemed intent on converting the historic zone around the Zócalo into a museum-shrine. This vast, sacred space, once indigenous, at times appears too solemn to be used for any kind of daily functional activities. The scale is too grand; the memories of events that have happened here are so powerful as to make everyday tasks seem beside the point. Yet, though few formal activities take place on the plaza, there are social protests, virtually on a daily basis. The symbolism and the weight of history draw urban dwellers to the plaza. Each afternoon hundreds of people per hour are likely to be found congregating in small groups to chat, or simply to walk across the plaza. The crowds that gather on the streets defining the perimeter of the plaza can easily double or triple the number of users on the space itself.

The Plaza Mayor is intensely alive with people. While its scale seems too large, perhaps that is only true if one is looking for the kind of neighborhood-scale plazas found in smaller towns and cities. This is a plaza for a nation, truly the national public space of the entire country. People seem to want to be near it, simply as a ritual act, much like visiting the Western Wall in Jerusalem or the Forbidden City in Beijing. Indeed, one of the biggest events in recent history, the arrival of the national indigenous solidarity movement leader, the Zapatista Subcomandante Marcos, after his one-month march across the country in the spring of 2001, attracted tens of thousands of Mexicans, and captured the attention of the nation and world for several weeks.

Humanity is, in effect, strongly and permanently tied to the plaza;

*The great Zócalo of Mexico City transcends the neighborhood and even the city; it is a plaza for the nation.*

people walk, chat, or watch the indigenous dancers who are permitted to perform here. Vendors, however, have recently been banned from the zone around the central plaza, making it all the more impressive that people continue to come here as a ritual act.

This is a square that transcends. It humbles the buildings that face it. It manifests the power of place, that force that makes a location more significant than the sum of the buildings around it. The Plaza Mayor is a place of history; its unique character is intensified by its imposing scale. The scale, after all, is part of what gives it power and attracts people to it, just as with Mesoamerican ceremonial cities. This is the power of urban design at its best, when people unconsciously respond to architecture and scale. People are drawn here, and they make their way toward the very center of the giant paved square where a large Mexican flag—red, white, and green—flies on a small pedestal, with the backdrop of the red-hued National Palace signifying national pride and patriotism. Seen from above, there is a harmony in this vast space: the green-and-white taxis flowing around the perimeter of the plaza combine with the red awnings on the National Palace to re-create the colors of Mexico in a flowing symphony of surroundings.

Thus, it is memory and ritual that define the great Zócalo of Mexico City. During the September pilgrimage to hear the president declare the nation's independence, these elements reach their maximum pitch, as in the words of one observer: "[T]here is no greater moment in which the Mexican feels the weight of his nationality, than when he comes to the plaza to participate in this ritual, which is repeated every year with the same gestures, and the same invocation of patriotism on the night of September 16."[70]

Ultimately, the Zócalo screams out for remodeling; indeed, the historic core desperately needs a new design plan that reorganizes the system of public spaces connected to the Plaza Mayor. But, thus far, the Mexican political system has been unable to address this critical urban need. No politician has been able to implement change, even though several design competitions have generated acceptable working design plans. *Sexenios* (six-year presidential terms) have come and gone, but no solution has been reached. Meanwhile, the central core's public spaces are left to the cultural whims of a system that allows open spaces to become contested by various interest groups—from street vendors to political movements seeking a place to protest. There is a kind of lawlessness that ebbs and flows across Mexican public spaces.

### Plaza Santo Domingo

Yet another historic plaza lying in the path of urban redevelopment is the colonial Plaza Santo Domingo, a church and neighborhood space lying adjacent to the convent of the same name. This 65,000-square-foot plaza remains one of the most dynamic public spaces in Mexico City today. The hustle and bustle of the nineteenth century has been partially preserved here. The square gives the impression of a space buffered from the protests, earthquake damage, demolition, and high-tech architecture that is sweeping through other parts of downtown Mexico City. The Portal de los Evangelistas (the portal of the scribes) continues to run the length of the main part of the plaza. Underneath the plaza more than one dozen printer operators produce everything from Christmas cards and calling cards to wedding invitations. At tables alongside, older men with pens, ink, paper, and typewriters wait for clients, whose thoughts they will transpose into love letters or business correspondence. Of course, globalization has penetrated this space, as starkly exhibited by the numerous computer-generated options advertised. The plaza also remains alive with book vendors, shoeshine stands, magazine and newspaper stands.

On a typical weekday afternoon, hundreds of people can be found sitting, or standing, or passing through the plaza, perhaps stopping to chat with a neighbor. Bicyclists make their way across the space, carrying bottles; people sit and eat ice cream or tacos; businessmen stop by to chat in their suits and ties; workers head home for lunch; men have their shoes shined, and street cleaners in orange coveralls sweep the plaza and nearby streets. In front of the Old Customs House, there is a student demonstration and a loudspeaker plays Andean folk music. In the fountain that anchors the center of the plaza is a monument to a woman, Josefa Ortiz de Domínguez, a former mayor (*corregidora*) of Querétaro, and one of the early organizers of the independence movement against Spain, which led to the Proclamation of Independence at Dolores Hidalgo in 1810. Thus, this dynamic plaza celebrates Mexican energy and community and the independence of a nation. Here, the same people come back each day, some to the scribes, others just to meet, and thus spontaneously create a vibrant street life in the center of the downtown of their largest city, just as they did a century ago.

### Alameda

This very large park-plaza (720,000 square feet) has retained much of its original colonial character, a place that inspired artists over several centuries. It is a space liberally sprinkled with wrought iron benches along its pathways, and fountains near both entrances as well as at the center. Inside are also a number of bronze monuments, including one of Beethoven. On one side of the park sits the monument to mid-nineteenth-century president Benito Juárez, the first indigenous president of Mexico. His statue sits at the center of a semicircular marble structure called the Hemiciclio. The Hemiciclio seems out of scale with the rest of the park. Given that it is the only green space in the center of downtown (with the large Chapultepec Park much farther to the west at the end of the Paseo de la Reforma), the Alameda serves an important function as both green space and social meeting place in the city center. During the earthquake of 1985, the Alameda became a campground for thousands of families, mainly from the popular sector, who had been displaced from their homes by the disaster.

For most of the remainder of the decade of the 1980s, and into the 1990s, the poor used makeshift shelters in the Alameda as a form of popular protest over the lack of government programs for provision of adequate housing. This became part of a larger national movement among the popular sector to use public space for the purpose of lobbying and protesting lack of government intervention to solve urban problems among the poor.[71] During holidays, especially Christmas, the Alameda comes alive with vendors of holiday-theme items, food, music, and festivals, in much the same way that the great plazas of Spain come alive for holiday seasons.

As mentioned earlier, the Alameda zone faces the most immediate prospect of dramatic change, as a number of key redevelopment projects—a high-rise hotel, commercial centers, and a convention center—begin to appear along the park's edge on Avenida Juárez. The challenge will be to plan urban development in such a way that it respects the sense of place and pedestrian scale so important to this district.

### The church plazas

Today two museums—the Franz Mayer, an art museum; and the National Museum of Engraving—are located on the Plaza Santa Veracruz. This small space (some 11,250 square feet) lies sunken below the level of pedestrians and passersby, and thus is not a heavily used plaza. As such, it has been preserved as an historic site, a museum space from which to contemplate two good examples of Baroque religious architecture, or across which one can enter one of two well-run museums. The plaza has been renovated and is in relatively good form, with three stone fountains, and 14 stone benches. Only a handful of people, between 5 and 20, can be found here on a typical weekday afternoon; obviously on weekends the churchgoers fill the space.

Nearby lies the Plaza de San Fernando, which in 1967 was widened and remodeled by the government. Today this 40,000-square-foot plaza remains popular, although it has a somewhat run-down quality to it. As a public space the plaza is noticeably weakened by the heavy traffic and noise of the adjacent, highly commercial Hidalgo Avenue. This corridor of noise, gas fumes, and heavy truck and automobile transit runs along the edge of the plaza, making it a far less tranquil public space than, say, the Alameda. However, to the credit of its designers, the plaza has a striking stone pergola with arched entrances, which creates a visual separation between the square and the busy commercial boulevard. This achieves a sense of place within the plaza, despite the nearby noise and commerce. Also, near the entrance an array of shoeshine stands, fruit and flower stands, trinket and souvenir vendors, and a newspaper and magazine kiosk can be found. These activities add vitality to the plaza and create a comfortable transition from busy Hidalgo Avenue to the quiet retreat found further in the interior of the plaza.

Landscape design within the plaza helps in making it more personable: by creating not one large space, but a number of smaller spaces separated by three-foot hedges or wrought iron fences, the plaza retains a sense of intimacy and a human scale. The wrought iron benches, elegant gardens, and stately trees add to this feeling of comfort and sociability. On typical weekday afternoons one finds more than a hundred people sitting, chatting, reading the newspaper, walking with children, or stopping on the way to the office.[72] The plaza has its seedy elements too—unemployed men getting drunk at midday—but they are balanced by the diversity of users and by the good design, which allows one to choose a different subarea of the plaza, if one is put off by less pleasant aspects. While this space may have lost some of its historic flavor to the density of activities around it, it has also retained that flavor by a combination of good landscape design, by the location of dynamic activities that attract users from the neighborhood, and by the more elusive fact that Mexicans simply like to use public spaces if given design incentives to do so.

### Plaza Manuel Tolsa

This small (27,000-square-foot) space lies in one of the most important architectural junctures of the historic downtown. It was created in 1982 by the government to "museumize" the historic center. It lies in front of the neo-Renaissance National Art Museum and across the street from the great neoclassic Palacio de Minería (Palace of Mining), with its dark granite facade and great Doric columns. Across the intersection sits the neo–Italian Renaissance Palacio de Correos (Central Post Office), possibly the most beautiful building in the downtown, and adjacent to that is the Palacio de Bellas Artes (Palace of Fine

Arts), a turn-of-the-century marble neoclassic monument to Mexico's European architectural links.

Thus, in many ways this vacant, paved plaza exists to accentuate the architecture around it. There are no trees or amenities, such as benches. Street vendors today are not allowed in this part of the city, so there are but one or two officially permitted vendors. The plaza is named to honor the Valencian neoclassic sculptor Manuel Tolsa, one of whose greatest works sits in the center of the Plaza: the equestrian bronze statue of King Charles IV, known popularly as "El Caballito." This square is like a mini version of the Zócalo: a space made more monumental by its being empty. The eye is therefore drawn to what is around it, in this case some of the best neoclassic buildings in downtown Mexico City. The plaza's emptiness draws one to the statue as well, and by evoking a feeling of unresolved mystery causes one to want to examine the contents of the surrounding place. Relative to the population density around the plaza, this is a little-used space. On a typical weekday afternoon, only a few people can be found sitting under the statue, and there may be between 75 and 100 people walking past the statue, often without stopping because there is nowhere to sit.

### Plaza Tlatelolco

This is another of Mexico City's monumental "museum" plazas. The Plaza Tlatelolco, or Plaza of Three Cultures, lies 12 kilometers (7.4 miles) north of the downtown Zócalo. It lies on the site of the former Aztec satellite community of Tlatelolco, which, among other things, had one of the largest open air markets in Mesoamerica. The Aztec ruins on the site have been preserved, as well as a colonial church. In the 1940s and 1950s the Mexican government hired well-known architect Mario Pani to build a massive city of public housing projects, using the ideas of the popular modernist architect Le Corbusier. The resulting "machine age" city of cubist tower blocks surrounded the original Plaza de Tlatelolco, creating a sweeping landscape of three layers of Mexican culture: Aztec, Spanish colonial, and modernist, hence the subtitle "Plaza of Three Cultures." This vast open space (more than 100,00 square feet) has become an archaeological site and park under the supervision of the Instituto Nacional de Antropología y Historia (INAH). It has lost its spontaneity as a neighborhood space, but perhaps that is a small price to pay in the interests of preserving this incredible overlap of historical layers of the urban fabric.

The Plaza Tlatelolco anchors what would otherwise be a drab example of the failures of modernist architecture. In 1968 it gathered fame as the site where government troops massacred hundreds of protesters prior to the Olympic Games. It has since become a kind of symbol of popular protest against the government. In 1985 the great earthquake damaged or destroyed about one-fourth of the 104 public housing buildings surrounding Plaza Tlatelolco. Several of Pani's apartment towers were either destroyed by the quake or damaged so severely that they needed to be demolished. Many people died or were injured here. Since 1985 the government has consolidated control over the plaza, making it a historic landmark that is carefully monitored and guarded. It has important symbolism both within the city and nationally, and is a powerful anchor for defining place and community in this part of the city.

### Plaza Garibaldi

At the other end of the spectrum lies the spontaneous, wild, and at times out of control Plaza Garibaldi. Lying only about eight blocks north of the Zócalo in the Lagunilla Market district, this public space is the product of folklore and tourism. It was created early in the twentieth century as a plaza of bars and mariachi singers. Around it were built simple stucco one- and two-story cantinas and restaurants with fake arches and faded pastel colors. The neo-colonial facades look like they belong in a northern Mexican border town. But the Plaza Garibaldi is perhaps typical of Mexico's ability to poke fun at itself through caricature, as its great postrevolutionary muralists—Rivera, Orozco, and Siqueiros—did.

Plaza Garibaldi is a deconstructed caricature of an imagined Mex-

*Plaza Tlatelolco's history as a symbol of popular protest contrasts with the otherwise drab landscape of modernist architecture that surrounds it.*

ico, a Disneyland of seedy bars, strolling mariachi bands with black uniforms and studded trousers, cantinas decorated with serapes, men drinking tequila out of the bottle and singing of lost love. The Plaza Garibaldi does not try to be more than what it is—a place to eat, drink, and hire a strolling mariachi band in an atmosphere of mild debauchery and wild bistros. The cantina dominates, and people come here for the atmosphere, which can be rowdy. On a given weekday late afternoon, drunken men are observed tossing bottles at each other; the crashing of glass on pavement resounds against the melodious mariachi songs. Typically, there might be more than 25 mariachi groups, totaling more than 100 singers (this number may more than double on weekends, or later at night).

In the center stands a large fountain; streams of water shoot up into the air. Statues to the left and right are monuments to former mariachis. Most of the cantinas have exotic or wild Mexican west–sounding names like Las Espuelas (the spurs), Tropicana, El Rincón del Mariachi (corner of the mariachi). This is not a daytime plaza where one goes for a stroll; nor is it a neighborhood-scale public space where people go to meet each other. It lies in the heart of a warehouse district of low-income residents, and according to some, it attracts a lot of criminals. This is a plaza of the night, which some Mexico City residents claim has become more dangerous, and thus is no longer frequented by locals as it was 20 years ago. It tends to mainly attract tourists, who wander here drawn by the myth of the place.

Plaza Garibaldi, for all its theatricality, has created a sense of place through its folklore. It is said, for example, that even an accompanied woman walking through the Plaza Garibaldi at night will have her derriere pinched. Whether this is actually true, it is the kind of thing to which intrepid travelers are drawn.

### THE FUTURE OF PUBLIC SPACES

The future of Mexico City's historic downtown offers a strange mix of political actors and planning issues. There is convincing evidence that the downtown community can build a power base, by organizing a coalition of residents, store owners, street vendors, and area workers. The Alameda example is persuasive. One government official, when asked why no Mexican investors were involved in the Alameda project in 1997, responded by hinting that they were put off by how much power the community has.[73] Other observers corroborated this. It appears that whatever the government chooses to do here will have to be acceptable to the community.

Cultural patrimony cannot be underestimated in the politics of downtown redevelopment in Mexico. Historic preservation appears as a goal in almost every design study and workshop held with community members. Clearly, residents, merchants, and other members of the community view the historic buildings as intrinsic to the neighborhood's value. This is not necessarily always the case among government officials, however. The former director of the Fideicomiso Alameda, when asked about the Art Deco buildings in the neighborhood, opined that "the government is not that concerned about Art Deco, and there aren't very many Art Deco buildings in the zone."[74] This is directly contradicted by most experts, and by on-site analysis, which shows a relatively significant number of Art Deco buildings in the Alameda district. In fact, the Instituto Nacional de Bellas Artes (INBA) is heavily involved in preserving Mexico City's Art Deco structures, including the ones in the Alameda District. More recently, the new director of the Fideicomiso Alameda stated that, after financing, "culture is the key variable that will make Alameda work."[75] This official, in fact, argued that "culture"—in the form of distinct culture zones for theater, dining and culinary arts, and ethnic groups like the Chinese, as well as the zone's history—would go a long way toward making the neighborhood successful for business.

In the realm of formal city planning, there appears to be a serious gap between the making of plans and what actually happens on the ground. It is not always clear that what is carried out in the name of planning is actually taken seriously by government officials at the point of implementation. Several examples from the Alameda case serve to question whether the public sector can be a reliable mediator of the redevelopment process. To begin with, the Salinas administration allowed premature redevelopment along Avenida Juárez, development that violated the design goals of the community, and that occurred within buildings that should not have been reoccupied so soon after the earthquake. Second, the Salinas administration issued an ill-timed decree on the eve of its departure, implementing a development plan that had already been rejected by the Federal District's planning office, and that was not being used by the trust office. This represented a serious betrayal of the planning process and threw into uncertainty all of the planning and negotiation that had taken place before. Third, the current megaprojects—convention center, hotel, and mixed-use commercial/office development—appear to have moved forward without any serious review of their connection to the community-approved plan.

One must therefore question the efficiency of government planning in and around the historic center. Evidence shows that it was the community itself that galvanized efforts to protect the value and ambience of the Alameda zone. Meanwhile, Mexico's national political system is in the midst of its greatest moment of change since the Revolution, change that will seriously redefine all levels of government. On the streets of the Alameda, crime and overcrowding continue to plague the neighborhood, and the destruction wrought by the 1985 earthquake is still evident. Change comes slowly.

Two key factors, globalization and politics, remain critical to any analysis of the planning of redevelopment for the historic core of the Western Hemisphere's largest metropolis. Both are broad, abstract constructs until one brings them to bear upon actual cases. Evidence of globalization abounds today in Mexico City; its high-tech skyscrapers march up the Paseo de la Reforma like soldiers of the twenty-first-century world economy. The high-rises stop short of the landmark historic center, but just barely. Geological limitations and historic preservation may keep the global skyline out of the centro historico.

Meanwhile, the most valuable and traditional public spaces—the Zócalo, the plazas, parks, and promenades—continue to give the city center its sense of history and identity. Yet, these spaces lie firmly in the path of downtown redevelopment. They are in danger of being overwhelmed by the magnitude of growth and change around the downtown. These spaces must be carefully studied, as part of a general plan for preserving pedestrian life in the historic center.

Politically, all eyes remain on the Alameda district, the true epicenter for NAFTA and the transformation of the downtown. Here, too, is where the political contest will be played out among competing actors: street vendors, car owners, investors, criminals, global capitalists, the municipal and national governments. Who will win? Certainly not the old political interests—the one-party system and the centralized bureaucracy. Local government is now firmly in the picture. The good news is that city planning has a better chance to be a significant part of the new politics of downtown Mexico City. The bad news is that it has not yet flexed its muscles.

### THE MANY DIMENSIONS OF PUBLIC SPACE

In studying the dynamics of public space in Mexico, it seems clear that complex factors shape it today. These factors can be summarized as follows:

### 1. Public space and memory

Mexicans have a great affection for their past. This has even been

institutionalized through the phrase "patrimonio cultural," which, until the early 1990s, was a term used by the government to protect historic spaces and buildings as part of the national interest. Public spaces—plazas, gardens, parks, patios, promenades—were considered fundamental to the cultural patrimony, and were protected, as if it was official public policy to connect the physical environment and open space with the well-being of the citizenry. Memory was part of the national obsession with identity, which became embedded in city places, and in the public life played out in these spaces.

## 2. Public space and nature

During the mid-nineteenth-century period of Emperor Maximilian and Duchess Carlota, ideas of European landscape architecture were brought into Mexico—in particular, the notion of transforming the unlandscaped zócalo into a lush garden of trees, grass, and flowers. This "greening" of public space has remained as a central element of Mexican urban design.

*The flag ceremony on the Zócalo is one of many rituals that anchor public spaces in Mexico.*

## 3. Public space and ritual

Being on the plaza, the street, or in the corner store has long been part of the daily ritual of Latino and Mexican culture. Unlike the urban experience of its northern neighbor, the street and the square remain central to daily life for millions of Mexican urban citizens.

### 4. Public space as contested space

One must acknowledge that in Mexican culture, public spaces are, in part, "up for grabs." The political system has tolerated the use of public space for political protest. It has seen interest groups—street vendors, store owners, residents—fighting for control of streets and plazas. The arrival of new global chain establishments (like McDonald's) at the plaza will raise new questions about how much change should occur in public places.

### 5. Public space as manipulated space

It has also been clear that during the twentieth century, the post-revolutionary Mexican government (through the PRI) utilized public spaces as places to manipulate public opinion in favor of the ruling party. Celebrations of national identity were always held in historic public places, and architecture/landscape thus became a vehicle for promoting the PRI agenda of staying in power.

### 6. Public space and art

Mexican culture has produced some of the greatest artists in the world, and many of these are globally recognized "icons"—Frida Kahlo, Diego Rivera, Luis Barragán, Manuel Álvarez Bravo. Art has always been a driving force in Mexican public space design, a quality that distinguishes it from other cultures. For example, the muralism movement is unique to Mexico, and involves embellishing public spaces with monumental works of art.

### 7. Globalization and public space

It would stereotypically be argued that public space in Mexico is altered by the United States, and not vice versa. In fact, the reality may be more complicated. The "Towers of Satellite," a sculptured public space at the entrance to the first 1950s megasuburb of Mexico City, were designed by Mattias Goerritz and Luis Barragán. The artists claim their inspiration came from visiting Manhattan (New York City) and observing its 1950s skyscrapers. The "Torres" were designed as hybrid "towers" that morphed into bright indigenous stone structures. These in turn have inspired artists and architects in their work in the United States, creating a series of cultural feedback loops between Mexico and

its northern neighbor. For example, the main square of downtown Los Angeles, Pershing Square, was redesigned during the 1990s. Its sense of color and celebration and its modernist design have a strong connection to the work of Luis Barragán. The principal architect of Pershing Square's revitalization was, in fact, a Mexican—Ricardo Legorreta, himself a strong disciple of Barragán.

While public space in Mexico City (and other large Mexican cities) is compromised by such globalizing influences as privatization and commodification, to date scholars have not adequately addressed the culturally unique practices that allow Mexican urban public space to retain some of its dynamic qualities. Mexican cities are inherently more walkable than U.S. cities. Mexican urban culture tends to emphasize a pedestrian-scale public life more so than its northern neighbor. Indeed, there are many positive forces at work that may keep public space thriving "south of the border" for years to come. Scholars and policy makers need to pay more attention to this. At the same time, it is critical that Mexicanist scholars also ask hard questions about the future impacts of globalization on Mexico's unique urbanism.

*Artistic expression is a critical part of Mexican public space: "El Caballito" sculpture, Paseo de la Reforma, Mexico City.*

—

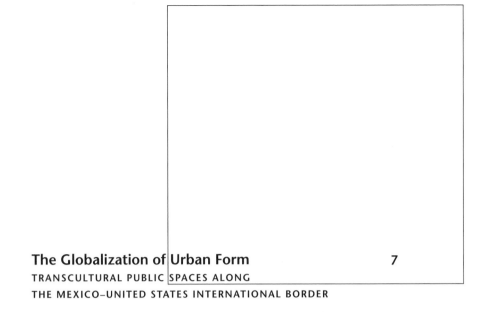

# The Globalization of Urban Form

## TRANSCULTURAL PUBLIC SPACES ALONG
## THE MEXICO–UNITED STATES INTERNATIONAL BORDER

Globalization will significantly alter Mexico's city-building practices in the twenty-first century. The question is: How will global forces reconfigure urban public spaces? In the new century, Mexico's cities will also be partly defined by their interactions with the culture, economy, and built environment of the United States, its all-important global economic partner. As the twentieth century ended Mexico emerged from its century-long era of nationalism and protectionism and began seriously to embrace its northern neighbor. The 1993 signing of the North American Free Trade Agreement (NAFTA) was a tangible and climactic expression of this shift in foreign policy. NAFTA opened the borders to more than investment and economic change; it heightened the neighboring nations' exposure to each other's mass media and culture. It opened the floodgates for a set of cross-border synergies that will permanently redefine the nature of regions and cities in both countries.

Globalization has been defined as "the growing interdependence of countries resulting from the integration of trade, finance, people, and ideas in one global marketplace."[1] This interdependence, as I have argued in earlier chapters, is so all-encompassing, it is now altering the physical form and social structure of our cities. In the Western Hemisphere, globalization is producing a juxtaposition of U.S. and Mexican urbanism—an overlap in styles and philosophies of city building.

Globalization can permanently alter the distinct traditions of urbanism and public space in each nation, producing new kinds of dynamic hybrid metropolitan forms.

The best laboratory for examining the ways in which globalization brings distinct streams of urbanism together is the region where the two cultures physically meet—the Mexico–United States border zone. Here the economies, social geographies, and distinct cultures overlap in a shared geographic space—the border zone. Here, too, the urban design implications of bicultural globalization are being previewed before a world audience. And here we can observe how those who shape the form and style of urban growth—politicians, investors, developers, builders, realtors, architects, and urban space consumers—increasingly operate in overlapping circuits within the "transfrontier" metropolitan living spaces along the Mexico-U.S. border.

Cities have grown dramatically in this region, especially in the post-1960 period.[2] In the early 2000s a half dozen border cities count a million or more inhabitants, while another dozen have over 300,000 people. This is one of the more rapidly urbanizing regions in the Western Hemisphere. It is also probably the fastest-growing international border region in the world.

Mexico's northern border zone lies more than 1,000 miles from the traditional heartland of the nation, the basin of Mexico City. To reach the borderlands from the capital an arduous journey must be made—across the chain of the Sierra Madre and through the fierce Chihuahuan and Sonoran deserts. But the connection between central Mexico and the north has not been inhibited solely by geography; it has also been held back by time. After the arrival of the Spanish colonists, it took nearly 400 years for the region to begin to integrate its northern territories into the center. During that time, Mexico lost large tracts of those territories through the Mexican-American War with the United States. That war led to the drawing of a new boundary in the middle of the nineteenth century, and the creation of the Mexico-U.S. frontier region.

Nearly 2,000 miles span the distance from the U.S. national capital (Washington, D.C.) to the "southwest borderlands." For America, incorporating the southwestern edges of the United States into the national political and economic power structure also required more than a century's journey through time. Following the Mexican-American War and the creation of a new boundary in 1848 through the Treaty of Guadalupe Hidalgo, it took more than 100 years for the southwestern United States to transcend historic inertia, and become a significant region within the nation. For decades, the federal government neglected the needs of the southwestern states; only a constellation of shifts in national politics combined with changing technology and new economic restructuring in the decades after 1960 allowed the once marginal Southwest to become more significant within the continental United States.

This chapter contrasts the urbanism of northern Mexico and the southwestern United States, with special attention to northern Baja California (Tijuana) and Southern California (San Diego). These comparisons serve as a prelude to exploring the globalization of Mexican-U.S. public space. Mexican urbanism embodies a distinct set of traditions and social values regarding the use of public space. Divergent forces shaped cities and public spaces on each side of the border. Yet, globalization has softened the boundary's shelter functions over time, leading to stark shifts in the form and functioning of urban spaces in the border region. The U.S.-Mexico border zone is becoming a testing ground in the shaping of a transcultural city; spaces are being gradually transformed into new hybrid forms that reflect the processes of global integration and the socioarchitectural and economic fusion of neighboring urban cultures.

## NORTHERN MEXICO

Isolated from mainstream Mexican culture by distance, the cities of the northern border region evolved under unique circumstances. Northern Mexico remained a marginal territory during most of the 300-year Spanish colonial rule (c. 1500–1800). The Spanish royal family concentrated on the collection of wealth in the mining regions of the Sierra Madre chain, and in the fertile agricultural basins of central Mexico. The arid northern borderlands were relatively sparsely explored and settled.

All of this began to change in the second half of the nineteenth century. The coming of steel rails and steam power technology opened up northern Mexico via a system of railroad linkages that connected the nation's center with emerging settlements in the north. During the American Civil War, towns like Matamoros, Monterrey, and Tampico were connected to the American South through an emerging transshipment network for delivery of goods and supplies across the border. This induced a robust entrepreneurial spirit in northern Mexico, along with a consciousness of the regional benefits of commerce with the United States. By the 1880s, America had entered a period of economic boom, and the new Mexican president, Porfirio Díaz, organized the first large-scale national effort to court foreign investment in

Mexico, and to open up the country to foreign trade. Northern Mexico benefited directly from these new policies. Thus began a new era of Mexico-U.S. regional economic relations.

Northern Mexico also experienced significant economic development for the first time in this period, as new technologies in irrigation created centers of agricultural wealth in the north, in cities like Chihuahua, Hermosillo, and Matamoros. By the early twentieth century commercial agriculture began to prosper, particularly in the northern and western states of Sonora, Sinaloa, and Baja California. Along the border itself, the government sought to create competitive advantages for border-town trade, by officially sponsoring free trade zones, where import duties would be eliminated within 12 miles of the international border. The first zonas libres (free zones) were created in the 1890s, although vigorously challenged by merchants on the U.S. side of the border. Some free zones, under political pressure, were withdrawn at the turn of the century.

But by the second and third decades of the twentieth century, the economy of Mexican border towns received an enormous boost with the emergence of a new economic sector—tourism. Before 1920 conservative religious groups forced racetrack and gambling interests out of the southwestern U.S. region; investors began to look at Mexico as a source of recreational tourism. When the U.S. Congress declared the prohibition of alcohol in 1919, the tourism economy of Mexican border towns was elevated to what some historians would later call their golden age. From 1920 until the early 1930s, gambling, drinking, prostitution, and the building of hotel spas and restaurants generated a huge multiplier effect that expanded the population and economy of the border towns. The Great Depression slowed down growth for a short time, but soon migrant workers were streaming toward the United States in the 1940s, under the binational Bracero program, which brought hundreds of thousands of Mexican workers to the U.S. agricultural sector. The border towns that served as conduits for these migrant streams received economic benefits, as all transit cities do.

Following the end of World War II, the economic boom in the United States once again sparked growth in the commercial sector along Mexico's northern border. By the 1960s the Mexican government was seeking to strengthen its northern border-town economies through the National Frontier Program (PRONAF), which would shore up the infrastructure and promote the image of border towns to attract investment and tourism. In the 1970s another colossal economic opportunity for border cities materialized in the form of foreign investments in assembly plants, or maquiladoras, providing huge revenues to northern

Mexico in the form of wages, rents on manufacturing space, and the growth of companion service industries to the assembly operations. By the early 2000s the maquiladora industry was bringing an estimated $6–8 billion annually to the Mexican economy and employing half a million workers, mainly along the border. More recently, the northern border region has seen a boom in land investment, tourism projects, local manufacturing, and agricultural development. The region has become one of Mexico's most productive. Its cities are among the fastest growing: several exceed 1 million inhabitants (Tijuana, Ciudad Juárez, Mexicali), and a host of others count more than 100,000 residents (Nogales, Matamoros, Nuevo Laredo, Tecate).

While border towns in Mexico can be discussed as a group sharing many common attributes due to geography and history, there are distinctions among them too.[3] One thing seems clear: Mexican border cities share a common morphology—which includes a traditional urban historic downtown (typically adjacent or very close to the international boundary line) that includes the tourism district, a modern suburbanizing periphery served by a highway system, and a peripheral industrial enclave where the maquiladoras are concentrated.

Mexican border cities have boomed since the 1960s; their expansion has been shaped both by traditional Mexican urban design influences as well as by those of the United States. Consider perhaps the largest city on the Mexican side of the border, Tijuana. To understand Tijuana's changing form, or the nature of its public spaces, one must sort out the varying and often conflicting impacts two different cultures—Mexican and Anglo-American—have had on this region.

Like other towns on Mexico's northern edge, Tijuana languished as a small, insignificant settlement, a cattle ranching village, well into the nineteenth century. Its birth as a town can be traced to the 1880s when, during the Southern California land boom, two wealthy Mexican families hired an engineer, Ricardo Orozco, to create the first urban plan. Orozco had worked for a California real estate company, and was clearly influenced by the U.S. design profession. So, it is not surprising that his 1889 plan of Tijuana combined the radial street designs in vogue in the rapidly growing western United States, or in Washington, D.C., with the traditional Mexican gridiron plan. The resulting hybrid urban design included one large central plaza and four smaller ones. The tradition of the Mexican "plaza mayor" was projected to continue along the northern border.

But Tijuana did not follow the urban design path of traditional Mexican cities. During the first three decades of its growth, it became clear that the 1889 plan, anchored by five central plazas, would not conform with the emerging commercial character of the city. By 1921 Tijuana had become a robust center of trade and tourism services oriented toward the Southern California market just north of the border. These influences caused the settlement to reconfigure itself. Commercial uses began to cluster in the northeastern corner of town, near the international border crossing, rather than around the main plaza that had been designated in the original plan. Radial streets leading out of town fell into disuse. So did the plazas.

The city's physical form favored both a compact geometry, which allowed the provision of tourism services in a concentrated, accessible space, and the formation of commercial ribbons—arteries that facilitated travel back and forth across the border. During the 1920s, Prohibition in the United States further accelerated Tijuana's evolution into a commercial center, by adding new cross-border attractions: gambling, bars, cabarets, etc. In the Tijuana of the Roaring Twenties, traditional Mexican public spaces were quickly forgotten, as the em-

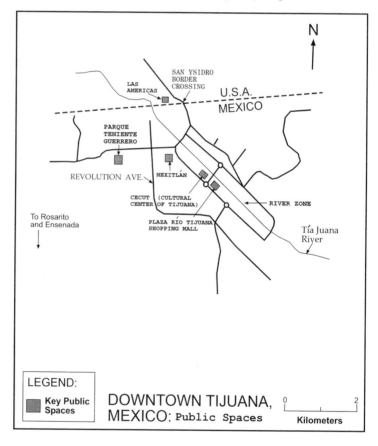

*Tijuana, Mexico: Public spaces.*

phasis shifted to the service economy and tourist circulation. Revolution Avenue, lined with wooden cantinas and dancing halls, became the functional center of town. The avenue originally connected two of Orozco's public plazas from the 1889 design plan. But now the plazas were disappearing and only one public space—a park called Plaza Teniente Guerrero, to the west of the downtown area—would survive the fervent tourism boom of the 1920s.

## CHANGING PUBLIC SPACE IN TIJUANA AND
## BAJA CALIFORNIA IN THE CONTEMPORARY ERA

Between 1950 and 2000 Tijuana was among the fastest-growing cities in the Americas, its population increasing from 65,364 in 1950 to nearly 1.5 million in 2000.[4] The expansion, mainly fueled by migration from within Mexico, placed enormous strains on the physical form of the city. By the 2000s spontaneous growth continued to produce a very spatially decentralized metropolis. Within this increasingly amorphous geometry, the city's physical form continued to favor the commercial economy, linked with the United States. Greater automobile ownership in the post-1950 era meant that Tijuana increasingly became a city oriented along radial commercial boulevards, or peripheral highways. Traditional urban spaces will find it difficult to survive in the twenty-first century.

### Old downtown plazas and parks

The main plazas or zócalos in Mexican border towns tend to have a number of common elements: they are often, but not always, adjacent to the port of entry; they are called parques; they tend to be rectangular and cover a complete city block; they are usually adorned with a gazebo, benches, fountains, monuments, and statues. Most of them are landscapes in a "plaza-garden" style, thus typifying the design developed during the mid-nineteenth century during the brief presence of the Emperor Maximilian. The plaza-garden grew out of the French and Italian romantic design approach that favored carefully landscaped city parks to symbolize humanity's ability to tame nature and create a new urban order.[5]

In downtown Tijuana the Parque Teniente Guerrero emerged near one of the original secondary plazas from the 1889 urban plan. It was set in a space that matched the traditional morphology of the colonial era—rectangular streets, interspersed with plazas.[6] The park was expanded to cover an entire city block early in the twentieth century; its radial pedestrian paths lead into a central square within the park mirroring the macro design of the larger town in its original urban plan. Today it stands as Tijuana's throwback to the colonial zócalos that grace Mexico's older cities. Its tall trees are formal, painted white on the bottom portion. A large kiosk in the center serves as a bandstand, and is surrounded by wrought iron benches in a circular space. Tree-lined promenades run along the edge of the plaza; a small library anchor's one end, a children's playground the other. Ornamental features include black iron lampposts, decorative paving, tile steps, and statues. The park's accessibility is enhanced by the traffic lights at each street corner on the four edges of the plaza, which regulate the flow

of autos and facilitate pedestrian crossing. The neoclassic Church of San Francisco across the street acts as a several-story-high landmark giving the plaza greater visibility, and fulfilling the traditional Mexican custom of locating churches on or near plazas. The park is also landscaped in a way that allows users to see the surrounding buildings, thus enhancing the park-community connection. Also, evidence of the cross-border "California connection" can be found in the visual landscape of the neighborhood around the plaza. Here one finds three-story older commercial or residential buildings, many of which were constructed during the 1920s and 1930s period when Mexico embraced "California style" architecture (Mission or Spanish Colonial Revival), the dominant architectural trend in the early twentieth century north of the border.

*Parque Teniente Guerrero is a traditional zócalo in the heart of downtown Tijuana.*

The park no longer serves the larger city, which has grown too large and too spatially decentralized to depend on open space near the old center. Teniente Guerrero remains, however, a well-maintained neighborhood public space, heavily used by residents of the downtown zone. Most impressive are the number and diversity of users: vendors selling ice cream, sweets, drinks, shaved ice, cotton candy, fruit cocktails, tacos, and balloons; elderly residents getting together to chat; married couples walking with children; young couples strolling, businesspeople reviewing paperwork in briefcases. There is a strong sense of community here, a friendly feeling that this is a place to meet neighbors, or just enjoy being in a typical Mexican zócalo. Along the edges of the park one finds predictable Mexican activities, such as an auto body salesman who drums up business by wielding his hammers in front of park users and passersby. Clients can sit in the plaza while he works on their cars. On an active weekday in the early evening, as many as 300 people can be seen gathering here at any one moment. At dusk the plaza comes alive with children on bicycles, young couples, pigeons, shoe-shine stands, and vendors selling elote (corn on the cob). In a city largely devoid of well-designed open spaces, this plaza is a welcome change.

Another more traditional plaza lies some 30 miles away in the center of the border town of Tecate. Tecate is mostly known as the place where the Mexican beer of the same name is produced at the Cuahtémoc Brewery. But it has expanded into a significant small-scale manufacturing center, as well as the location of a well-known health spa (Rancho La Puerta) for affluent foreigners. Its population is near 80,000, although the official census claims it is lower. Not historically seen as a tourist center, Tecate has a much more traditional ambience; it is not a loud and commercial Americanized border town. Here one finds such small town behavior as men walking with loudspeakers advertising their wares. In the center of town lies one of the most traditional Mexican zócalos along the entire 2,000-mile border, the Lázaro Cárdenas Park, typical of the shady, tree-lined plazas that became popular in late-nineteenth- and early-twentieth-century Mexico. Because the scale of Tecate is small, traffic is limited, and thus pedestrian access to the plaza is excellent.

Inside the main Tecate plaza stands a kiosk with four pathways leading into it. There are abundant trees for shade, rose bushes, and green iron benches. A statue of one of Mexico's greatest presidents, Lázaro Cardenas, anchors one side. There is also the ubiquitous plaza fountain. Around the space are taxi stands, shoe-shine boys, and vendors selling cotton candy or ice cream. City hall and the tourism office are located on the plaza. Most of the surrounding buildings are commercial, small in scale, and one to two stories tall; some have red brick arches, wrought iron bars, and Spanish tile on slanting roofs. On a normal weekend day as many as 100 people can be found at any given time on the plaza sitting, eating, reading, or chatting. On weekends a crafts market brings hundreds more to the plaza.

In most larger Mexican border towns, the plaza does not dominate the life of the city. Even in a smaller city like Tecate, the plaza is not the sole attraction. It has been pointed out that "[a]s a tree-shaded, flower-graced urban oasis, it [the plaza] is a complement to, and separate from, el centro."[7] So the plaza is not the dominant element in border-town urban core areas. This is especially true in Tijuana.

### Enter the new "plazas"

In most of Mexico's border cities, post-1960 development and urban form have followed the path of the automobile, the highway, the suburban-style residence, and the great twentieth-century public gathering mecca—the shopping mall. Ironically, the current Mexican word for shopping mall, plaza, is derived from the earlier term for town square, plaza mayor. Of course, the two places could not be more different. The traditional plaza was the outdoor living room of the town, a place of discourse, serendipity, and free access to all. The shopping plazas are privately owned, rigidly controlled, and frequently indoor spaces.

Indeed, most of the inland border cities, located in the semi-arid desert, have built large-scale, indoor air-conditioned malls. In Mexicali, the capital of the state of Baja California, the largest mall is called the Plaza Cachanilla, which from the outside appears to be a cheerful, postmodern, playful design, near the city's new downtown Civic Center. Its interior consists of two major public areas—one a food court; the other an open plaza used for public events, art shows, and other civic activities. Cascaded around the two public areas are a series of rectangular walkways lined with stores. This popular plaza mirrors the designs of malls north of the border. It has therefore been fairly successful in attracting customers, although the proximity of less expensive "big box" stores just north of the border in Calexico and El Centro, California, compromise some of the mall's selling potential.

In Tijuana the largest and most visited urban commercial node is a private outdoor shopping mall called Plaza Rio Tijuana, completed in 1982. Built along the lines of a modernist Southern California regional shopping mall, it is anchored by three large department stores (two of which are Mexican companies, the other being a Sears), a multiplex movie theater, restaurants, and an array of smaller shops that sell everything from designer clothing, books, and records to shoes, athletic equipment, and pastries. The design of the mall allows mostly middle- and upper-class shoppers, who arrive mainly by car, to actively utilize open-air public spaces within the shopping center. These spaces consist of sunken plazas. The plants, shrubs, and flowers are neatly cut and well kept. There are fountains and shade trees. The spaces are carefully maintained and tend to be heavily used for casual eating, with food supplied by numerous concessions.

It should be noted that Plaza Rio Tijuana's tremendous success

may have less to do with its design, than with the fact that it offers the kind of stores and quality of goods that Mexican consumers learned to prefer from their shopping experiences in the United States. Nevertheless, this is a highly sociable space, where people engage in window shopping and purchasing, as well as sitting, talking, haggling with numerous merchants who own small carts that line the walkway and sell candy, T-shirts, and other "hook items." Occasionally, musicians wander through the outdoor mall, but there is always plenty of music emanating from the music stores with their outdoor speakers. Approximately 85 percent of the shoppers are Mexican.

In the United States, over the last decade, shopping mall development has experienced a dramatic restructuring. Malls have had to reinvent themselves to keep customers. A competitive atmosphere between

*Commerce permeates the landscape of Mexican border cities.*

regional malls has led to massive reconstruction and mall revitalization, with malls building newer, larger multiplex movie theaters, restaurant complexes, playgrounds, community centers, fitness facilities, and other amenities in order to make the mall the true community gathering place of the city.

Globalization is causing this investment tactic to shift south of the border. Developers tried building specialized shopping malls in Tijuana with mixed results. One example, Plaza Fiesta, was completed in 1986 in the heavily traveled River Zone, a linear wedge of office buildings and shopping centers with high speed traffic corridors running through it. Plaza Fiesta's designers sought to re-create the ambience of a colonial town in a space dominated by outdoor cafés and restaurants. Some say they tried to resurrect the feeling of Guanajuato, Mexico, one of the country's greatest colonial cities. The buildings are of white stucco, with pseudo-arcaded facades and second-floor balconies with iron railings and lanterns. The public areas have fake kiosks and fountains. There is very little public seating provided; users of these spaces are primarily those who sit at costly outdoor cafés or restaurants.

The designers of this commercial center envisioned a lively ambience; they placed brightly colored awnings and umbrellas in front of the many restaurants serving international cuisine—Greek, Italian, French, and Yugoslavian. The center offers live entertainment in the evenings. But it has become a largely underutilized, claustrophobic, and not very public place. It is cut off from the rest of the city by boulevards with heavy automobile traffic surrounding it. It is a commercial island filled with provocative colonial signage that fosters neither a sense of place nor a feeling of community.

### Politics, public art, and ceremonial public space

Modernist architects in Mexico have sought to adorn the contemporary urban landscape with ritual public squares constructed with the most advanced materials and architectural techniques, but in a style and scale that brings to mind the Mesoamerican plaza of precolonial times. Examples of these grand modernist spaces in Mexico City include the Plaza of Three Cultures at Tlatelolco, the INFONAVIT (National Workers' Housing Institute) building plaza, and the Anthropology Museum central patio. In Mexico's third-largest city, Monterrey, the "MacroPlaza" is an example of a modern public space built at a grand indigenous scale, but surrounded by modernist buildings.

The most salient example of this kind of avant-garde ceremonial public space in Tijuana is found in the River Zone—at the outdoor plaza of the landmark CECUT Cultural Center (Centro Cultural de Tijuana) building, the cultural museum complex designed in 1982 by the nationally known architect Pedro Ramirez Vazquez and local designer Manuel Rosen. The designers believed the museum would be more exciting if it included a usable outdoor space: "We created a great plaza, so you could feel the openness, which is something we inherited from our pre-Columbian ancestors, and from the Spanish."[8] The plaza they created has touches of the indigenous ceremonial plaza, empowered by the massive concrete walls of the museum and a globe-shaped amphitheater. The space is generously used by pedes-

trians, schoolchildren, and museum visitors. While there are no actual chairs, ledges along the building provide ample space to sit. Taxis make stops nearby, while vendors sell tacos, hot dogs, sandwiches, ice cream, and juices. Unfortunately, the center is mainly utilized as a function of the presence of the museum, and of its numerous scheduled events. It does not generate spontaneous pedestrian use, partly because access for people on foot is made difficult by the major thoroughfares running along three sides. It lies in the city's River Zone.

The plaza at Tijuana's Cultural Center (CECUT) is an avant-garde ceremonial space that fuses modernist and indigenous design principles.

In the fall of 1997, during an international art festival called INSite 97, one artist created a temporary exhibition entitled "Century 21" (Siglo XXI). The artist cleverly located the performance sculpture on the plaza of the CECUT building. The sculpture consisted of a re-creation of an actual shanty residence, built of corrugated metal, wood and cardboard. It was surrounded by discarded oil cans, drums once used to store toxic chemicals used in the maquiladora factories. The irony and symbolism of the exhibit were quite powerful—"Century 21" is also the name of a global real estate corporation that personifies private land investment in Baja. The exhibit was actually a spoof—it created a fictional real estate project in which all the shanties were being marketed by a developer, much like actual subdivision housing. The exhibit challenged viewers to understand that even poor people deserve to live in an organized, legitimate housing complex. The use of the name of a U.S.-based real estate company also implied that U.S. and global capital ought to get involved in helping Mexico with its housing crisis.

On-site documents at the exhibit recorded a wave of outrage by many Mexican visitors with this public art project. They wondered why anyone would want to "invade" the sanctum of a museum. One Saturday evening, shortly after the exhibit had opened, elegantly dressed couples were arriving for the Ballet Folklórico performance—the men in French-cut suits and Italian leather shoes, the women wearing European perfumes and expensive jewelry. Apparently, many of the attendees were shocked to see what appeared to be a makeshift squatter house on the CECUT esplanade. They may have thought poor immigrants who normally lived in irregular settlements far outside the city, often on land they illegally occupied, were now invading the city's Cultural Center. When they later discovered it was a piece of performance art, they, too, were outraged, believing the gesture to be inappropriate to the setting. Yet, because the CECUT location is symbolic of the new Mexico, it was precisely the strategy of the artist to express these confrontational sentiments on a public space that is perhaps the most visible and visited public place in the region.

### Commercial streets and promenades

In downtown Tijuana Avenida Revolución (Revolution Avenue) is the quintessential hybrid border "main street," a popular, if somewhat mythologized pedestrian space. It is heavily used by tourists, shoppers, service-economy employees, street vendors, Mexican teenagers, and nearby elderly residents. It became a much more pleasant and vibrant public space after the government remodeled it in the early 1980s, mainly to enhance tourist appeal. The remodeling was effective; the original flavor of its playful buildings was left intact. Sidewalks and the street itself were widened, iron benches installed, trees planted, colorful flags hung, special bus stops built; some buildings were modernized, their facades repainted in bright pastel shades, while a few new glass box–style banks and office buildings were constructed.

There is nothing pretentious about Revolution Street; it is first and foremost a tourist space. Its curio shops sell leather, jewelry, knives, blankets, and cigarettes. It has bars, discos, restaurants, and nude dancing revues. Taxi drivers wait at every other street corner; also present are hot dog vendors, photographers with striped donkey carts, and "greeters" in front of each bar trying to coax people in. Buildings speak of an impending carnival: large signs in English read "Margaritaville"; an actual-size yellow school bus is appended to the second floor of a bar; balloons are everywhere.

The scale of the street is intimate enough to make the pedestrian feel stimulated, yet ample enough for people not to feel claustrophobic. There is traditional Mexican music alongside American rock and roll, the rattling of souvenirs, and the constant chatter of greeters ushering tourists into their clubs. Adjacent to the old Spanish Colonial Revival buildings, or the ticky-tack facades, one finds the emerging icons of globalization: Jack in the Box, Carl's Jr., the Hard Rock Cafe. Revolution Avenue has always been a bubble of American culture. In the age of NAFTA the bubble is expanding.

A similar atmosphere is found in downtown Mexicali, Tecate, Ensenada, and other border towns. Most border towns have a main street corridor that runs through the older part of the city and continues to be a magnet for tourists and border visitors. In many Mexican

*Tijuana's Revolution Avenue is a metaphor for globalization along the border: discotheques, fast food, all the trappings of American culture.*

border towns these spaces have experienced enormous physical deterioration, to the point where they are no longer viable to the tourism economy. Mexicali is a good example. Its old downtown commercial streets lie adjacent to the boundary line at Calexico. On both sides of the border, streets lined with portals define the geography of commerce. Yet, on both sides of the boundary the portals are run-down, buildings are severely blighted, and for the most part, the commercial activities are poorly maintained. Few tourists will venture into these areas on a regular basis, and since most of the stores are unspectacular, this sustains a vicious cycle of disinvestment and economic decline of the streetscapes. These commercial main streets are desperately in need of some form of revitalization, or they will continue to fall into disarray, and ultimately be abandoned.

One big project most municipal governments are taking on is redevelopment of the old commercial centers through public space improvements. Tijuana is an excellent example. It is the most visited border city in North America. With so many Americans walking across the border, the Mexican government has realized that it needs to better channel this traffic to tourism destinations. Ambitious public space redevelopment strategies are being discussed with the goal of better accommodating the flow of consumers in the NAFTA era. For example, one might envision a complete overhaul of the old Zona Norte red-light district, and its conversion into a kind of New Orleans French Quarter district. Better direct access to the zone, via a pedestrian access bridge built to connect visitors from California directly into the heart of downtown Tijuana would be strategic. It would allow visitors to bypass the currently unpleasant concrete channel section of the River Zone.[9]

### The privatization of public space

One of the many side effects of globalization is a shift in the balance between public and private life. A disturbing trend is the attempt to privatize the experience of public encounters. The combined effects of cities defined by automobiles, increasingly decentralized suburban housing construction, and technology (computer, fax, telephone, etc.) diminish face-to-face encounters, and thus encourage the privatization of urban space. Along the Mexico-U.S. border this trend toward privatization of space takes on several forms.

One border prototype lies in what we might term the "new auto-oriented tourism corridor," a postmodern version of the 1950s roadside strip development. The small city of Rosarito, 15 miles south of Tijuana, offers a lesson on the future of the street and the square along the Mexican border. Rosarito is a classic "strip development town"—several miles of restaurants, hotels, and drive-in stores that follow the old, toll freeway along the coast. Not unlike a frontier town, the development falls off quickly as one moves away from the main strip. Rosarito is, in every sense, a highway town, a modern town, a U.S.-oriented tourism corridor. There are no central plazas or pedestrian gathering spaces here. The plazas have been replaced by indoor patios wedged inside of luxury hotels. The main walking spaces lie hidden along the sides of the coastal highway, which is completely dominated by cars, angled parking, and the road itself. The newest additions to the landscape of the coastal highway in Rosarito are postmodern hotels that celebrate the view from the automobile, the prime vehicle from which to experience this space.

A second form of privatized border space is the "global tourism promenade." Part of the NAFTA process in Mexico has been the shift toward privatization of economic sectors that were once controlled by the government: telecommunications, transport, and tourism. Large-scale public infrastructure—parks, promenades, ports, airports—are gradually converted to private enterprise. An excellent example lies in the privatization of the port of Ensenada. Ensenada has long been a key to Baja California's economic development. It is one of the best deepwater ports on the Pacific coast of North America. The highly centralized Mexican political system tended to favor infrastructure in the central regions of the nation; for decades Ensenada's promise as a major port was held back. The decade of the 1990s saw the emergence of Ensenada in an atmosphere of decentralized authority and NAFTA. The Mexican government has been gradually privatizing the operations of the port. The goals are to dredge the harbor; expand shipping, trade, and the tourism economy; and clean up the environment. One piece of this larger plan was the creation and expansion of public spaces along the waterfront. By the early 2000s a network of new promenades had been constructed along the harbor, in tandem with housing, parking garages, and commercial development projects.

### International border crossings as public space

In a globalizing world international border zones can no longer be thought of merely as buffer spaces, defensive edges, or appendages to nations. In a world of emerging free trade zones, common markets, and global exchange, border regions are urbanizing. Nations now understand that border zones can house people, industry, trade infrastructure, and other economic activities. Borders, therefore, can physically become more than "pass through" spaces. They can transcend their previous limitations as mere connectors for the regional economies. Border zones can become destinations in their own right, dynamic urban centers or satellite villages near major population agglomerations. The enormous density of flows of pedestrian visitors and automobiles through border zones offers a ready market for trade and tourism to flourish.

An excellent example is the San Ysidro–Tijuana border crossing, the main gateway between Mexico and the United States in the most heavily populated border metropolis in the world (some 5–6 million people), and the most dynamic NAFTA nexus in North America. The town of San Ysidro, California, has a population of about 20,000 in-

*The San Ysidro–Tijuana border crossing has traditionally been a "pass through" space; but the huge daily flow—of vehicles and pedestrians— offers the possibility for a high-density, pedestrian-scale urban village at the border.*

habitants; about 90 percent are of Mexican origin. The social character of the town ranges from working and middle class to poor; statistically it is one of the poorer subregions of San Diego. Downtown Tijuana, which lies a few hundred yards to the south of the San Ysidro border crossing, houses more than 100,000 inhabitants within a radius of one mile of the border. Obviously, for Tijuana the density of residential and commercial activity around the border crossing area is far greater than for San Ysidro.

Approximately 34 million vehicles and more than 7 million pedestrians pass through this gate each year. But the port of entry and surrounding zone on both sides of the border is fragmented by a variety of urban design problems: traffic congestion, poor circulation routes, disorganized land uses, conflicts between local interests, crime and public safety concerns, and unresolved land development plans.

San Ysidro–Tijuana has been saddled with an abundance of "negative" land uses, including activities of border security agencies such
as the U.S. Border Patrol and Customs, as well as warehousing and
automobile parking. The zone is also dominated by fences. If there is
one single characteristic of the San Ysidro–Tijuana crossing zone, it
is its noxious image. Speaking of the San Ysidro border crossing, one
former city council member stated: "Few would disagree that its iron
bars, concrete walls and blighted surroundings are an unsightly dis-
grace to our regional dignity."[10] A former chairman of the City of San
Diego Planning Commission commented: "The border entrance is a
very seedy kind of place. There is no elegance to it. When you cross
the border into Mexico, you feel like you are going into a second-rate
place. And it really shouldn't be."[11]

In the late 1990s a number of investors, community advocates, and
others believed it might be possible to create an urban village at the
San Ysidro–Tijuana border crossing. Border monitoring would continue to have a function within the district, but steps might also be
taken to create better public places within a more cosmopolitan setting supported by careful landscape design. These groups began to
discuss the idea of reinventing the San Ysidro border crossing zone.
They asked: How can this seemingly dead space be brought to life as
a new hybrid global investment center and downtown lying between
two traditional urban centers?

Adjacent to the San Ysidro crossing, one private firm purchased
large tracts of land, and with the Redevelopment Authority of the city
of San Diego, it put together a large-scale commercial development
called "Las Americas." The plan saw itself as a metaphor for the future
of land along the border—an integration of pedestrian walkways, gardens, plazas with private retail, entertainment, hotel, and office buildings. The initial idea was to create a complex of mixed and retail uses,
a public plaza, a landmark pedestrian bridge linked to a new pedestrian crossing, a world trade center, a market facility, and links to a
regional trolley, as well as across the border to Tijuana's downtown
artery, Revolution Avenue.[12] Here was recognition that the boundary
itself could be a space of community life, rather than a space of instability, conflict, and smuggling. It also reinforced the pattern of creating new public spaces via the private sector, and in the long run creating a border zone that is a privatized place.

Simultaneously, a second project also contemplated ways of reinventing this troubled border crossing. The regional transit planning
agency, the Metropolitan Transit Development Board (MTDB), developed a new transit complex to replace the existing trolley station

at San Ysidro. That station had long suffered from poor circulation patterns and confusion among competing transit users (autos, pedestrians, trolley riders, taxis, buses, etc.) around the facility. The main goals of the project include: (a) limit the movement of private vehicles from the trolley, bus, and taxi zones; (b) create a pedestrian plaza space; (c) separate boarding areas for public and private transit; (d) minimize walking, by providing clear and direct access between different modes of transit.[13] Ultimately, MTDB officials envision an interface with a Tijuana light-rail system across the border.

Yet another project added to the economic development momentum of this zone. For many years commerce either clustered in Tijuana or located farther north. The construction of a Duty-Free Center at San Ysidro, in the parking area adjacent to southbound pedestrian entry, west of the freeway, changed this. This 15,000-square-foot retail facility was completed in early 2001. It allows traffic to flow and utilize the duty-free shopping area, then continue circulation south into Mexico. The designers for the center suggest their design plan will facilitate a pedestrian-oriented experience, by screening the parking space from the store.[14]

A reinvented and well-planned San Ysidro gateway could ignite a regional reconfiguration in the distribution of wealth. As San Ysidro becomes a destination in itself, more tourists and local residents may simply come to the border, and not necessarily cross it. Like Old Town in San Diego, San Ysidro and the surrounding south bay could become a surrogate for a "Mexican border cultural experience," where consumers would feel comfortable coming to the border, without having to deal with the perceived inconveniences of crossing into Tijuana. While previous studies of San Ysidro's economic potential have mentioned tourism development, one can argue that this potential has been underestimated. For example, a major study of the San Ysidro economy in the 1980s buried the tourism and visitor potential in a larger model that cast a much wider development net, covering commercial development for Mexican nationals and local residents.[15] However, if pedestrian bridges and other new infrastructure make it easier to cross back and forth into Tijuana, the "border urban village" would benefit the economies on both sides.

This could be the setting for new innovative globalized public spaces. But they will have to overcome two immediate concerns. First, in the post-9/11 atmosphere of greater attention to security along borders, those spaces will have to find ways to face the realities of antiterrorism screening along borders as well as serve the needs of an emerging "village" atmosphere. Second, the development of a true village setting will require direct input from designers and city officials. Left to private land investors, these spaces could quickly become suburban, big-box commercial centers or cookie-cutter shopping malls. To achieve a high-density village morphology with pedestrian-scale public spaces will require significant planning input. For example, by 2004 the early returns on the "Las Americas" project suggested that some of its image as a progressive border "village" was manufactured through a publicity campaign by investors aimed at maximizing profit on the property. There is a danger in converting parts of the border into a "theme park" of artificial, consumer-oriented public spaces. This has occurred elsewhere, as I discuss later in this chapter.

### PUBLIC SPACE AND MEXICAN CULTURE: THE SOUTHWEST UNITED STATES BORDER REGION

The United States made significant strides in developing its southwestern border region in the second half of the twentieth century. Rail technologies had linked the two coasts in the late nineteenth century. But heavy manufacturing favored the traditional industrial centers of the Northeast and Midwest. The locational costs associated with moving raw materials and final products from the distant Southwest made large-scale restructuring of the North American economy unlikely; the Southwest region thus remained marginal. Los Angeles in the first decades of the twentieth century was only beginning to forge a strategy for making itself into a booming metropolis. It needed water and an economic development plan.[16]

After World War II things fell into place for the southwestern United States, and especially for Southern California. New strategies of defense and military technology meant that U.S. military air bases would relocate to the open spaces of the southwestern desert. New military bases attracted manufacturing activities centered on the production of aerospace weapons. Southern California became one of the major beneficiaries. The Southwest was further aided by the completion of the federal interstate highway system, which linked cities across the continent, and by the amplification of air travel, which allowed business interests to move quickly across the nation.

The restructuring of the American economy after 1950 was perhaps the most significant factor, as the nation moved toward tertiary (service, trade) and quaternary (computer, information) sectors. Research and development spawned major growth centers in places like Silicon Valley, and elsewhere across the Southwest. Technology (especially air conditioning) and the defense industry were two key forces that brought growth; others included the real estate boom, and the tourism and leisure industries. The cumulative effect in a short period of time was that a new dynamic region, the Sunbelt, emerged, with new centers of power—Los Angeles, Dallas, Phoenix. The Sunbelt would begin to rival the so-called Frostbelt. Its growth would be further fueled by migration (the arrival of retirees, amenity-seeking residents and businesses, the armed forces), by lower land and energy costs, by supportive federal government policies, and by the expansion of new markets into the southwestern region.

In the realm of architecture, even the casual observer cannot miss the obvious Latino/Mexican elements imprinted on the landscape of the southwestern border region: red tile roofs, adobe/stucco pueblo-style walls, bell towers and archways from Spanish missions, porticoes reminiscent of plazas in faraway Spain or central Mexico. Despite the clear imprint of Latino cultural influences in southwestern architecture, surprisingly few books have been written on the subject.[17] Given such limited attention, I find it hardly surprising that little has been written about the impact of Latino/Mexican culture on public space in the southwestern United States.[18] As mentioned, I believe southwestern U.S. cities will benefit by more fully embracing this important theme. To do so will require a reflection on the past, and on how lessons of design history can be recycled into the future.

### Anasazi-Pueblo culture

The Anasazi-Pueblo culture arrived in what is now the southwestern United States around AD 700, centuries before the Spanish/Mexican period. Because its influence spread and later mixed with Mexican building styles in the present-day American Southwest, its role in shaping landscapes deserves recognition.

Anasazi-Pueblo culture was driven by its strong connection to the natural environment. The physical landscape of arid desert valleys, arroyos, red rock canyons, rocky cliffs, and mesas dictated the built environment of their settlements. Indeed, Anasazi-Pueblo building systems followed the cyclical patterns of nature, alternating between settlements that hugged the fertile canyons and valleys of the desert ecosystems and cliff-oriented cities that cantilevered themselves along steep canyon walls. These divergent shifts in settlement location and architecture partly responded to the long-term natural cycles in the region that altered between periods of rain and flooding and seasons of drought. Heavy rains in one generation might drive the settlers into the mountains, if the flooding threatened canyon lands; severe droughts would bring them back to the water-friendly valleys.

In the 1500s the Spanish king dictated a set of rules about city building—rules based on studying Roman military towns as well as patterns of climate and wind. But Anasazi-Pueblo city building was truly organic, strongly tied to the regional ecology. In the Spanish colonial town plan, the central public space of the city was defined by the main plaza, which anchored the town physically and functionally. Anasazi culture had no such definitive political or functional central public space. The Anasazi were a peaceful, artistic culture of farmers. Their built environment reflected their main purpose—to survive in a challenging landscape. Their main spaces were outdoor spaces of

work and the interior space of religious worship—the "kiva," often a sunken interior room attached to houses in the village.

During the peak period of Anasazi town building, the main settlements dominated what we call today the "Four Corners" region of the American Southwest (where the present-day states of Arizona, New Mexico, Colorado, and Utah meet). Here is where the Anasazi-Pueblo peoples, as mentioned above, fluctuated between building canyon-bottom towns and cliff-dwelling settlements with cave spaces on the elevated slopes of the mountain chains that cut across the great deserts. While these shifts, as mentioned, were partly driven by the cycles of nature, they also were responses to the threats posed by marauding tribes of outside indigenous cultures that periodically appeared in the region.[19]

*Anasazi-Pueblo cities did not emphasize public life in the European sense, but rather hard work, survival, and spiritual calm: Taos Pueblo, New Mexico.*

Although Anasazi-Pueblo culture did not emphasize the central public plaza in the spatial life of its towns, there were outdoor public places in these settlements. They typically included either work areas where laborers interacted during rest periods or ceremonial plazas where religious and other festivals took place.[20] Hard work, survival, and religious ceremony came together to form a coherent, peaceful settlement landscape. Yet ultimately it was the elements of defense and nature that defined the physical form and urban design of these built villages.

It is striking, for example, that most of these towns often lacked public streets. In cliff-dwelling villages like Mesa Verde, people walked from one roof to another to move through the complexes. Even when a public place was created, such as the central plaza at Chaco Canyon, which was surrounded by "great houses"—terraced communal structures—the plaza was oriented toward the sun for religious reasons, and apparently did not have a social or interactive function.[21] Ultimately, as one observer has noted, the main purpose of Anasazi building was "imitation of natural forms by human beings who seek, thereby, to fit themselves safely into nature's order."[22]

### Spanish colonial city building

Where Anasazi town building responded to the dictates of nature, colonial Spain choose a different path. Spain, a Roman Catholic nation, and one of the leading powers of the world in the seventeenth century, believed that its urbanizing culture could conquer nature, and could impose the power of the Church and the imperial government (the Spanish royal family) over the natural order. The transition from indigenous architecture to Spanish colonial town building is therefore visually striking. The Spanish royal family constructed a city-building ideology derived from the vision of a culture wedded to the power of its ideas and religious beliefs over the natural environment.

Despite the hopes of the king of Spain and his royal court to build a new world order in their own image, the colonists did not always carry the royal family banner directly into the town-building process. The town builders of the New World may have acknowledged the laws written by the king of Spain, but they did not always follow them. The Spanish settlers also came to respect the labors of their indigenous predecessors in the northern regions of Spanish America, as they did elsewhere in Latin America. We shall see that in various places, the Anasazi-Pueblo architectural style and philosophy are incorporated into Spanish colonial architecture and town building.

The Spanish imperial urban design approach did begin to dominate the creation of very different kinds of cities. One useful barometer lies in the way Spanish colonial city builders imagined a city, and the role they assigned to public spaces in their urban designs. Public spaces, in effect, were highly valued as symbolic icons that reminded citizens of the power of the Spanish monarchy; in time they also became the functional lifelines and hierarchical centers of political and

economic power as Spain slowly established itself as a world power in the sixteenth and seventeenth centuries. The power of Spain and its royal family over city building shows up even on the distant plains of the arid, relatively untouched landscape of the present-day American Southwest. Each subregion of this borderlands region absorbed these ideas and invented an urbanism in slightly different ways, even if they were, in the end, variations on a similar theme.

*The Spanish colonial approach to city building brought a very different aesthetic to the borderlands region: scene from San Miguel de Allende, one of Mexico's best-preserved colonial cities.*

### New Mexico

If there is one quintessential definitive historic place in the southwestern United States that celebrates Spanish/Mexican urban design and great public spaces, it would be the city of Santa Fe, New Mexico. Santa Fe, founded in 1609, was the first important border settlement constructed by the Spanish colonial regime north of the present-day boundary between Mexico and the United States. Santa Fe's design plan followed the principles of the Royal Ordinances prescribed by the king of Spain in his late-sixteenth-century Laws of the Indies. These included detailed instructions on how colonial engineers were to lay out new towns.

Santa Fe's town plan was true to the model described in the Royal Ordinances: a large central plaza bordered by one-story structures with porticoes and arched doorways. Prestigious buildings faced the plaza, including the stately Governor's Palace. The main plaza was sited at the center of a rectangular gridiron street design typical of the kind that characterized so many colonial cities in Mexico and Latin America. The square was the physical center of the design plan; it also quickly became the economic and social activity center of the town: "All the business of the little settlement of Santa Fe took place at the Plaza Mayor—commerce, politics, marketing, religious processions and entertainment."[23] Not only was the plaza a center for commercial, political, and spiritual pursuits, it was also in the direct line of movement of people and vehicles: "the plaza was, in a very real sense, the thoroughfare of the city."[24]

Santa Fe remained an isolated town after the Spanish colonial period, largely because it was far enough north that the nineteenth-century railroad-driven development of the Southwest passed it by. To the south, the city of Albuquerque became the rail terminus and ultimately the capital and main economic nexus of the state of New Mexico. Santa Fe evolved into a kind of cultural and urban design icon—the best-preserved major Spanish colonial settlement in the southwestern United States. Santa Fe was discovered by artists and intellectuals at the turn of the twentieth century, and subsequently became a mecca for photographers, painters, and writers. Its citizens soon realized that the best way to preserve its unique heritage was to build the city's economy around the Spanish-Pueblo architectural theme. In 1958 the municipal code was adapted to preserve the Spanish-Pueblo cultural landscape.

An essential component of Santa Fe's design is its "walkability" and traditional public life, including the downtown plaza with one of the nation's most pedestrian-friendly historic spaces under its porticoes. However, its beauty and authenticity would also become the very ingredients that threatened its decline. So many people moved to Santa Fe in the post-1970 period that it is in danger of becoming too culturally defined, to the point that its history is becoming overblown and trivialized.[25]

If Santa Fe is the historic soul of New Mexico, then the heart of the state's modern urbanism lies in the capital and largest city, Albuquerque. Albuquerque's evolution stands in stark contrast to Santa Fe.

Albuquerque's original Old Town, its early Mexican settlement, was eclipsed by the arrival of the railroads in the late nineteenth century, which brought subsequent growth that turned the city into an administrative and economic/industrial metropolis. The city's late-twentieth-century growth was energized by the location of military facilities as well as the nuclear power industry. It boomed from 1960 to 2000, becoming a modern urban center, characterized by suburban sprawl surrounding a struggling inner city.

Santa Fe's public spaces evoke a sense of the past, a world of convivial interaction in public plazas and gardens and on quiet streets. Albuquerque's public life is fragmented, like so many large metropolitan regions in America today. It is a car-oriented city, with few great civic spaces to allow for a pedestrian-scale public life. For example, the city tried to create a civic plaza downtown, but that space continues to be poorly used, and is surrounded by harsh and uninviting modernist office buildings. "Our public life and our public spaces are almost non-existent," claims one critic.[26]

Yet, even here, both the Mexican and the Anasazi-Pueblo cultures impress a sense of the past on the contemporary landscape. For all its problems as a modern business and industrial center, Albuquerque still retains a certain regional authenticity. A Mexican sense of place pervades the Latino barrios around the Old Town and in south Albuquerque. Visually, Mexican/Anasazi-Pueblo architectural elements abound in the region, whether in the form of actual adobe structures, or modern designs that borrow heavily from indigenous styles of architecture. One of the most striking is the University of New Mexico at Albuquerque, a campus built in part to honor and reinvent the Pueblo/Mexican heritage of the region. It is a place that truly achieves a sense of the past without trivializing it.

### Texas

After New Mexico, the second most important example of Mexican influence in the southwestern United States is Texas, especially the southern part of the state. "South Texas" is probably a more distinct cultural region than "Southern California." It is roughly bordered by the Rio Grande to the south and west, the Gulf of Mexico to the southeast and east, and the hilly terrain to the north.[27]

A critical feature of the built landscape and design of cities and towns in South Texas is the plaza or town square, a distinctly Spanish/Mexican urban design element. One comprehensive study of townscape design in this region shows that 20 of the most important towns all have traditional plazas, with 2 originally built in the eighteenth century, 10 in the nineteenth century, and 8 in the twentieth century.[28] Like their Mexican counterparts, many of these towns had multiple plazas.

Mexican town squares left a powerful imprint on urbanism in South Texas, even as the cities around them modernized and grew toward the suburbs, and even as downtown pedestrian life became eclipsed by the automobile, the shopping mall, telecommunications, and the Internet. Of the 20 South Texas towns with plazas, 12 continue to have churches on present-day squares and 16 have kiosks where music is played on weekends or at special festivals. Of course, traditions like the "paseo" (couples promenading around the squares) have all but disappeared, and even many of the festivals, especially the religious fiestas patrias (holidays), are also falling by the wayside.

Still, much like in Santa Fe, New Mexico, the plazas in South Texas symbolize historic heritage that is being recycled into the new modes of self-promotion that small towns must use to survive in an increasingly competitive global and regional economy. For example, in Laredo, a border town, the San Augustín Plaza, nearly two and a half centuries old, has virtually abandoned its original functions as a social node. "In Laredo, the new plaza is a regional shopping space, Mall del Norte, some ten miles distant from San Augustín plaza," states one publication.[29] Yet, with the expansion of U.S.-Mexico tourism in the NAFTA era, the Laredo–Nuevo Laredo region has become a major tourism gateway for those heading into or out of Mexico. Laredo now has an upscale hotel, La Posada Hotel, which lies adjacent to the Plaza San Augustín. Self-guided tourism brochures in Laredo (and other South Texas cities) highlight the traditional plazas as landmarks on their tours. Thus, although one set of plaza-driven traditions may have faded away, the past has been recycled and may serve not only to preserve these historic spaces but also to utilize them as levers for economic growth through tourism and historic-heritage marketing of commercial and residential real estate.

The anchor of historic heritage in South Texas is, of course, San Antonio. San Antonio was settled as early as 1718 and was formally designated by the king of Spain as a presidio/mission town in 1731. It served a key administrative function in the northeast frontier region of New Spain. San Antonio was originally laid out with the standard rectangular gridiron plan typical of all Spanish colonial urbanism. Yet, its growth in the nineteenth century as an important Anglo center of economic growth caused it to significantly reinvent its form. By the early twentieth century there were, in fact, two separate downtowns (similar to what happened in Albuquerque, New Mexico)—one Mexican, the other Anglo.[30] The Mexican quarter continues to proudly display its symbolic cultural identity, an identity that architecturally reemerges in the barrio's plazas and public places, such as Market Square, or in community spaces like the nearby westside barrio.

While the Mexican quarter of downtown San Antonio has maintained a strong sense of place, the Anglo side of town fell completely flat in the twentieth century. It was rescued when the city discovered the value of the river flowing through it, unleashing a successful boom in hotels, restaurants, convention center, tourism, and real estate development. San Antonio's Mexican origins may have played the most important role in the economic success of the downtown. As early as 1879 a historic preservation movement was started; its main focus was to rescue and preserve the Alamo and its adjacent public square, as well as the main plaza and market squares of the Mexican quarter. This movement succeeded in conserving the zone and much of the original architecture in it.[31]

South Texas is but one cultural layer in a much larger, more complex state. One could argue that Texas is also a powerfully Anglo state that has not necessarily embraced all of its Latino origins. Indeed, after the mid-nineteenth century, the cultural landscape of Texas tilted toward the Anglo domain. Cities like Houston and Dallas offer the best evidence of this. There are almost no Hispanic/Mexican-scaled public spaces in either city—no plaza morphology, no church squares, no porticoes. The state capital is Austin, a town created in the nineteenth century to celebrate architecturally everything Anglo and European about Texas—its Greek Revival and Victorian mansions, its frontier-log structures, and its Beaux Arts buildings and spaces, including the prestigious University of Texas campus. All of these architectural elements speak to the eclipse of the Mexican past in the state's cultural landscape, and the ascendance of Anglo political and economic culture.

### Arizona

The whims of geography left present-day Arizona as the least settled subregion of what is now the southwestern United States. The river valleys of New Mexico and Texas and the coastal region of California were far more compelling as places for the Spanish king to set up missions, presidios, and pueblos. The arid desert dominated Arizona, and only the valleys near the Salt River (Phoenix) and the Gila River (Tucson) attracted Spanish colonial interest.

Phoenix was a latecomer to city building and, like Albuquerque, has a far more Anglo rhythm to its urbanism. Mexican heritage is more concentrated in the present-day city of Tucson. Tucson began as a fort (presidio) built in 1775 near the Gila River. Just south was the San Javier Mission. Tucson's fort provided shelter and protection for settlers; the original Mexican "Old Town" was enclosed by barricades for defense against attacks by marauding Apache warriors.

Old Town was built again according to the Royal Ordinances of the Spanish imperial government. It was physically structured around its rectangular grid of streets, which were linked to the central plaza. This plan has been preserved in the modern era, with some modifications. The main plaza is now called El Presidio Park and serves as a tourist district tied to art and to the surrounding pueblo-style architecture. Much like in Santa Fe, Old Town Tucson has been converted into a "commodified" consumer space. It seeks to evoke the visual architectural romance of the past as a way of attracting clients to restaurants, hotels, and other commercial activities. Because Tucson's marketability to tourists and visitors lies in its exotic past, it has tried to reinvent itself as a dynamic tourist space. For example, its strong cultural ties to art and architecture led to the creation of a one-square-block adobe restoration zone called "Old Town Artisans."

But unlike earlier periods when its public life spilled naturally out into streets and plazas, aside from Presidio Park, much of Old Town has become privatized. For example, the "walking tour" organized by the Visitor's Bureau features mostly private homes, whose open spaces consist of interior patios, completely walled off from the community.

The irony of a place called "Old Tucson" cannot be missed. "Old Tucson" is a stage set lying in the mountains west of the city. It was built in 1929 as a location for making films about the "Wild West." Over 100 Westerns have been filmed there. Today it is a prime tourist site and a reminder that sometimes the imagined place holds more interest to visitors than the real place.

## MIXING CULTURE AND PUBLIC SPACE:
## THE CONTEXT OF SOUTHERN CALIFORNIA

Southern California has been referred to as the capital of the Sunbelt. It is certainly the metropolitan region that grew the most during the Sunbelt boom. Metropolitan Los Angeles grew from 237,000 inhabitants in 1900 to 11 million in 1980.[32] The San Diego metropolitan area's population expanded from 35,100 in 1900 to more than 3 million in 2000. The region's economy has expanded around high technology, defense, and trade. The economic and population boom led to massive physical expansion, with the urbanized regions extending thousands of square miles into the San Gabriel Mountains and Mojave Desert to the east, north along the coast toward Santa Barbara, and south to the Mexican border. It is a sprawling, diffuse array of subdivisions, shopping districts, and planned unit developments snaking through canyons, over mesas and mountains, and along valleys. It is the most decentralized, freeway-dominated, exogenous metropolitan region in the United States. It may also be on the cutting edge of future trends in urban planning and design that are needed to deal with the many problems occurring here.

Over the last three decades a growing body of literature crystallized around the subject of Southern California urbanism. In the early 1970s Los Angeles was celebrated as a new prototype of urban ecology, highlighted by rapid movement (via the automobile), modern freeway systems, and innovative architecture.[33] Freeway morphology in new Sunbelt cities stood in stark contrast to the high-density, pedestrian scale of older U.S. cities—an urbanism traditionally promoted by important scholars and practitioners.[34] But the old school was now being challenged by a shift in paradigms toward postmodern cities like Las Vegas.[35] Writers argued that the automobile scale of cities called for a new urban landscape, where the architecture would provide visual information needed by car-oriented consumers. This new approach embraced strip development, a design element that had been anathema to architecture before this. Some now saw Las Vegas as a new paradigm for urban design.

The debate, however was far from over. While modernists struggled with skyscrapers and the meaning of suburbs, Los Angeles grew. By the 1990s a "Los Angeles" school, a distinct set of studies and discourses on the nature of the metropolis, began to emerge.[36] Much of the literature had in common an attempt to sort out the meaning of Los Angeles–style urban growth. Not only had the metropolitan region boomed demographically, it was an important cultural icon for North America, being at the center of the production of images for film and television. Los Angeles cried out for attention as a significant urban prototype. In keeping with intellectual trends more generally, Los Angeles was adopted by the postmodern movement as the capital of "postmodern" cities—a polycentric, polycultural, polyglot; a place that challenges the way we think about cities.[37]

A number of common themes emerged out of the so-called L.A. school. First was the theme of "trouble in paradise."[38] Los Angeles had built its real estate boom early in the twentieth century by selling itself as a land of paradise, with palm trees, lovely sunsets, and idyllic climate. But by the 1990s the sheer magnitude of growth—some 12 million people in the basin—had generated severe urban diseconomies:

traffic gridlock on freeways, overpriced housing, smog, crime, and increased incidence of psychological disorders. The myth of paradise was crumbling. The threat of earthquakes and racial tension only added to the sentiment that this earthly paradise needed to be rethought.

A second common theme centered on the physical design of Los Angeles. In many ways L.A. transcends physical space; its sprawl is so vast as to render conventional notions about intraurban travel obsolete. Physical travel slowly gives way to the movement of electronic data and information, yielding to the birth of "cyburbia," a sea of suburban realms linked by telecommunications and the computer.[39] The massive decentralization of the metropolis led observers to identify new spatial behaviors; traditional downtown-periphery relations disappeared, and a new independent suburban world was being created. The suburbs had become their own centers, forging what one observer referred to as a "new exopolis lifestyle."[40] Suburban life was viewed as individual oriented, leading to new and more vitriolic forms of suburban separatism—a "militarization of space" and obsession with keeping society out, generating an urban "fortress mentality."[41] Once ensconced in their suburban enclaves, residents were determined either to use zoning to keep unwanted people out of their towns or to fortify their own homes and gated communities against outsiders.

All of this has given greater Los Angeles a distinct look, and a distinct and somewhat bizarre kind of public life. Its image is not so much that of a city with unique regional qualities and a distinct identity, but rather of a city of simulated places—futuristic downtown glass towers, Hollywood "stage set" residential developments,[42] and air-conditioned shopping malls. In the end, the "theme park" becomes a norm for urban development. In Los Angeles, high profile examples abound. Of course, everything about Los Angeles city building is high profile—as the city becomes a metaphor for trendiness in an urban culture that worships trends. "CityWalk," a commercial center in Hollywood, epitomizes this trend. It is an artificial downtown, a pedestrian-scale, private commercial site, with postmodern re-creations of theme architecture and design elements from the region. It does not connect to surrounding neighborhoods; it was simply plunked onto the landscape, like Disneyland, by a developer. Suddenly there were boutiques and ice cream shops and movie theaters, and a feeling of a mall disguised as a small main street in some downtown somewhere.

Los Angeles offers a model of a new kind of increasingly antigeographic city. The "100-mile city"[43] is too spread out to accommodate earlier urban forms. Yet, its suburban form creates social tension. The movie *Blade Runner* offers a dark prediction of the future Los Angeles, an urban landscape of alienated individuals in fragmented spaces.[44] Los Angeles is seen as becoming so individualized and so separatist that public space rapidly gives way to privatized space. Observers speak of the decline of the "Olmstedian" vision of public space, the notion that public spaces could generate a sense of community and public goodwill.[45]

The private shopping mall has eclipsed the public square and the promenade as the main social gathering place of contemporary Southern California. But the privatized spaces carefully screen their occupants; if you're not dressed properly or doing something other than shopping or browsing, the message is that you don't belong here. Student researchers in an urban planning class taking photographs at an outdoor shopping mall have been turned away by security guards and told that photos are not permitted. The privatized shopping mall may be imagined to be the new downtown of America, but only if you are there to consume. Public space in Southern California will struggle to survive under these conditions.

*"CityWalk" reveals the kind of artificiality and lack of identity associated with public spaces in Southern California.*

There is an enormous range of types of public spaces in Southern California: traditional public squares and parks, shopping malls, simulated spaces like CityWalk, neotraditional community spaces, and ethnic public spaces. These spaces offer a set of metaphors indicative of changes occurring in the contemporary urban culture.

### Traditional squares

Most of the traditional public squares in Southern California have either fallen into serious disrepair or become overshadowed by surrounding private developments. Traditional civic plazas like Pershing Square in downtown Los Angeles or Pantoja Park in downtown San Diego are typically located in historic spaces in the older districts of town that have either deteriorated or undergone urban redevelopment. In most cases, when this occurs, the original squares do not necessarily fit prominently into redevelopment plans, which typically favor automobile-oriented uses, or projects that turn their back on the streets. U.S. redevelopment projects and plans, especially in Southern California, have not been particularly friendly to public space. In downtown Los Angeles, for example, many of the redevelopment efforts of the 1970s and 1980s, created privatized spaces apart from the street. The St. Bonaventure hotel complex is a small indoor autonomous community for tourists and visitors, air-conditioned and cut off from the street. The Museum of Contemporary Art project also created a raised environment separate from the life of the street. Pantoja Park in downtown San Diego is one of the oldest public spaces in the city; it was laid out in 1850, a square-block civic space. As the surrounding lots were redeveloped in the 1980s and 1990s, Pantoja Park was virtually ignored. Rather than allowing it to serve the public, it was surrounded on three sides by condominium residential developments or commercial structures. The result is that it has been turned from a vital civic space into a hidden, forgotten park.

### Recycled spaces

The example of Pershing Square in downtown Los Angeles illustrates the challenges facing designers who seek to revitalize century-old town squares in American central business districts. By the 1980s Pershing Square's deterioration was a metaphor for the nature of urban life in Southern California. The urban experience has become largely a private experience; most urban dwellers no longer gathered regularly on public squares to socialize. For several decades Pershing Square had served as the community nexus for elderly downtown residents, homeless squatters, and drug dealers and other criminals. Yet, in Southern California, and across the nation, a restlessness was emerging among city residents to invent a more public life amidst the spatial alienation they face each day, enclosed in their cars, offices, or homes, or in front of television sets and computer screens.

This search for more community-oriented experiences coincided with a movement in many cities to find and recreate better public spaces. About this time, the city of Los Angeles raised some $14.7 million to remodel Pershing Square. They hired a team of architects, including the high-profile Mexican architect Ricardo Legorreta, as well as local designers. The architects were faced with the task of cre-

The remodeling of Pershing Square injected a more Latino flavor onto a struggling public place in downtown Los Angeles.

ating a space that was both exciting and secure, not easy to achieve in downtown Los Angeles. The resulting design plan borrows from the "hard architecture" paradigm of public space planning in Spain—where many remodeled plaza designs emphasize the use of pavement, minimal trees, and few amenities. The new plan for Pershing Square is open and has easy sight lines (for security). It resembles the new design of Bryant Park in New York City, which effectively created a more secure space in Manhattan's midtown by getting rid of potential hiding spots.[46]

Legorreta brought a Mexican sensibility to Pershing Square, and this is most obvious in his choice of color—the square uses strong earth tones, suggesting the texture of adobe, and also draws from the modern emphasis in Mexico on bright colors, such as striking purple and tan. The tall purple tower creates a distinct landmark that can be seen from a distance. A circular tidal pool fed by an aqueduct injects a Mediterranean element—water—into the space. The pool creates a soothing sound of flowing water, reminiscent of the plazas of Spain, as well as Mexico.

Still, the square is set in the midst of high-density, modernist office towers, such as the Sanyo Bank Tower and Wells Fargo corporate center. One critic described the ambience as seeming desolate.[47] While some attempt has been made to create activities that will attract people to the square, the fact is that Pershing Square is a much less popular gathering place than the beach boardwalks, shopping malls, or interiors of hotel complexes. Legorreta, the optimistic Mexican, notes that "the tradition of public spaces is just starting in Los Angeles."[48] That remains to be seen.

### Malls and artificial spaces

Shopping malls have become, in Southern California and elsewhere in the United States, the new "public realm" for many urban residents. But to call these the "new American downtowns"[49] may be misleading. Shopping malls are enclosed, privatized, "commodified" spaces. They are neither spontaneous nor freely available to the public at large. Attempts have been made to create shopping malls that are both more innovative and more linked to urban life. One example is the Horton Plaza in downtown San Diego. Designed by architect Jon Jerde and completed in the late 1980s, this $40-million postmodern four-story mall with an outdoor central courtyard and balcony walkways has been successful as a business venture, and it won awards for its innovative design.

Set in the heart of a revitalizing downtown San Diego, Horton Plaza successfully established itself as an activity node. Its bright pastel colors, giant flags and banners, and upscale stores, restaurants, movie theater, and stage make for an entertaining experience for shoppers. Yet, one could argue that the "plaza" is nothing more than a media creation. It advertises itself as a "vibrant European marketplace" in tourist brochures, and also as a "sun-drenched square." However, in some manner it is rather inaccessible, a walled fortress that is only entered at street level by foot in two places, and is mainly reached by car. Patrons drive in and park inside, then walk from the parking lot directly into the plaza at whatever level they have parked. It is truly a controlled environment.

Ironically, the original "Horton Plaza," a turn-of-the-century square with a Victorian fountain designed by the great architect Irving Gill, sits sadly forgotten alongside the shopping mall. After redesigning the space, it was opened in 1993, with virtually no places to sit! City officials wanted to discourage loitering by homeless people, so they removed all seating benches. The flower beds and palm trees make for a potentially pleasant space, but without seating, the plaza is nearly always empty. More ironic still, only the homeless are seen lingering here on the edges of the flower beds, which themselves have been lined with chicken wire to keep people from entering them.

If Horton Plaza is a simulated shopping mall, another well known and successful simulated space in Southern California is the Third Street Promenade in downtown Santa Monica. Anchored on one end by a shopping mall, this five-block pedestrian street has become a

*One of the many attempts to innovatively design a shopping mall in Southern California.*

gathering place for Angelinos, demonstrating the degree to which the public savors a place to gather that is more spontaneous than a mall. In fact, the shopping mall is usually much more empty than the street. The actual pedestrian space is a street that has been closed to traffic for several blocks, landscaped with trees and plants, and covered with decorated brick tile. The commercial buildings that were once struggling for clients now have upscale restaurants, bookstores, cafés, a movie theater, clothing stores, and other pedestrian-scale uses. Some benches have been installed, and numerous "street entertainers" are seen. Most impressive are the wide range of users here: Blacks, Asians, Latinos; young "punkers," yuppies, older couples, musicians.

Perhaps the epitome of late-twentieth-century Southern California public space is the "Universal CityWalk," a themed entertainment complex built in 1992 in a parking lot at Universal Studios about 10 miles northwest of downtown L.A. CityWalk's theme is "the city." It seeks to create a feeling of downtown in a simulated space operated by private developers. Not lost is the irony of re-creating downtown in center-less Los Angeles, by what is the largest Hollywood corporate stage set design firm—Universal Studios. CityWalk has had some success as a public space, although in the fall of 1994 gang violence spilled briefly into the project, and private interests were quick to call in more security. It is possible that projects like CityWalk are doomed by their false sense of place.

### Latino public space

One of the critical and least studied elements of public space is the cultural/ethnic connection. We can learn a great deal from ethnic communities' use of public space. In Southern California the most important regional ethnic public spaces are to be found in the Latino community. East Los Angeles, the largest Mexican American residential enclave in the country, has a distinct cultural landscape, which in subtle ways adds to the barrio's sense of community. For example, seemingly undistinguished small cottages are brought alive by the design and use of the street ambience. The street is lined with vendors of many types; front yards are outdoor oriented; murals, graffiti, and other innovative visual material adorn the street space.[50] Trucks park to create a makeshift market; abandoned gas stations are redesigned into taco stands.

Latinos regularly create vital public spaces through vernacular design. In East Los Angeles, the sense of community is bolstered by pedestrian-scale avenues lined with small markets, bakeries, and restaurants, and by people using the benches along the streets. The sense of community is perhaps most strengthened by the sense of barrio unity that allows the Latino community to come together. For example, the East Los Angeles community fought for historic spaces, such as the Golden Gate Theater or the Ruben Salazar Park symbolizing battles between the community and the police.[51] Clearly, Latinos value social space.

There is such a thing as "Latino street culture."[52] It is about people interacting in a spontaneous way on the streets. Even along automobile-oriented Whittier Boulevard, a human scale has been preserved by the landscape of neighborhood businesses (furniture stores, secondhand clothing stores), or by the numerous street vendors. The popular activity of cruising or "low riding" by car along Whittier Boulevard may be more than just a form of moving about in the car culture of L.A.; it may pay homage to the sense of community that Whittier Boulevard symbolically communicates, since East L.A. arguably has become a state of mind for all Latinos in the region, even those who have moved away.[53]

Meanwhile, other vital Latino public spaces can be found. Many people decry downtown Los Angeles as unsafe and filled with homeless people. But in the Latino section of Broadway Street, the old Broadway neighborhood of theaters, Art Deco and Moderne architecture has been absorbed by Mexican residents and commercial users and transformed into a center of Latin culture, with its street-scale vendors, small retail businesses, and numerous pedestrians. Meanwhile, if we travel some 100 miles south to the Mexican border, the U.S. town of San Ysidro is an emerging excellent example of a Latino space in Southern California. While the town serves as the border gate into Mexico, it retains a sense of community enhanced by small businesses, pedestrians, and people constantly interacting spontaneously in public space. Abundant pedestrian-oriented elements attest to the street life: from ATM machines to ticket booths, newspaper stands, shaded benches, and small shops, San Ysidro is a place where one can get around on foot, and interact with people in public. It is also very accessible by mass transit.

Some Latino barrios have also re-created the traditional Mesoamerican plaza in their community. "Chicano Park" in San Diego's Barrio Logan is a case in point. Chicano Park lies under the Coronado Bridge, which slices through the heart of San Diego's oldest Mexican American barrio. It is surrounded by a collection of waterfront industries that include shipbuilding, auto and metal recycling yards, and chemical storage. Despite the concentration of neighboring heavy industrial uses, Barrio Logan has remained a vital Latino residential community. When the California Highway Patrol tried to build a police station under the Coronado Bridge in the 1970s, the community responded with an on-site protest, effectively shutting down construction. Ultimately, the community negotiated the city's cancellation of the police station project, replacing it with a community park, later named "Chicano Park." By the late 1970s and early 1980s, award-winning murals had

been painted on the pillars of the bridge, and a striking indigenous-style platform and kiosk were built at the park's center. The park has become symbolic of the Mexican American community's struggle for neighborhood preservation.

*Latino public spaces in barrios across the south-western United States reflect the excitement and energy of streets and squares in Mexico: a barrio mural.*

## SUMMARY

The theme of privatization dominates the late-twentieth-century transformation of Mexican public space along the northern border with the United States. Privatization is an underlying theme in the NAFTA regime as well. Public space along the Mexico-U.S. cultural frontier is a study in contrasts as well as globalization. Traditions of public space design south of the border are quite distinct from those in the United States. Mexicans have more history on their side—hundreds of years of Spanish colonial tradition, with its emphasis on community and public space. Even when creating an artificial promenade, such as Revolution Avenue in Tijuana, Mexico brings distinct design standards. Revolution Avenue has ended up being pedestrian friendly, but not pretentious.

Time is a differentiating factor on both sides of the border. There are age-old cliches about time in Mexico, but one should recognize the obvious: Mexicans are less frenetic in moving about their cities. People seem to linger on public squares or streets. They interact more. Public spaces are more alive. In the United States public space experiences are more private—people by themselves watching, reading, but not necessarily interacting with each other. Public safety and security also distinguish the two societies and their public spaces. Mexicans feel secure in public places; they generally are not afraid of crime.[54] In the United States the biggest obstacle to public life is fear: managing crime and the perception of crime. Some people fail to use public spaces because they believe crimes will occur there.

All of this is, of course, changing. NAFTA is speeding up Mexico's path to global economic development. One finds fewer people lingering in the old plazas and parks, as new forms of technology change urban life. Crime rates are increasing in Mexican cities. Privatization is the buzzword of the new century.

In the United States, in Southern California, we find public spaces in the midst of a crisis, which is part of the larger crisis of public life in the city. The nineteenth-century landscape architects' vision of public space and urban reform has given way to a new millennium of privatized cities. Southern California epitomizes the private, fragmented nature of U.S. cities—a world of cars, suburbs, offices, and human interaction mainly in private settings, usually places where people are consumers. Under these conditions the only way public places have been able to be reborn or preserved is as "spectacles," locales of high-profile experiences that draw people lured by the idea of some amusement or entertainment awaiting them, or by the prospect of pleasant consumption. This may be the future that is slowly redefining urban space along Mexico's side of the border as well.

An intriguing possibility lies in observing the hybridized, globalized spaces that will result when Mexican and U.S. investors, designers, developers, and planners begin to overlap in their city-building practices. Not all forms of globalization are necessarily bad. In its early stages globalization challenged the virtues of tradition in Mexico, bringing privatization, NAFTA, and even suburban models of urban development. But the exciting long-term prospect of the U.S.-Mexico border is that it can become a living laboratory of discovery, a place to invent hew hybrid forms of city building that merge the best elements of U.S. and Mexican design. The "transfrontier metropolis" offers a chance to create a multicultural urban prototype. Urban designers have the opportunity to invent a new kind of global urban space that allows people to live, work, and interact literally on and across international borders. In a world where political boundaries are changing, such acts of innovative city building will be critical. Places like Tijuana-San Diego will move to center stage as global experts study what goes on in these bicultural laboratories for urbanism in the new millennium.

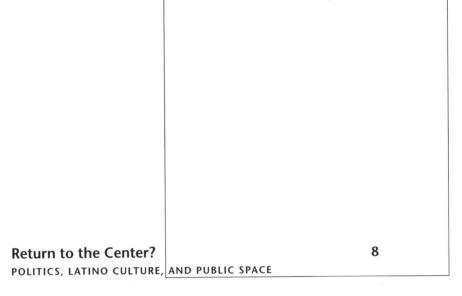

## Return to the Center?

**8**

POLITICS, LATINO CULTURE, AND PUBLIC SPACE

Even in cultures with deeply entrenched traditions of public life—like those of Spain and Mexico—conditions in the new millennium will not be favorable to the preservation of historic public space. City life will increasingly become more nonspatial and virtual. Some public spaces—like the plazas, promenades, and town squares examined in this book—will either fall into a state of decline, disappear, or be substantially altered.

Scholars, members of the design community, planners, and policy makers will need to rethink the term *public space*. To begin with, it will be necessary to critically evaluate the categories of "public" and "private" in contemporary cities. For example, it is no longer accurate to consider streets, town squares, or parks as "unconstrained spaces," entirely public and available to all citizens.[1] Many so-called public spaces are hardly public at all: parks regulate which groups may enter and which may not; streets within gated communities are carefully monitored; even downtown squares screen users. In many cities the places people go for public experiences—festival marketplaces, theme parks, stadiums, shopping malls—are actually not public at all. Rather, they are privately owned sites whose management team makes its own rules about the kind of public experience it wants users to have. In short, urban space has become more politicized then ever before in history. Corporations or governments increasingly dictate the form and use of civic spaces.

It may also be useful to consider the nonspatial character of "public space." Scholars have long regarded the "public domain"[2] as a nineteenth-century phenomenon: the amalgam of media forms that allowed the public to engage in dialogue without being face to face. Today the public domain has come to include such nongeographic forms of interaction as modern-day mass media, fax machines, Web sites, and e-mail. Cyberspace has become the postmodern incarnation of the "public square."

Technology has dramatically transformed city form, consistently eclipsing public spaces from previous eras. For example, transport technologies—mainly the automobile—made possible the massive urban exodus and decentralization of cities. Plazas and public gathering places dramatically declined by the end of the twentieth century, in a world where urban dwellers traveled at high speeds between point of origin and destination. Spatial decentralization has the simple effect of increasing the amount of time it takes for city residents to perform daily activities (journey to work, shop, visit friends, etc.). Time spent in automobiles leaves less time for face-to-face interaction on streets and in public squares. Residents accept the transplantation of their public lives to the supermarket, the shopping mall, the airport, or the parking garage. Telecommunications advances and e-mail add to the impending decline of pedestrian-scale spaces in cities.

Given the constraints on human interaction imposed by postmodern, sprawling metropolitan life, it is not surprising that alternative media have materialized to serve as substitutes for traditional public life in cities. Media such as television and computers have become surrogates for the traditional physical communities that existed in earlier centuries. Lacking a civic place to gather in their neighborhood, many urban dwellers seek refuge in the artificial world of electronic entertainment. Alternately, they venture out into privately controlled, seductive urban consumer spaces—the shopping malls. One might choose to walk the streets in a neighborhood, but in suburban cul-de-sac morphology, the streets have little to offer by way of stimuli or public experiences. Yet, neither the shopping mall nor the television can adequately replace the traditional experiences of public life—the spontaneity of commercial streets, the civic squares and gardens, the overflowing promenades.

### CULTURE, PUBLIC SPACE, AND PLACE: THE IMPORTANCE OF CONTEXT

I have argued in this book, however, that despite the debilitating effects of globalization, technology, and privatization on cities, the battle for recapturing public life is far from over. Indeed, I have suggested that culture is a powerful mediating force—in this case Latino culture primarily, illustrated mainly from the examples of Spanish and Mexican cities. Viewed through this lens, public space narratives still offer glittering possibilities and valuable lessons about saving urban identity and recapturing the spirit of cities.

High-tech urban life faces a crisis of fragmentation, alienation, and cultural landscape homogenization, or "McDonaldization,"[3] across much of the planet. But there is evidence that people are resisting these trends. In Spain, in Mexico, and elsewhere around the globe, one is struck by the number of people in the streets of the urban core

areas. Urban dwellers make a point of going to urban centers, to bask in the thrill of crowds or to be a part of the ancient Greek vision of urban public life: the place where one experiences democratic tolerance of strangers.

How do we explain the apparent contradiction between increasing corporate control and privatization of urban space, or the technologically facilitated retreat of people into homes, often behind the walls of gated communities, on the one hand, and the millions of people coming back into the downtown zones and public spaces of American and foreign cities, on the other? I have suggested in this book that one part

*"Corporatization" of public space: entrance to a new shopping mall in downtown Rotterdam, Netherlands.*

of the answer lies in exploring the ways distinct cultures embrace public spaces. One might term this approach "contextual" in that it argues that national and local culture serve to define distinct places within cities. It is these discrete places, the memories and heritage they evoke, and the behaviors they catalyze that bring urban residents back to the city centers, to walk its public passageways, to experience city life among strangers. It is also these spaces, contrary to conventional wisdom, that could become the anchors for successful downtown economic redevelopment in the twenty-first century.

Spanish and Mexican cities are anchored by public spaces rooted in historic context and place identity. The main chapters in the book have reconstructed "public space narratives" for Spain and Mexico, in effect outlining the ways public spaces changed over time as politics shifted, memory either thrived or waned, and surrounding conditions evolved. These chapters also seek to analyze the meanings of selected public places for the larger city. I argue that many traditional niches continue to possess a magnetism, or what has been termed a "power of place."[4] The power of a given place is best understood in its unique cultural and political context.

In Madrid we encountered a badly fragmented, congested, deteriorating historic core. Some of its contemporary public spaces are underutilized, converted to parking lots and traffic circles, or taken over by drug dealers. While surrounding neighborhoods are rapidly experiencing land-use change (from residential to tertiary districts), those who visit downtown increasingly perceive its public plazas to be in decline. Madrid's political climate strongly shaped the plight of its public spaces. City leaders lacked the political will to promote an urban design vision for the city or to craft a policy that will protect it. Meanwhile, Madrileños hold dearly to the post-Franco notion that in a democracy automobiles should be allowed free access anywhere in the old city, while elected officials routinely avoid any policies that support pedestrian-only use of inner-city land.

In spite of these constraints Madrid's historic district contains a rich stock of public spaces. Its tight, uneven grid is still favored by pedestrians. Some plazas in the downtown core evoke strong attachments to urban space and place. Despite numerous alterations in the twentieth century, the Plaza Mayor continues to be a noble space, not only the national symbol of the Renaissance plaza's role in Spanish urban history but also a reminder that such spaces can continue to thrive—in weekend philatelic markets, seasonal fairs and celebrations, or such daily rituals as the paseo that bring pedestrians onto the main square. The Plaza Mayor should be the heart and soul of any redevelopment plan for downtown Madrid.

If the Plaza Mayor is a museum of the Spanish royal family, the Puerta del Sol is a shrine of popular protest. Here the *sindicatos* (unions) and other social movements find a place of expression, as they have throughout Spain's history. While Madrileños look at the Plaza Mayor as the symbolic historic center of Renaissance Spain, they see the Puerta del Sol as the functional, political, and spiritual center. Here is where all roads meet; it is also where people meet. It is not uncommon to hear in Madrid "Meet me at the Puerta del Sol."

In Barcelona we encounter a different situation. Barcelona, although not as politically influential as the nation's capital, Madrid, has nevertheless rocketed past its Castilian neighbor when it comes to innovation in urban design. In the past two decades, while Madrid wallowed in uncertainty and political infighting, Barcelona found a coherent urban redevelopment strategy acceptable to most political coalitions: revitalize the waterfront, strengthen neighborhoods, and reroute traffic away from the historic center. It adopted an urban design strategy that featured public spaces as the catalysts for revitalizing neighborhood identity and upgrading community well-being. Barcelona became a virtual laboratory of successful open space projects, from renovated parks, recycled slaughterhouses, and reclaimed quarries to reinvented promenades. Barcelona gained international recognition as a shining example of what good urban design can produce—a global business center with very high marks for quality of life. The lessons of Barcelona lie in the ability of a local/regional political coalition to implement a new strategy of urban design, based on the importance of public space traditions in defining a city center.

At first glance Mexico City brings to mind some of the inner-city dilemmas observed in Madrid. The historic quarter is extremely fragmented and under siege by the forces of growth, which threaten to smother it. With a population of more than 20 million, and one of the fastest urban growth rates on the planet, Mexico City is struggling to find a design strategy and urban planning model that can accommodate its gargantuan population. The downtown must carve out a niche for itself within the rapidly decentralizing urban region. Politically, it appears that the fate of downtown will be to house tourism and high-end commerce. Meanwhile, the residents and users of the inner city face a severe quality-of-life crisis. Unemployment is high; housing is in short supply. Air pollution, noise, and rising crime rates tend to keep people inside during leisure time (watching television increasingly), or cause them to flee the city on weekends. The future sustainability of the historic core remains in doubt.

Yet, like Madrid, in material terms Mexico City's central historic district contains one of the most abundant collections of colonial-era buildings and spaces in Latin America. The downtown streets attract a large number of users, for both functional reasons (shopping, work) and for aesthetic ones. Downtown Mexico City, despite the air pollution and crime, somehow continues to remain a vital "people place." The public spaces, particularly the civic plazas, are one reason for this. The Zócalo anchors the downtown both symbolically and geographi-

*In Mexico public spaces can be mysterious and poetic: patio in a housing complex, Querétaro, Mexico.*

cally. It is the national shrine of Mexico, an expression of the basic mix of indigenous and colonial influences on Mexican culture. The Zócalo is Mesoamerican in scale, surrounded by a landscape of colonial buildings—the National Palace, the Cathedral, and so forth. It is a metaphor for Mexico's centralized political system, stamped with a Kremlin-like feel of a bureaucratic managerial state watching over an austere space. It is the Tiananmen Square of Mesoamerica. The weight of historic events—from the seventeenth-century tribunals of the Spanish Inquisition to the outbreak of early-twentieth-century revolution—can never quite leave this vast plaza.

Just as Madrid has its yin/yang of public spaces, official and popular, so, too, does Mexico City. If the Zócalo is the shrine of official

Mexico, the Plaza Santo Domingo is the plaza of organic neighborhood life. Created more than a century ago as a place for the illiterate to hire writers, the "Portals of the Scribes" has become a permanent institution imbedded upon this inner-city space. In the nearby Alameda the sacred paseo continues to exist amidst a green space of fountains and statues that have inspired Mexican artists for several centuries. Some of Mexico City's squares serve more as demarcations in the urban fabric—monuments to revolutions, fallen heroes, churches, or political symbols. One place where memory and conflict overlap is on the Plaza de Tres Culturas at Tlatelolco. Here is a historic site where three layers of Mexico's past—indigenous, colonial, and modern—overlap architecturally. But here also is where a contemporary nightmare of government repression took place—the 1968 massacre of hundreds of student protestors—which still has not been erased from Mexicans' memories.

### POLITICS AND CONTESTED PUBLIC SPACE

What seems clear in both urban Spain and Mexico is that public plazas and other public spaces in downtown historic districts are no longer completely free from the competitive bidding that occurs among interest groups for inner-city real estate. As land becomes more valuable in these districts, different users compete for access to the best outcome in the changing use of space. Even the once sacred historic plazas are subject to contention among competing interests. Public space has become embedded in the larger debates about the future of downtown. We find many examples of contestation among competing interests over the use of public squares in Madrid, Barcelona, Mexico City, and Mexico's northern border region.

In Madrid perhaps the most visible example of this process is the conflict over the future use of the Plaza de Oriente, the public plaza-garden across the street from the Royal Palace. One interest group, aligned with the conservative political party called the Partido Popular, advocated reconfiguration of the plaza to include closing the main streets around it and putting in underground parking and a cultural center. Supporters of PSOE (Socialist Workers Party of Spain) loudly objected to this vision. They claimed that the plan was really designed for the wealthy residents who owned land near the Royal Palace. They also believed that the monies used to reconfigure the plaza would be better spent on building housing for low-income families, or doing better ecological planning, such as planting more trees in downtown.

Mexican public spaces are equally politicized. It must be recalled that indigenous public spaces were often ceremonial spaces used for brutal human sacrifice. Yet, they also transcended the secular—by connecting outdoor ceremony with nature, through ritual plaza spaces. Colonial public spaces, like the plaza mayor, are arguably reflections of a totalitarian system of imperial control imposed on the Americas by the king of Spain and the royal family. Modern public spaces continue to reflect the power of the state, not only in managing people's lives, but in dictating how culture is defined.

In the modern period, however, Mexican public spaces also reflect the importance of popular protest. Many scholars who study urban popular movements are finding that in Mexico popular factions rely on streets and public spaces as places to protest state repression. For example, in the 1990s the well-known figure "Superbarrio," who posed as a masked superhero, used public appearances to protest the plight of the poor in urban Mexico. One study of the city of Monterrey showed how Mexican women utilized public places—streets, plazas, and public fountains in front of government offices—to stage protests against government-imposed water shortages that were mainly affecting the low-income neighborhoods in the city. The author argues that these protests embarrassed officials and led to major changes in water allocation policy.[5]

In Mexico City, as mentioned earlier, it is striking that in one year (1992) more than 2,000 marches and demonstrations took place on or near the Zócalo. Protests range from the national (the plight of indigenous people, unemployment, inflation) to the local (lack of services, housing shortages, and poor quality of life). The example of the Alameda district is particularly revealing. The "Plan Alameda" pits local residents who want to preserve their formerly prosperous Art Deco neighborhood against a coalition of global investors aligned with the national and local government. The investors and the government would convert the Alameda district into a tourism/luxury housing zone, thus threatening the existing sense of place in the district.

A second example of contested space lies in the government's continuing policy of "museumization" of downtown public places. The government and the merchants of downtown are pitted in a conflict with popular street vendors who believe they have a right to use the streets for spontaneous marketing. Much of the inner core of Mexico City has been cleared of street vendors, and some public places seem strikingly empty of the kind of vital life necessary to make the inner city alive. This problem has been well documented in the Federal District[6] as well as in other cities like Puebla[7] or in the northern border region.[8] At the same time, some inner-city streets and squares are overrun by itinerant vendors selling pirated DVDs, CDs, and computer software. One also sees examples of artificial landscapes imposed on public places. In Mexico City the Plaza Garibaldi is a theatrical space of arcaded cantinas that looks more like a border town than a colonial district.

The northern Mexican border region is embroiled in a campaign to reinvent frontier cities and thus break the century-old image of the border as "dead space," a "no-man's-land" between two nations. The border cities are gradually being reclaimed by their communities, with local government joining in. In the cross-border metropolitan region of Tijuana–San Diego, this process includes the actual construction of a small urban village on the political boundary itself, and the creation of public spaces nearby. Such a project could combine the best elements of Mexican public space traditions with those of the United States, or it might yield to the least common denominator of suburban shopping mall design.

### REINVENTING SPACE IN THE URBAN DOWNTOWN

In rapidly decentralizing, postindustrial, postmodern cities, the role of downtown remains as a central debate for urbanists and urban professionals. In cities in different parts of the world, from Los Angeles to Berlin to New York, downtown redevelopment occurs in different cultural, political, architectural, and economic contexts, yet the themes are remarkably similar.

In Los Angeles the traditional center is suffering what one observer has called "a crisis of identity."[9] Downtown Los Angeles in the post-1950 period tried to fashion itself as a monolithic, corporate, modernist command center for Southern California, a high-tech space of giant corporate skyscrapers, hotels, and museums, all interconnected and apart from the streets below. Glass and steel megastructures were built, to the tune of billions of dollars; older neighborhoods, like Bunker Hill, began to wither away. By the 1980s downtown L.A. was on its way to becoming the kind of place depicted in the film *Blade Runner:* a polarized space of glass towers housing the moguls of corporate capitalism on one side of town, while on the other, run-down districts bubbled over with a growing class of homeless and marginal poor on the "mean streets."[10] Ironically, some of these megatowers were found to be seismically deficient, and needed expensive retrofitting; a socioeconomic earthquake came in the form of the L.A. riots of 1992, which represented a wake-up call, reminding the region of social and ethnic divisions. It is now clear that a corporate financial-administrative

downtown won't work. What is needed is a diverse downtown core: one that combines the commercial functions of skyscrapers, with a human element, a sense of community, within a properly scaled pedestrian space, and amidst a built environment similar to turn-of-the-century downtown Los Angeles. In short, it will take a return to the past to bring Los Angeles into the future.

In a completely different cultural and geographic setting, Germany, this same theme is encountered for the case of Berlin. One of Germany's great cities, Berlin is an old city with a bizarre spatial pattern: its historic center is virtually empty, demolished first by Allied bombers during World War II, and later by East German state planners who removed the old urban fabric and replaced it with the Berlin Wall. Early in the 1990s the once thriving, historic public square, the Potsdamer Platz, sat literally in the midst of 17 vacant acres, perhaps the most valuable piece of downtown real estate in central Europe before the postmodern plaza redevelopment scheme was finally put into place. Great attention throughout Europe and the world has been focused on the revitalization of downtown Berlin. Berlin is poised to become the new economic capital of Europe, and may even supplant Paris as its cultural capital. Within Germany a great debate centered around

*Disney Music Hall (Frank Gehry, architect) has begun to inject a sense of excitement to the streets of downtown Los Angeles.*

the Berlin downtown. Artists, architects, and futurists want Berlin to be a focus of avant-garde creativity, with the downtown serving as a kind of giant laboratory for deconstructivism and postmodern design. Postmodern designs and sleek skyscrapers have emerged around the main square. But some in the urban planning sector believe that downtown Berlin can only thrive if it maintains the overall scale and structure of its pre-1920s era. It needs low-density, pedestrian-scale morphology, with traditional street grids and public squares.[11]

## GLOBALIZING PUBLIC SPACE: GROUND ZERO, NEW YORK CITY

If any city in North America, or indeed the world, can be called the symbol of twentieth-century modernism, it is New York. Some contemporary urbanists, myself included, entered the profession as a result of the magnetism of a childhood spent gazing in awe at the Manhattan skyline. New York has ridden the roller coaster of the twentieth-century central business district political economy: from the skyscraper office building boom of the first 30 years, through the Depression, to urban renewal, the financial crisis of the 1970s, the revitalization of the 1980s and 1990s, and finally the response to the tragedy of 9/11 in the new millennium. Despite its remarkably high density, and the gargantuan skyscrapers, it has been shown that Manhattan works best if the spaces between the towers—the streets and public spaces—can be transformed into livable spaces for city dwellers.[12] But still, in this age of information and suburbs, places like Lower Manhattan are in danger of becoming corporate "Jurassic Parks," zones of outmoded skyscrapers abandoned and left behind as fossils from a previous era. The only way to save Lower Manhattan is to reinvent it as a desirable place to conduct business and to live. This can be said to be true for most of downtown New York City. The solution lies not merely in fixing up buildings, which is what architects do, or even in making buildings attractive to business; rather, the answer lies in crafting a larger urban vision for the entire setting—the spaces within which the skyscrapers sit.

Such ideas are made even more critical by the events surrounding the tragic destruction of the Twin Towers of the World Trade Center in Lower Manhattan on September 11, 2001. The debates about how to rebuild this critical space will no doubt carry on over the next decade.[13] An important component of the rebuilt environment will be the new public spaces, which will serve as memorials to the victims of the tragedy, as well as mechanisms to invigorate the human spirit in this important zone of lower New York City.[14] Indeed, the World Trade Center Towers site could become one of the greatest public spaces on the planet, if it is carefully and sensitively designed.

Ground Zero's future design is complex, however. Few urban design projects in the twentieth century resonated around the world as strongly as the proposed future redevelopment of Ground Zero. The world knows this space—it witnessed live telecasts of the Twin Towers' collapse. The global community waits to see what kind of grand gesture will put a permanent mark on this site of sadness.

For Ground Zero, imagination is everything when it comes to designing a space so fraught with symbolism and emotion, and so impli-

cated in global conflict. Therefore, how to invent a memorial site fitted to the complex emotional, social, political, and architectural implications of September 11? First, Ground Zero needs a monumental community space. However, the United States does not have a particularly good track record here. In America "monumental architecture" is frequently viewed as archaic—the pyramids of Egypt, the Eiffel Tower, the Taj Mahal, the great Inca city of Macchu Pichu. Buildings here have become like consumer products—designed to have a short shelf life. We no longer construct our cities to last for centuries.

*Great public places anchor and give meaning to urban space: under the Eiffel Tower, Paris.*

Ground Zero needs a transcendental public plaza to honor the meaning now attached to the site. But great plazas have never been America's forte. Resplendent urban squares are found in other countries—in Venice (Piazza San Marcos), Rome (St. Peter's Square),

Moscow (Red Square), London (Trafalgar Square), or Beijing (Tiananmen Square). The greatness of squares across the globe lies in the way they evoke a feeling of mystery and grandeur, a sense of place, and a connection to the past, somehow embedded in a real place in a city with memory, with architectural tradition.

We can learn about such places of memory from our closest southern neighbor, Mexico. Mexicans love their plazas, as we have seen in this book. But where to look in the United States for inspiration? I suggest the Vietnam Veterans Memorial in Washington, D.C., perhaps the greatest modern-day public monument north of the Mexican border. Consider the difficult task facing architect Maya Lin—how to commemorate a war that had profoundly divided the nation, and left behind a troubled legacy. But Lin imagined how the site could both embrace history and transcend it. "I thought about what death is, what a loss is," she notes. "A sharp pain that lessens with time, but can never quite heal over. A scar. The idea occurred to me there on the site. Take a knife and cut open the earth, and with time, the grass would heal it. As if you open the rock and polish it."[15]

To enter the site of the Vietnam Veterans Memorial, you descend into the earth, below ground level, cut off from sight of the streets and from urban noise. Suddenly there are black marble walls and silence. The design jolts one's awareness; it forces upon the viewer contemplation of the past: death, life, change. Ground Zero needs delicate urban surgery—implant an urban context that is functional, but monumental in its gesture toward tragedy. The site must be integrated into the urban core; however, at least part of it, the memorial space, must also be detached. The site should be both quiet (like the Vietnam Veterans Memorial) and busy, like a Mexican plaza. It should be alive, connected, and spontaneous, but it should also speak of memory, however painful that is.[16]

### GLOBALIZING THE PLAZA: THE BATTLE IN OAXACA, MEXICO

An important but virtually unseen battle over public space with global ramifications was quietly fought in Mexico during the final months of 2002. It pitted one of the world's largest and most powerful corporations—McDonald's—against the preservers of Mexico's past. McDonald's had a seemingly innocent plan—to build a fast-food franchise on the main square of the city of Oaxaca, one of Mexico's sacred historic colonial centers.

The international fast-food giant already owns 270 franchises in Mexico. It plans to build 100 more in the next two years.[17] Most of the

McDonald's restaurants tend to be located in the suburbs, in shopping malls—or near other commercial centers. It is one thing to build a fast-food chain on the outskirts of town (such a franchise already exists on the edge of Oaxaca); it is quite another to wedge a McDonald's into the tightly knit fabric of one of Mexico's most beautiful colonial squares.

But McDonald's Corporation was determined to install its Golden Arches right on the nearly 500-year-old plaza mayor (main square) of Oaxaca, in a historic district that has been declared a World Heritage Site by UNESCO. Critics cried foul. One respected scholar and community leader told citizens in a public forum that "[t]his is nothing less than a cultural conquest."[18] A popular protest movement emerged, led by national and local artists, writers, intellectuals, and environmentalists, and backed by world-renowned figures—from former first lady of France Danielle Mitterand to Diana Kennedy, international author of books on Mexican cuisine.

In early December 2002 the Oaxaca City Council, under pressure and worldwide scrutiny, voted to deny McDonald's permission to build on the plaza. At stake was the cultural heritage of Oaxaca's downtown historic district. But the battle was symbolic of the struggle between global corporatization and the preservation of precious historic resources, which, like the earth itself, once destroyed cannot be recovered. In Oaxaca you hardly need a guide to find the historic center. Just breathe in and let your sense of smell lead you: to pungent tamales with shrimp and pumpkin seeds baked in banana leaves, greasy *chapulines* (deep fried grasshoppers), spicy chile powder spread over *cacahuetes* (peanuts) and lime juice—and richly aromatic *mole* sauce. This savory montage and the buzz of vendors and people circling through the narrow streets and across the ancient plaza are part of the authenticity that makes historic Oaxaca unique.

How different the world looks from the sleek, glass, high-rise office towers of the accountants, financial consultants, investment bankers, marketing experts, risk analysts, cost estimators, and design consultants hired by global companies to make decisions about new investment sites. For them there is simply no way to measure the alchemy of sound, smell, time, and architecture that embody a place. It cannot be translated into economic value. Historic buildings and spaces are viewed as mere backdrops in the inevitable spread of the global marketplace.

For a country like Mexico the value of its unique historic districts cannot be underestimated. After oil the tourism industry in Mexico rivals the manufacturing assembly sector as the second-largest source of foreign export revenue, generating $8–10 billion per year.

McDonald's (and other megaretail chains) is more than a mere fast-food franchise. It represents a cultural paradigm of globalization. McDonald's is a symbol of rationality, assembly-line production, efficiency—and homogeneity. Everything about the experience of eating in a McDonald's is about sameness and predictability. The portions are calculated. The ingredients are uniform. The interior design is virtually the same—and the experience of eating faster and more impersonal.[19]

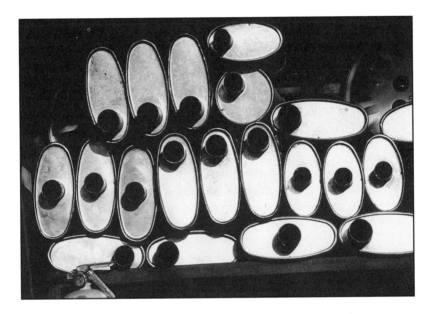

This goes against the grain in every sense of the rhythm of Mexican historic centers anchored around their *zócalos*, like the one in Oaxaca. "Oaxaca's center is part of who we are," Alejandro de Avila, who directs a botanical garden near the Regional Museum of Oaxaca, told the media. "It gives us a very special sense of place. McDonald's does not correspond to that sense of place."[20]

At some point, a historic place loses its meaning (and value) as it is overrun with fast-food chains, malls, supermarkets, and global video outlets. In a sea of sameness—for tourists and locals—how can city planners preserve a distinct sense of different locales? Should government step in and protect not only the buildings but also the sense of place embedded in a historic zone? Mexico will continue to see more McDonald's and other fast-food operations built. The question is not whether they should come, but where to put them. Should they be allowed to perforate the sanctity of sacred plazas and historic spaces? The City of Oaxaca offered its answer in 2002: No.

*In Mexico the creativity of a vernacular streetscape can spring from individual storefront designs: muffler shop in Tijuana.*

## THE FUTURE OF PLAZAS

What is clear in all of the cases reviewed in this book is that public spaces—streets, squares, parks—can enhance the experience of place and assist in keeping the inner city densely populated and livable. Public places are a vital resource in the redevelopment of the central city. While public life has suffered in the decentralized metropolis of the late twentieth century, some scholars, writers, and design/planning practitioners are pointing to ways to recover it. Public spaces anchor and give coherence to intensively urbanized inner-city areas. Some of the cutting-edge revitalization plans for cities like Barcelona, London, Frankfurt, or New York City are putting more and more emphasis on the importance of a network of public spaces in creating identity, and in providing a stage for pedestrian and public life, which in turn anchors the ability of urban core areas to house larger residential populations, while expanding their economic base around sectors such as tourism, commerce, and education.

In Spain and Mexico streets, promenades, gardens, parks, and squares form part of the rich tradition of public life that makes cities vital. In particular, the plaza—a multicultural product derived from Moorish, Spanish colonial, and, in Mexico, Mesoamerican influences—is a vital element of the historic urban patrimony. Spanish and Mexican plazas have been the site of many key historic moments. Plazas bring together important buildings, institutions, and landscapes fundamental to Spanish and Mexican society. Plazas embody the exuberant public spirit of these cultures, as well as the crisis of state and economy. They are essential to social meaning in Spain and Mexico.

While many plazas in Madrid, Barcelona, Mexico City, and other Latino cities were compromised by modernization, most of the vibrant public squares have, surprisingly, been protected. They are recognized as being national treasures. Many are surrounded by small businesses typically patronized by pedestrians—cafés, bars, bakeries, and restaurants. But because these spaces lie on increasingly valuable real estate, city planners must find ways to both preserve them and make them contribute to the urban economy. One way of preserving them is by carefully researching and recording their history, and their importance in enhancing neighborhood identity and the experience of place, something that is valuable to all city dwellers, though not easily measured in economic terms.

Spain, with its Islamic patios and Renaissance plazas, and Mexico, with her Pre-Columbian ceremonial spaces and colonial squares, offer invaluable narratives around which to construct models for creating

downtown redevelopment through the use of public space. In Barcelona, Spain, for example, this notion has been put into practice with admirable results.

As mentioned in Chapter 4, Barcelona, during the 1970s was a city whose historic core had become deteriorated and in a state of severe disorder. Businesses were moving away. The Franco regime neglected the Catalonia region because it had remained so independent. This fortunately left the historic center intact, albeit in disrepair. When Franco died in 1975, the new local government immediately organized a renewal plan for the inner city. This plan involved a strong alliance between the government and the business community. Barcelona invested in the renewal of the city's cultural patrimony—its historic buildings, parks, neighborhoods, and public spaces. The city tied its economic and business development strategies to the physical renewal of the city, and to its quality of life. Among the revitalized areas were the Barrio Gótico (Gothic Quarter), the oldest district in the

*The choreography of people in public places is a product of culture, politics, and history; it is a subtle but powerful element of good urban design: Atocha Train Station, Madrid, Spain.*

city dating to the late Middle Ages; the port and seaside districts, old industrial areas that had been abandoned; and the core zones around downtown. More than 160 major renovation projects were completed, including commercial centers, housing projects, office buildings, sports complexes, new transport lines, parks, town squares, promenades, civic monuments, and communication towers.

For Mexico the future lies in its embrace with the United States and Canada through the North American Free Trade Agreement (NAFTA). Cultural integration finds its expression in the border region where the two nations' territories meet. Mexico has the opportunity to offer to the United States some lessons on a different kind of urban design, one rooted in the civic spirit expressed in physical space through the plaza, or the commercial street.

If physical, material space is to continue to have meaning in cities, it may be the public places that serve best to encapsulate the significance of particular fragments of urban territory. While there is a certain romanticism in imagining a Baroque city of promenades and parks, such a vision is obviously not realistic for the twenty-first century. Any public place that is preserved will be so only through negotiation within the competitive arena of urban politics. Yet, if the spatial terrain of urban life is to be more than simply a "pass through" zone as city dwellers move from one privatized space to another, it will be necessary for urban dwellers to defend the places they value, and where necessary, to invent new ones. Thriving city centers will still need their plazas.

# Notes

**PREFACE**

1. Dear 2000; Garreau 1991; W. Mitchell 1995; Soja 1989.

2. Rybczynski 1996.

3. See Dear 2000; Dear, Schockman, and Hise 1996; Scott and Soja 1996.

4. See, for example, W. Mitchell 1995.

5. The story of planning and design at Ground Zero is brilliantly narrated in Paul Goldberger's new book, *Up from Zero* (see Goldberger 2004).

6. Zellner 2004.

7. "Third places" form the basis of Oldenburg's clever book on declining public life in urban America (see Oldenburg 1989). Sucher writes about "City Comforts" in a well-crafted recent volume (see Sucher 2003).

8. Mansnerus 2004.

9. This point is illustrated in Banerjee 2001; A. Jacobs 1993; Girouard 1985.

10. Lewis 2001.

11. Davis 1990.

12. An excellent study of the vitality of historic downtowns in Latin America can be found in Scarpaci 2005.

13. Low 2000.

14. This point is vindicated by the recent publication of a second major work on public space and historic preservation in Latin American inner cities; see Scarpaci 2005.

15. See, for example, Simon 1997.

16. This idea is explored in Herzog 1999; 1997.

# CHAPTER ONE

1. Rybczynski 1996.
2. Dear 2000.
3. W. Mitchell 1995.
4. See Dear 2000; Sandercock 1998.
5. Dear 2000.
6. Ibid.
7. There are others who believe that American urbanism must also embrace its past in the form of the New England town or colonial village; see Calthorpe 1993.
8. Sorkin 1992, Introduction, xi–xv.
9. This point is argued in Hiss 1991.
10. Harvey 1989.
11. *Oxford English Dictionary* 1971.
12. Lynch 1960.
13. Hiss 1991.
14. Jackson 1994.
15. Barthes 1982.
16. Krampen 1979.
17. J. Jacobs 1961.
18. Venturi, Scott, and Izenour 1972.
19. Soja 1989; Dear 2000.
20. Lofland 1973.
21. See the evocative writing in Orwell 1933.
22. Sennett 1976.
23. J. Jacobs 1961.
24. Brill 1989.
25. Rybczynski 1993.
26. See, for example, Sorkin 1992.
27. D. Mitchell 1995.
28. See Lofland 1998.
29. Whyte's work (1988) on public spaces pointed to examples where homeless people were either entertaining or helped give identity and character to a street or public place.
30. See Davis 1990.
31. See Lofland 1998, 162–168.
32. Oldenburg 1989.
33. Cranz 1982.
34. Webb 1990; Zucker 1959.
35. Zucker 1959.
36. Jackson 1987, 121.
37. Mumford 1961.
38. Kostoff 1992.
39. Zucker 1959.

40. Kostoff 1992.

41. Kato 1980.

42. Webb 1990.

43. Zucker 1959.

44. Kostoff 1992, 181.

45. See, for example, Girouard 1985; A. Jacobs 1993.

46. Zucker 1959.

47. See Cranz 1982.

48. Webb 1990.

49. Glazer and Lilla 1987, 119.

50. Brill 1989.

51. Jackson 1987.

52. Whyte 1980.

53. Project for Public Spaces 1984; Francis 1989.

54. Chidister 1986.

55. Carr et al. 1992; Cooper Marcus and Francis 1990.

56. Carr et al. 1992.

57. See, for example, Blake 1993.

58. Safdie 1997, 21.

59. Ibid.

60. Blake 1993, xvi.

61. Ibid.

62. Wright 1953, 57.

63. Hughes 1991, 188.

64. Ibid., 187.

65. Wright 1953, 57.

66. Ibid.

67. Rybczynski 1996, 229.

68. Ibid.

69. Ibid., 130.

70. This point is cleverly analyzed in Sklair 1991, 75–77.

71. See, for example, reviews in Huxtable 1986a; 1986b; or Stern 1986.

72. Jencks 1977.

73. Hughes 1991, 207.

74. Goldberger 1979.

75. Goldberger 1983.

76. Hughes 1991, 211.

77. W. Mitchell 1995.

78. Ibid., 7.

79. This is a paraphrased summary of one theme in written columns by *New York Times* architecture critic Herbert Muschamp during the 1990s.

80. W. Mitchell 1995.

81. See Girouard 1985 for one of the best narratives of how people historically transformed urban landscape in different cultural settings. Kostoff's two

volumes on urban history offer many useful insights into the role of public space in urban design across space and time (see Kostoff 1992).

82. Newton 1971.
83. Garrett Eckbo, quoted in Laurie 1976, 9.
84. Sklair 1991.
85. Ibid.
86. Ritzer 1996; Herzog 1999.
87. Harvey 1989.
88. Hiss 1991.
89. Rogers 1994.
90. See Whyte 1980; 1988.
91. Webb 1990, 105.
92. Rapoport 1969.

### CHAPTER TWO

1. See Torres Balbas 1987.
2. Ibid.
3. Ibid.
4. Cervera Vera 1990.
5. Ibid.
6. Torres Balbas 1987.
7. Cervera Vera 1990.
8. Torres Balbas 1987.
9. Ibid.
10. Bonet Correa 1991.
11. Navajas 1983.
12. Terán 1993.
13. Bonet Correa 1980.
14. Corral 1987.
15. Ibid., 19.
16. Bonet Correa 1980.
17. Morris 1979, 9–10.
18. Girouard 1985, 223–225.
19. Semler 1993.
20. Ibid.
21. Torres Balbas 1987.
22. See Terán 1993.
23. Busquets 1994.
24. SPYOT 1985.
25. Terán 1993.
26. Corral 1987, 30.
27. Corral 1987.
28. Pérez Galdós, in Thomas 1988, 140.
29. Thomas 1988, 145.

30. Miguel 1976.

31. See Hooper 1986.

32. SPYOT 1985, 113.

33. Semler 1993.

34. SPYOT 1985, 116.

35. Fernández de los Ríos 1989, 154–155.

36. Semler 1993, 206.

37. Terán 1993.

38. Hooper 1986.

39. Buchanan 1984. See Chapter 4 for a complete discussion of Barcelona's evolution in the late twentieth century.

40. Fernández Galiano 1992c.

### CHAPTER THREE

1. Rivas 1992.

2. Shubert 1990.

3. Terán 1978.

4. Castells 1990.

5. Estebañez 1990.

6. COPLACO 1980; Castells 1990; Ayuntamiento de Madrid 1993a, 1993b.

7. Fernández Galiano 1993.

8. Ibid.

9. Isasi 1992.

10. Ingersoll 1992.

11. Two more beltways, concentrically further from the center, are projected—the M-40, already under construction, and the M-50 beyond that.

12. Ayuntamiento de Madrid 1993a, 1993b.

13. Moya González 1987.

14. Villasante 1989.

15. Fernández Galiano 1992b.

16. Brandis 1975.

17. The example of Plaza Colón in Madrid is instructive; one can simply not cross the street in a safe way to get to this plaza, even though it is popular in the neighborhood.

18. Ramón Moliner 1992, 238.

19. Fernández Galiano 1992b.

20. Hauser 1991.

21. Ibid.

22. Hooper 1986.

23. Ibid., 91.

24. Ibid.

25. Ibid.

26. Ibid.

27. Villasante 1989.

28. Cortés 1992.

29. Villasante 1992.

30. Moya González 1987.

31. Hernández and Velásquez 1985.

32. Ayuntamiento de Madrid 1993a, 1993b.

33. Comunidad de Madrid 1992.

34. Cabezas 1989. 130.

35. Harvey 1989.

36. This point is based on impromptu interviews carried out by the author with local users on the plaza, as well as interviews with Madrid architects.

37. This plaza was observed systematically by the author during six months of field research from August to December 1993, and again during a one-week return visit in June 2003.

38. Mora Carbonell 1980, 1613.

39. Ibid.

40. Ibid., 1618.

41. Colegio Oficial de Arquitectos de Madrid 1987.

42. During the mid-1990s, an average of only 90 people were observed using this space at different times; on some days there were only 8 or 10 people in the entire space, even during lunchtime.

43. Blanco González, in Fundación Caja Madrid 1992, 73.

44. Ridruejo 1993.

45. Recall that the *ensanche* was the first rectangular, gridded addition to Madrid as it grew in the middle and late nineteenth century.

46. Ayuntamiento de Madrid 1985.

47. Ridruejo 1993.

48. Venturi, Scott, and Izenour 1972.

49. Zucker 1959.

50. Fernández Galiano 1993.

51. De La Hoz 1993.

52. Fernández Galiano 1993.

53. These figures are extracted from the author's observations during the mid-1990s, and have been corroborated by planners and architects in Madrid.

54. Fernández Galiano 1993.

55. Oriol 1993.

56. Ibid.

57. Ibid.

58. These points were made in several interviews. See Ridruejo 1993; Fernández Galiano 1993.

59. Ayuntamiento de Madrid 1993a, 1993b.

60. Gómez de la Serna 1988, 122.

61. Thomas 1988, 151, 154.

62. Ibid. 1988, 73.

63. Gómez de la Serna 1988.

64. M. N. Roy, *Memoirs* (Bombay 1964), cited in Thomas 1988, 154.

65. V. S. Pritchett, *The Spanish Temper* (London 1959), 107–109, cited in Thomas 1988, 159.

66. This rumor was confirmed in interviews with politicians and journalists in Madrid, December 1993.

67. Ayuntamiento de Madrid 1982.

68. Fernández Galiano 1993; Echenegary 1993.

69. Gómez de la Serna 1988, 151.

70. Ridruejo 1993.

71. Fernández Galiano 1993.

### CHAPTER FOUR

1. Ferrer 1997.

2. Sudjic 1992, 32.

3. This was actually the title of a popular 1994 book by that journalist. See Moix 1994.

4. Busquets 1994.

5. Terms like *llotja* and *drassanes* are Catalan words; where possible I try to include these since Catalan remains the official language of Barcelona. I have also mixed in the use of Spanish terms and place-names, to capture the feeling of both languages (Catalan, Spanish) in the urban culture of Barcelona as I experienced it during my field research and numerous subsequent visits between 1993 and 2003.

6. Ibid., 58.

7. Hughes 1993.

8. Center for Contemporary Culture 1994.

9. Hughes 1993, 285.

10. Calavita and Ferrer 2000.

11. Moix 1994.

12. Hughes 1993.

13. Ibid., 37.

14. Moix 1994, 78.

15. P. Cabrera 1997.

16. Ajuntament de Barcelona 1999; recall that the importance of design is discussed in a key book written about the city's reawakening titled *City of Architects* (see Moix 1994).

17. Calvet 1997.

18. Calavita and Ferrer 2000.

19. Ferrer 1997.

20. Hughes 1993, 41.

21. Ibid.

22. Borja 1996.

23. Ajuntament de Barcelona 1999.

24. Ibid.

25. Borja 1996.

26. Ibid.

27. García and Claver 2000.

28. Hughes 1993, 43.

29. Ferrer 1997.

30. Ajuntament de Barcelona 1987.

31. P. Cabrera 1997.

32. Corominas 1997.

33. Moix 1994.

34. Cited in Moix 1994, 62.

35. Ibid., 63.

36. Ferrer 1997.

37. Ibid., 64.

38. Ajuntament de Barcelona 1999.

39. The notion of defensible space, and the use of design to lower crime rates, has become an important subfield in the design profession. See Newman 1973.

40. Hughes 1993.

41. Moix 1994.

### CHAPTER FIVE

1. For a description of the fall of Tenochtitlán, see Díaz del Castillo 1963; Kandell 1988.

2. Hardoy 1968.

3. Ibid., 23.

4. Heyden and Gendrop 1980.

5. Ibid.

6. Hardoy 1968, 33.

7. This figure is cited in A. Morris 1974, but demographers have debated its accuracy. What is clear is that this was one of the largest urban concentrations in pre-Columbian North America.

8. Kandell 1988.

9. León Cázares 1980.

10. Ward 1990.

11. Díaz del Castillo 1963.

12. Lombardo 1987.

13. Kandell 1988.

14. Ibid.,127.

15. Kandell 1988, 129.

16. Stanislawski 1947.

17. Stanislawski 1946.

18. Nelson 1963.

19. Suisman 1993.
20. Webb 1990.
21. Bonet Correa 1991, 185.
22. Suisman 1993, 8.
23. Nuttall 1922.
24. Ibid.
25. Suisman 1993.
26. Kandell 1988, 129.
27. León Cázares 1980.
28. Rojas-Mix 1978.
29. Ricaud 1950.
30. Rangel 1989.
31. Kandell 1988.
32. Comisión Estatal de Vivienda, Querétaro 1994.
33. Arvizu 1994.
34. Tostado 1998.
35. Suisman 1993, 6.
36. Nelson 1963.
37. Arreola and Curtis 1993.
38. Ibid.
39. Payne 1968.
40. Ibid., 109.
41. León Cázares 1980.
42. *Enciclopedia de Mexico* 1985.
43. León Cázares 1980.
44. González Obregón 1991.
45. Ibid., 212.
46. León Cázares 1980.
47. Álvarez y Gasca 1971.
48. Ibid., 61.
49. Álvarez y Gasca 1971, 77.
50. *Artes de Mexico* 1968, 60.
51. De La Maza 1968, 23.
52. Valle Arizpe 1946.
53. Ibid., 493.

### CHAPTER SIX

1. Elbow 1975.
2. Richardson 1982.
3. Robertson 1978.
4. Ibid., 214.
5. See Chapter 4 of this volume.
6. Robertson 1978.
7. Ward 1990.

8. Kandell 1988.

9. Ibid.

10. Cervantes 1991.

11. Canclini 1993.

12. Ibid., 9.

13. Gans 1977.

14. Frieden and Sagalyn 1989.

15. Ward 1993.

16. Ibid., 1149–1153.

17. Jones and Varley 1994.

18. Arvizu 2001.

19. A. Cabrera 2001.

20. Municipalidad de Querétaro 2000.

21. A. Cabrera 2001.

22. Ibid.

23. Pedro Ramirez Vázquez is one of Mexico's leading modern architects. His works include the Museum of Anthropology, Mexico City; the Mexicana Airlines building, Mexico City; the Sports Palace, Mexico City; as well as museums, hospitals, housing projects, and numerous other commissions.

24. A. Cabrera 2001.

25. Population projections for Mexico City are complicated by the accuracy of the census in exurban locations. Some have argued that São Paulo, Brazil, is larger than Mexico City (see Gilbert 1996). But most demographic projections put the greater Mexico City urban region at close to 20 million, thus making it the largest urban agglomeration in the Americas.

26. Chanfón Olmos 1987.

27. Ibid.

28. Monnet 1995.

29. Butina Watson 1995.

30. Pradilla Cobos 1993.

31. Coulomb 2000.

32. Cox 1973; Herzog 1983; 1990.

33. Bennett 1995.

34. Porras Robles 1992.

35. Rosas Mantecón 1990.

36. Ibid., 15.

37. Pradilla Cobos 1993.

38. Ward 1990, 35.

39. Mercado y Asociados 1997, 4.

40. Tomás 1991.

41. Lezama 1991.

42. Ibid.

43. Foote 1997.

44. See also Cross 1998.

45. Mercado y Asociados 1997.

46. Fideicomiso del Centro Histórico 1998.

47. Coulomb 1998.

48. Departamento del Distrito Federal 1996.

49. Butina Watson 1995.

50. Villalpando 1997.

51. Departamento del Distrito Federal 1996.

52. Butina Watson 1995.

53. Mercado 1997.

54. Mercado 1997; Eibenshutz 1997.

55. Mercado 1997.

56. Bianco 1997.

57. Butina Watson 1995.

58. Mercado 1997.

59. Perlo 1998.

60. Cardenas 1997.

61. Mercado y Asociados 1997.

62. Ozorno 1998.

63. Gutiérrez Kirchener 1998.

64. Mercado 1998.

65. See, for example, ACSP 1994; Sassen 1994; 1991.

66. See, for example, Rowland and Gordon 1996.

67. Herzog 1999.

68. *Enciclopedia de México* 1985, 215.

69. See, for example, Monnet 1995.

70. León Cázares 1980, 164.

71. See Bennett 1995.

72. Author's field observations during visits between 1993 and 2003.

73. Villalpando 1997.

74. Ibid.

75. Gutiérrez Kirchener 1998.

## CHAPTER SEVEN

1. Scarpaci 2005.

2. Herzog 1990.

3. These differences are wisely explored in Arreola and Curtis 1993.

4. Official estimates by Mexico's statistical bureau, INEGI, routinely undercount the populations of border cities like Tijuana. INEGI's estimate of 1,275,000 inhabitants for Tijuana in 2000 fails to include numerous "illegal" squatter communities that census takers either ignored or were unable to fully cover. Further, it is well known that the Mexican government may want to undercount border-city populations as a way of minimizing the number of migrants heading north toward the United States.

5. Arreola and Curtis 1993.

6. Ibid.

7. Ibid.

8. Rosen 1991.

9. As I discuss later in this chapter, plans are afoot to build a new pedestrian bridge across the border, forging a direct connection from San Diego into downtown Tijuana.

10. Vargas 1999.

11. Mark Steele, cited in Herzog 1998b.

12. Land Grant Development 1997.

13. Estrada Land Planning 1998.

14. Martinez and Cutri 1999.

15. See R/UDAT Briefing Book 1987.

16. For an excellent narrative on the evolution of Los Angeles as a global city, see Erie 2004.

17. A few authors have tackled this theme: see, for example, Herzog 1999; Leclerc, Villa, and Dear 1999; Villa 2000.

18. One exception is the superb work of Arreola and Curtis 1993 and Arreola 2002.

19. Mays 1982.

20. Bunting 1976.

21. Rybczynski 1996, 55.

22. Vincent Scully, cited in ibid., 56.

23. Crouch, Garr, and Mundingo 1982, 77.

24. Ibid., 79.

25. Price 2003.

26. Ibid., 100.

27. For a more complete geographic definition of South Texas, see Arreola 2002.

28. Ibid.

29. Ibid., 82.

30. Ibid.

31. Fisher 1996.

32. Nelson 1983., 180.

33. Banham 1971.

34. See, for example, J. Jacobs 1961.

35. Venturi, Scott, and Izenour 1972.

36. See, for example, Davis 1990; Soja 1989; Dear 2000; Dear, Schockman, and Hise 1996; Reid 1992; Scott and Soja 1996; Sorkin 1992.

37. Dear 2000.

38. Reid 1992.

39. Sorkin 1992.

40. Soja 1989.

41. Davis 1990.

42. Mission Viejo in Orange County is a good example of a simulated community. Its designers deliberately chose to create a stage set of Mexican missions within an upper-income non-Mexican enclave.

43. See the book by Sudjic (1992).

44. Harvey 1989, 315.

45. Davis 1990, 226–227.

46. Gordon 1994.

47. Whiteson 1994.

48. Gordon 1994.

49. Rybczynski 1993.

50. Rojas 1993.

51. Diaz 1993.

52. Ibid.

53. Ibid., 32.

54. The exception is Mexico City, where crime has increased to the point at which city dwellers are very worried about it.

### CHAPTER EIGHT

1. D. Mitchell 1995.

2. Habermas 1989.

3. Ritzer 1996.

4. Hayden 1995.

5. Bennett 1995.

6. Cross 1998.

7. Jones and Varley 1994.

8. Staudt 1996.

9. Starr 1996.

10. Davis 1990.

11. Goldberger 1995.

12. Whyte 1988.

13. See the excellent journal narratives from a local designer's perspective in Sorkin 2003.

14. See, for example, the excellent report "New York, New Visions" 2002.

15. See Herzog 2002b.

16. Ibid.

17. Herzog 2002a.

18. Ibid.

19. See Ritzer 1996.

20. Herzog 2002a.

# References

*Note: All quotes from interviews are author's translations from field interviews carried out in Spanish during the fall and winter of 1993–1994.*

ACSP (American Collegiate Schools of Planning). 1994. *Globalizing North American Planning Education.* ACSP Commission on Global Approaches to Planning Education.

Ajuntament de Barcelona. 1999. *Urbanismo en Barcelona.* Barcelona.

———. 1987. *Barcelona: Espais i escultures (1982–1986).* Barcelona: Fundación Joan Miró.

Alexander, Christopher, Sara Ishikawa, and Murray Silverstein. 1977. *A Pattern Language.* New York: Oxford University Press.

Altman, Irwin, and Setha Low. 1992. *Place Attachment.* New York: Plenum Press.

Altman, Irwin, and Ervin Zube. 1989. *Public Places and Spaces.* New York: Plenum Press.

Álvarez Mora, Alonso. 1978. *La remodelación del centro de Madrid.* Madrid: Editorial Ayuso.

Álvarez y Gasca, Pedro. 1971. *La plaza de Santo Domingo.* Mexico City: INAH.

Amestoy, D. Santos. 1985. "La Puerta del Sol en primavera." *Alfoz* 18/19 (July/Aug.): 73–76.

Arreola, Daniel. 2002. *Tejano South Texas.* Austin: University of Texas Press.

Arreola, Daniel, and James Curtis. 1993. *The Mexican Border Cities.* Tucson: University of Arizona Press.

*Artes de Mexico.* 1968. "Santo Domingo's Plaza." 110:59–63.

Arvizu, Carlos. 2001. Field interview. Querétaro, Mexico.

———. 1994. *Capitulaciones de Querétaro.* 1655. Ayuntamiento de Querétaro.

Ayuntamiento de Madrid. 1993a. *Revisión del plan general de ordenación urbana de Madrid,* Madrid: Oficina Municipal del Plan.

———. 1993b. *Un Madrid para vivir: Nuevo plan general.* Madrid.

———. 1985. *12 actuaciones para Madrid.* Madrid.

———. 1982. *Recuperar Madrid.* Madrid.

Banerjee, Tridib. 2001."The Future of Public Space: Beyond Invented Streets and Reinvented Places." *Journal of the American Planning Association* 67, no. 1: 9–24.

Banham, Reyner. 1971. *Los Angeles.* New York: Penguin.

Barthes, Roland. 1982. *Empire of Signs.* New York: Hill and Wang.

Bennett, Vivienne. 1995. *The Politics of Water.* Pittsburgh: University of Pittsburgh Press.

Bianco, A. 1997. "Faith and Fortune." *BusinessWeek.* January 20.

Blake, Peter. 1993. *No Place like Utopia.* New York: Alfred Knopf.

Bonet Correa, Antonio. 1991. *El urbanismo en España e HispanoAmerica.* Madrid: Ediciones Catedra.

———. 1980. "Plaza Mayor." In *Madrid,* 41-60. Madrid: Espasa-Calpe.

Borja, Jordi. 1996. *Barcelona: An Urban Transformation Model.* Quito: World Bank/Urban Management Program.

Boyer, M. Christina. 1995. *Cyber Cities.* Princeton: Princeton University Press.

Brandis, Dolores. 1975. "Forma y función de las plazas de Madrid." *Estudios Geográficos* 36 (Feb.–May): 125-155.

Brill, Michael. 1989. "Transformation, Nostalgia, and Illusion in Public Life and Public Place." In *Public Places and Spaces,* ed. Irwin Altman and Ervin Zube. New York: Plenum Press.

Buchanan, Peter. 1984. "Regenerating Barcelona with Parks and Plazas." *Architectural Review* 175 (June): 32–36.

Bunting, Bainbridge. 1976. *Early Architecture in New Mexico.* Albuquerque: University of New Mexico Press.

Busquets, Joan. 1994. *Barcelona.* Barcelona: Editorial Mapre.

———. 1992. "Evolución del planeamiento urbanístico en los años ochenta en Barcelona." *Ciudad y Territorio* 93:31–51.

Butina Watson, G. 1995. "Public Participation and the Urban Regeneration Process." Paper presented at the annual meeting of the Environmental Design Research Association, Boston, March.

Cabezas, Juan Antonio. 1989. *Diccionario de Madrid.* Madrid: Avapies.

Cabrera, Alejandro. 2001. Field interview, Querétaro, Mexico.

Cabrera, Pera. 1997. Field interview. Barcelona.

Calavita, Nico, and Amador Ferrer. 2000. "Behind Barcelona's Success Story." *Journal of Urban History* 26, no. 6: 793-807.

Calthorpe, Peter. 1993. *The Next American Metropolis*. New York: Princeton Architectural Press.

Calvert, A. F. 1908. *Southern Spain*. London: A. C. & Black.

Calvet, Luis. 1997. Field interview. Barcelona.

Canclini, Néstor García. 1993. "Mexico: La globalización cultural de una ciudad que se desintegra." *Ciudades* 20:3–12.

Canter, David. 1977. *The Psychology of Place*. London: Architectural Press.

Cárdenas, Cuahtémoc. 1997. *Una ciudad para todos: D.F. 1997–2000*. Mexico City.

Carr, Stephen, Mark Francis, Leanne Rivlin, and Andrew Stone. 1992. *Public Space*. Cambridge, England: Cambridge University Press.

Carrete Parrando, Juan. 1980. "Puerta del Sol." In *Madrid*. Madrid: Espasa-Calpe.

Castells, Manuel. 1990. "Oportunidades y estrangulamientos." *Alfoz* 74/75 (June): 36–39.

CEHOPU (Centro de Estudios Históricos de Obras Públicas y Urbanismo). 1989. *La ciudad hispanoamericano, El sueño de un orden Madrid*. Madrid: MOPU (Ministerio de Obras Públicas y Urbanismo).

Center for Contemporary Culture. 1994. *Contemporary Barcelona*. Barcelona: Diputación de Barcelona.

Cervantes, Enrique S. 1991. "Transport in the Mexico City Metropolitan Area." *Cuadernos de Urbanismo* 2:90–94.

Cervera Vera, Luis. 1990. *Plazas mayores de España*. Madrid: Espasa-Calpe.

Chanfón Olmos, Carlos. 1987. "El centro histórico de la Ciudad de México." In *Atlas de la Ciudad de México*, ed. Gustavo Garza, 240-244. México City. Departamento del Distrito Federal and Colegio de México.

Chidister, Mark. 1986. "The Effect of Context on the Use of Urban Plazas." *Landscape Journal* 5 (fall): 115–127.

Chueca Goitia, Fernando. 1974. *Madrid, ciudad con vocación de capital*. Santiago de Compostela: Editorial Pico Sacro.

Citta 3. 1999. *Plan de desarrollo turístico integral del estado de Querétaro*. Querétaro: Secretaría de Turismo.

Colegio de Arquitectos de Madrid. 1987. *Guía de arquitectura y urbanismo de Madrid*. Madrid.

Comisión Estatal de Vivienda, Querétaro. 1994. *Volver a nuestras calles*. Querétaro, Mexico.

Comunidad de Madrid. 1992. *El espacio renovado*. Madrid.

Cooper Marcus, Clare, and Carolyn Francis, eds. 1990. *People Places*. New York: Van Nostrand Rheinhold.

COPLACO (Comisión de Planeamiento y Coordinación del Área Metropolitano de Madrid). 1980. *Informe sobre ordenación del territorio en el área metropolitano de Madrid*. Madrid.

———. 1978. *Que hacer con Madrid*. Madrid.

Corominas, Miguel. 1997. Field interview. Barcelona.

Corral, Jose del. 1987. *La plaza mayor de Madrid*. Madrid: Méndez y Molina.

Cortés, Juan Antonio. 1992. *El racionalismo madrileño*. Madrid: Colegio de Arquitectos.

Coulomb, René. 2000. "El centro histórico de la Ciudad de México." In *La Ciudad de México en el Fin del Segundo Milenio*, ed. Gustavo Garza, 530–537. Mexico City: Colegio de Mexico.

———. 1998. Field interview. Mexico City.

Cox, K. 1973. *Conflict, Power, and Politics in the City*. New York: McGraw Hill.

Cranz, Galen. 1982. *The Politics of Park Design*. Cambridge: MIT Press.

Cross, John. 1998. *Informal Politics: Street Vendors and the State in Mexico City*. Palo Alto: Stanford University Press.

Crouch, Dora, Daniel Garr, and Alex Mundingo. 1982. *Spanish City Planning in North America*. Cambridge: MIT Press.

Curtiss, Aaron. 1994. "Grand Hopes for City Core." *Los Angeles Times,* September 12.

Davis, Mike. 1990. *City of Quartz*. New York: Verso.

Dear, Michael. 2000. *The Postmodern Urban Condition*. Oxford: Blackwell.

Dear, Michael, Eric Schockman, and Greg Hise, eds. 1996. *Rethinking Los Angeles*. Beverly Hills: Sage.

De La Hoz, Rafael. 1993. Field interview. Madrid.

De La Maza, Francisco. 1968. "Historical Sketch of Santo Domingo Plaza." *Artes de Mexico* 110:16–31.

Departamento del Distrito Federal. 1996. *Programa de mejoramiento urbano de la zona sur de la Alameda*. Mexico City: Fideicomiso Alameda.

Diaz, David. 1993. "The Free Life: The Street Culture of East L.A." *Places* 8 (spring): 30–37.

Díaz del Castillo, Bernal. 1963. *The Conquest of New Spain,* trans. J. M. Cohen. London: Penguin.

Echenagusia, Javier. 1985. "La Plaza Mayor." *Alfoz* 14 (March): 16–17.

Echenegary, Javier. 1993. Field interview. Madrid.

Eibenshutz, Roberto. 1997. Field interview. Mexico City.

Elbow, Gary. 1975. "Factors in the Differentiation of Guatemalan Town Squares." *Growth and Change* 6, no. 2: 14–18.

*Enciclopedia de Mexico*. 1985. "Imagen de la Gran Capital México, D.F."

Erie, Steven P. 2004. *Globalizing L.A.* Palo Alto: Stanford University Press.

Espiago González, Javier, and Rafael Más Hernández. 1985. "El centro comercial AZCA, Madrid." In *Urbanismo y hacienda en el mundo hispano*, 1367–1385. Madrid: Universidad Complutense.

Estebañez Alvarez, José, ed. 1990. *Madrid: Presente y futuro*. Madrid: Akal.

Estrada Land Planning. 1998. *The San Ysidro Intermodal Transportation Center*. San Diego: Metropolitan Transit Development Board.

Fernández de los Ríos, Angel. 1989. *El futuro Madrid* Reprint. Madrid: Libros de la Frontera.

Fernández Galiano, Luis. 1993. "Madrid madriguera." *El País*. November.

———. 1992a. "*Almendra con guirnalda.*" *El País*.

———. 1992b. "El espacio público: Físico y virtual." *El País*.

———. 1992c. "Viaje a Icaria." *Arquitectura y Vivienda* 37:4.

Ferrer, Amador. 1997. Field interview. Barcelona.

Fideicomiso del Centro Histórico. 1998. *Plan estratégico para la regeneración y el desarrollo integral del centro histórico de La Ciudad de México*. Federal District.

Fisher, Lewis. 1996. *Saving San Antonio*. Lubbock: Texas Tech University Press.

Fletcher, Richard. 1992. *Moorish Spain*. Berkeley: University of California Press.

Foote, W. 1997. "Mexico City's Street Vendors Have Big Brothers." *Wall Street Journal*. February 14.

Ford, Larry. 1994. *Cities and Buildings*. Baltimore: Johns Hopkins University Press.

Francis, Mark. 1989. "Control as a Dimension of Public Space Quality." In *Public Places and Spaces,* ed. Irwin Altman and Ervin Zube, 147–172. New York: Plenum Press.

Frieden, Bernard, and Lynne Sagalyn. 1989. *Downtown, Inc.* Cambridge: MIT Press.

Fundación Caja Madrid. 1992. *Madrid más alto: La Castellana*. Madrid: Ediciones la Librería.

Gans, Herbert. 1977. *The Levittowners*. London: Allen Lane.

García, Soledad, and Nuria Claver. 2000. "After 1992: Some Outcomes of the New Tourism Landscape in Barcelona." Paper presented at the International Tourism Research Group Conference, Barcelona, January.

Garreau, Joel. 1991. *Edge City*. New York: Doubleday.

Garza, Gustavo. 1992. "Evolución de la Ciudad de México en el siglo XX." *Documentos de trabajo el Colegio de México*. Centro de Demografía y Desarrollo Urbano (CEDDU).

Gilbert, Alan, ed. 1996. *The Mega-City in Latin America*. Tokyo: United Nations University Press.

Girouard, Mark. 1985. *Cities and People*. New Haven: Yale University Press.

Glazer, Nathan, and Mark Lilla, eds. 1987. *The Public Face of Architecture*. New York: Free Press.

Goldberger, Paul. 2004. *Up from Zero*. New York: Random House.

———. 1995. "Reimagining Berlin." *New York Times Magazine*. February, 45–53.

———. 1983. *On the Rise*. New York: Times Books.

———. 1979. *The City Observed: New York*. New York: Vintage Books.

Gómez de la Serna, Ramón. 1988. *Elucidario de Madrid,* Reprint. Madrid: Comunidad de Madrid.

González Obregón, Luis. 1991. *Las calles de México*. Mexico City: Alianza.

Gordon, Larry. 1994. "A Push to Take Back the Parks." *Los Angeles Times.* January 29.

Gutiérrez Kirchener, A. 1998. Field interview. Mexico City.

Habermas, Jurgen. 1989. *The Structural Transformation of the Public Sphere,* trans. Thomas Burger. Cambridge: MIT Press.

Hardoy, Jorge. 1968. *Urban Planning in Pre-Columbian America.* New York: George Braziller.

Harvey, David. 1989. *The Condition of Post Modernity.* Oxford: Blackwell.

Hauser, Dominique. 1991. "Ritmos e intensidades de frecuentación en los espacios públicos de las áreas interiores urbanos: el caso de Madrid." In *Seminario Hispano-Portugués Sobre Jardines y Espacios Abiertos.* Paper presented at UNESCO meeting. Madrid: Auryn.

Hayden, Dolores. 1995. *The Power of Place.* Cambridge: MIT Press.

Hernández Aja, Agustín, and Isabel Velásquez Aloria. 1985. "La recuperación del espacio público de los pueblos madrileños." *Alfoz* 20 (Sept.): 23–26.

Herzog, Lawrence A. 2003. "Global Tijuana." In *Postborder City: Cultural Spaces of Bajalta California,* ed. Michael Dear and Gustavo Leclerc, 119–142. New York: Routledge.

———. 2002a. "McDonald's vs. Mexico." theglobalist.com Web magazine. <www.globalist.com>. Posted December 16.

———. 2002b. "Rebuilding at Ground Zero: A Global Urban Design Project." Opinion Essay, *San Diego Union Tribune,* September 13.

———. 1999. *From Aztec to High Tech: Architecture and Landscape across the Mexico–United States Border.* Baltimore: Johns Hopkins University Press.

———. 1998a. "Border Urbanism." In *Encyclopedia of Mexico: History, Society, and Culture,* ed. M. Werner, 1505–1511. Chicago: Fitzroy Dearborn.

———. 1998b. "A New Tijuana Needs a New Image." *San Diego Union Tribune,* March 1.

———. 1997. "The Transfrontier Metropolis." *Harvard Design Magazine* 1 (winter-spring): 16–19.

———. 1992. "Between Cultures: Public Space in Tijuana." *Places* 8 (spring): 54–61.

———. 1990. *Where North Meets South: Cities, Space, and Politics on the U.S.-Mexican Border.* Austin: University of Texas Press/Center for Mexican American Studies.

———. 1983. "Politics and the Role of the State in Land Use Change." *International Journal of Urban and Regional Research* 7:93–113.

Heyden, Doris, and Paul Gendrop. 1980. *Pre-Columbian Architecture of Mesoamerica.* New York: Electa/Rizzoli.

Hiss, Tony. 1991. *The Experience of Place.* New York: Vintage Books.

Holden, Robert. 1988. "Barcelona Revitalized." *Landscape Architecture* 78:60–63.

Hooper, John. 1986. *The Spaniards*. London: Penguin.

Hopkins, Adam. 1993. *Spanish Journeys*. London: Penguin.

Hughes, Robert. 1993. *Barcelona*. New York: Vintage Books.

———. 1991. *The Shock of the New*. New York: McGraw Hill.

Huxtable, Ada L. 1986a. *Architecture Anyone?* Berkeley: University of California Press.

———. 1986b. *Goodbye History, Hello Hamburger*. Washington, DC: The Preservation Press.

Ingersoll, Richard. 1992. "La jungla de asfalto." *Arquitectura Viva* 27 (Nov.-Dec.): 9-17.

Isasi, Justo. 1992. "Madrid a la baja." *Arquitectura Viva* 27 (Nov.-Dec.): 5-8.

Jackson, J. B. 1994. *A Sense of Place, a Sense of Time*. New Haven: Yale University Press.

———. 1987. "Forum Follows Function." In *The Public Face of Architecture*, ed. Nathan Glazer and Mark Lilla. New York: Free Press.

Jacobs, Allan B. 1993. *Great Streets*. Cambridge: MIT Press.

Jacobs, Jane. 1961. *The Death and Life of Great American Cities*. New York: Random House.

Jencks, Charles. 1977. *The Language of Post Modern Architecture*. New York: Rizzoli.

Jiménez, Margarita. 1973. *Madrid en sus plazas, parques y jardines*. Madrid: Abaco Ediciones.

Jones, Gareth, and Ann Varley. 1994. "The Contest for the City Centre: Street Traders versus Buildings." *Bulletin of Latin American Research* 13:27-44.

Kandell, Jonathan. 1988. *La Capital: The Biography of Mexico City*. New York: Henry Holt.

Kato, Akinori. 1980. "The Plaza in Italian Culture." *Process Architecture* 16 (July): 5-24.

Kostoff, Spiro. 1992. *The City Assembled*. London: Thames and Hudson.

Krampen, M. 1979. *Meaning in the Urban Environment*. London: Pion.

Kunstler, James. 1993. *The Geography of Nowhere*. New York: Touchstone.

Land Grant Development. 1997. *International Gateway of the Americas*. Project Proposal. San Diego.

Laurie, Michael. 1976. *An Introduction to Landscape Architecture*. New York: American Elsevier.

Leclerc, Gustavo, Raul Villa, and Michael Dear. 1999. *Urban Latino Culture*. Thousand Oaks, CA: Sage.

León Cázares, María del Carmen. 1980. *La plaza mayor de la Ciudad de México en la vida cotidiana de sus habitantes*. Mexico City: Instituto de Estudios y Documentos Históricos.

Lewis, David. 2001. Lecture. Tecnológico de Monterrey, Querétaro campus, Department of Architecture. Video simulcast.

Lezama, J. L. 1991. "Ciudad y conflicto: Usos del suelo y comercio ambulante en la Ciudad de México." In *Espacio y vivienda en la Ciudad de México,* ed. M. Schteingart, 121–135. Mexico City: Colegio de Mexico.

Lofland, Lyn. 1998. *The Public Realm.* New York: Aldine de Gruyter.

———. 1973. *A World of Strangers: Order and Action in Urban Public Space.* New York: Basic Books.

Lombardo, Sonia. 1987. "México-Tenochtitlán en 1519." In *Atlas de la Ciudad de México,* ed. Gustavo Garza, 47–57. México City: Departamento del Distrito Federal and Colegio de México.

Low, Setha. 2000. *On the Plaza: The Politics of Public Space and Culture.* Austin: University of Texas Press.

Lynch, Kevin. 1972. *What Time Is This Place?* Cambridge: MIT Press.

———. 1960. *The Image of the City.* Cambridge: MIT Press.

Macedo, Luis Ortiz. 1993. "Mexico City: Its Historical Development and Future Expectations." *Cuadernos de Urbanismo* 4:75–79.

Mansnerus, Laura. 2004. "Suburban Sprawl? That's So 1990's, Study Says." *New York Times,* May 21.

Martinez, Joseph, and Anthony Cutri. 1999. *UETA Duty Free: Design Prospectus.* San Diego.

Más Hernández, Rafael. 1982. *El barrio de Salamanca.* Madrid: Instituto de Estudios de Administración Local.

Mays, Buddy. 1982. *Ancient Cities of the Southwest.* San Francisco: Chronicle Books.

Mercado, A. 1998. Field interview, Mexico City.

———. 1997. Field interview. Mexico City.

Mercado y Asociados. 1997. *Proyecto centro histórico, Ciudad de México.* Mexico City: Asamblea de Representantes.

Miguel, Carlos de. 1976. *Madrid: Plazas y plazuelas.* Madrid: Graficas Lorca.

Mitchell, Don. 1995. "The End of Public Space? People's Park, Definitions of the Public and Democracy." *Annals of the Association of American Geographers* 85:108–133.

Mitchell, William. 1995. *City of Bits: Space, Place, and the Infobahn.* Cambridge: MIT Press.

Moix, Llatzer. 1994. *La ciudad de los arquitectos* (*City of Architects*). Barcelona: Editorial Anagrama.

Monnet, Jerome. 1995. *Usos e imagenes del centro histórico de La Ciudad de México.* Mexico City: Departamento del Distrito Federal.

Mora Carbonell, Vicente. 1980. "Plaza de España." *Madrid.* Madrid: Espasa-Calpe.

Morris, A. E. J. 1974. *History of Urban Form.* New York: John Wiley and Sons.

Morris, Jan. 1979. *Spain.* London: Penguin.

Moya González, Luis. 1987. "Lo construido en la operación de remodelación." *Alfoz* 39 (April): 33–38.

Municipalidad de Querétaro. 2000. *Plan parcial de desarrollo urbano—delegación centro histórico.* Querétaro.

Mumford, Lewis. 1961. *The City in History.* New York: Harcourt Brace.

Navajas, Pablo. 1983. *La arquitectura vernácula en el territorio de Madrid.* Madrid: Diputación de Madrid.

Nelson, Howard. 1983. *The Los Angeles Metropolis.* Dubuque, IA: Kendall Hunt.

———. 1963. "Townscapes of Mexico." *Economic Geography* 39:74–83.

Newman, Oscar. 1973. *Defensible Space.* New York: Macmillan.

Newton, Norman. 1971. *Design on the Land.* Cambridge: Harvard University Press.

"New York, New Visions." 2002. In *Principles for the Rebuilding of Lower Manhattan.* New York. <www.nynv.aiga.org>.

Nuttall, Zelia. 1922. "Royal Ordinances Concerning the Laying Out of New Towns." *Hispanic American Historical Review* 5:249–254.

Oldenburg, Ray. 1989. *The Great Good Place.* New York: Marlowe and Co.

Oriol e Ybarra, Miguel de. 1993. Field interview. Madrid.

———. 1990. *Madrid a pie, una utopia.* Madrid: Real Academia de Bellas Artes de San Fernando.

Orwell, George. 1933. *Down and Out in Paris and London.* New York: Harcourt, Brace, Jovanovich.

*Oxford English Dictionary.* 1971. Oxford University Press.

Ozorno, Jorge. 1998. Field interview. Mexico City.

Payne, Robert. 1968. *Mexico City.* New York: Harcourt, Brace and World, Inc.

Perlo, Manuel. 1998. Field interview. Mexico City.

Porras Robles, Angel. 1992. "El D.F.: Acosado por marchas y plantones." *Uno Más Uno,* November 14.

Pradilla Cobos, Emilio. 1993. "Reconstrucción del centro histórico de la Ciudad de Mexico." *Ciudades* 17:14–21.

Price, V. B. 2003. *Albuquerque: A City at the End of the World.* 2nd ed. Albuquerque: University of New Mexico Press.

Project for Public Spaces. 1984. *Managing Downtown Public Spaces.* Washington, DC: American Planning Association.

Quesada Martini, María Jesús. "Olavide." In *Madrid.* Madrid: Espasa-Calpe.

Ramón Moliner, Fernando. 1992. "Automóvil privado y espacio público." *Ciudad y Territorio* 91/92 (Jan.–June): 233–238.

Rangel, Rafael López, ed. 1989. *Las ciudades latinoamericanas.* Mexico City: Plaza y Valdés.

Rapoport, Amos. 1969. *House Form and Culture.* Englewood Cliffs, NJ: Prentice Hall.

Reid, David, ed. 1992. *Sex, Death, and God in L.A.* New York: Random House.

Repide, Pedro de. 1985. *Las calles de Madrid.* Madrid: Afrodisio Aguado.

Ricaud, Robert. 1950. "La plaza mayor en España y en America Española." *Estudios Geográficos* 11:321–327.

Richardson, Miles. 1982. "Being in the Market versus Being in the Plaza." *American Ethnologist* 9, no. 2: 421–436.

Ridruejo, Juan. 1993. Field interview. Madrid.

Ritzer, George. 1996. *The McDonaldization of Society.* Thousand Oaks, CA: Pine Forge Press.

Rivas, Juan Luis de. 1992. *El espacio como lugar.* Valladolid: Universidad de Valladolid.

Robertson, Douglas. 1978. "A Behavioral Portrait of the Mexican Plaza Principal." Ph.D. diss., Syracuse University.

Rogers, Richard. 1994. Public lecture. Columbia University, Graduate School of Architecture, New York, February 17.

Rojas, James. 1993. "The Enacted Environment of East L.A." *Places* 8 (spring): 42–53.

Rojas-Mix, Miguel. 1978. *La plaza mayor: El urbanismo--instrumento de dominio colonial.* Barcelona: Muchnik.

Rosas Mantecón, Ana María. 1990. "Rescatar el centro, preservar la historia." *Ciudades* 8:15–21.

Roseman, Curtis, and J. Diego Vigil. 1993. "From Broadway to Latinoway." *Places* 8 (spring): 20–29.

Rosen, Manuel. 1991. Field interview. San Diego.

Rowland, A., and P. Gordon. 1996. "Mexico City: No Longer a Leviathan?" In *The Mega-City in Latin America,* ed. Alan Gilbert, 173–202. Tokyo: United Nations University Press.

R/UDAT (Regional Urban Design Assistant Team) Briefing Book, 1987. Summary of San Ysidro Community Revitalization Study. San Diego. Typescript.

Rybczynski, Witold. 1996. *City Life.* New York: Touchstone.

———. 1993. "The New Downtowns." *Atlantic Monthly* (May): 98–106.

Safdie, Moshe. 1997. *The City after the Automobile.* Boulder, CO: Westview Press.

Salazar, Sergio, Marco Ugalde, and Fabio Espinoza. 1994. *Volver a nuestras calles.* Querétaro: Gobierno del Estado.

Sandercock, Leoni. 1998. *Towards Cosmopolis: Planning for Multicultural Cities.* Chichester, England: John Wiley.

Sassen, Saskia. 1994. *Cities in a World Economy.* London: Pine Forge Press.

———. 1991. *The Global City.* Princeton: Princeton University Press.

Scarpaci, Joseph. 2005. *Plazas and Barrios.* Tucson: University of Arizona Press.

Scobie, Alex. 1990. *Hitler's State Architecture: The Impact of Classical Antiquity.* University Park: Penn State University Press.

Scott, Alan, and Edward Soja, eds. 1996. *The City: Los Angeles and Urban Theory at the End of the Twentieth Century.* Berkeley: University of California Press.

Secretaría de Desarrollo Urbano y Obras Públicas Municipales. Dirección de Desarrollo Urbano. 1995. *Propuesta de un programa de ordenamiento del comercio informal en la ciudad de Querétaro.* Querétaro: Presidencia Municipal.

Semler, George. 1993. *Madrid Walks.* New York: Henry Holt.

Sennett, Richard. 1976. *The Fall of Public Man.* New York: Alfred Knopf.

Shubert, Adrian. 1990. *A Social History of Spain.* London: Unwin Hyman.

Simon, Joel. 1997. *Endangered Mexico: An Environment on the Edge.* San Francisco: Sierra Club.

Sklair, Leslie. 1991. *Sociology of the Global System.* Baltimore: Johns Hopkins University Press.

Soja, Edward. 1989. *Post Modern Geographies.* New York: Verso.

Sorkin, Michael. 2003. *Starting from Ground Zero: Reconstructing Downtown New York.* New York: Routledge.

———, ed. 1992. *Variations on a Theme Park.* New York: Hill and Wang.

SPYOT (Seminario del Planeamiento y Ordenación del Territorio). 1985. *Espacios públicos en el casco histórico de Madrid.* Madrid: Colegio de Arquitectos.

Stanislawski, Dan. 1947. "Early Spanish Town Planning in the New World." *Geographical Review* 37, no. 1: 94–105.

———. 1946. "The Origin and Spread of the Grid Pattern Town." *Geographical Review* 36, no. 1: 105–120.

Starr, Kevin. 1996. "Downtown: Back to the Future." *Los Angeles Times,* February.

Staudt, Kathleen. 1996. "Struggles in Urban Space: Street Vendors in El Paso and Ciudad Juarez." *Urban Affairs Review* 31 (March): 435–454.

Stern, Robert. 1986. *Pride of Place.* New York: Houghton Mifflin.

Sucher, David. 2003. *City Comforts.* Seattle: City Comforts, Inc.

Sudjic, Deyan. 1992. *The 100 Mile City.* Orlando: Harcourt, Brace and Co.

Suisman, Douglas. 1993. "Plaza mexicana." *Places* 8, no. 3: 4–19.

Terán, Fernando de. 1993. *Madrid.* Madrid: Mapre.

———. 1978. *Planeamiento urbano en la España contemporánea: Historia de un proceso imposible.* Barcelona: Gustavo Gill.

Thomas, Hugh. 1988. *Madrid: A Traveller's Companion.* London: Constable and Co.

Tomás, F. 1991. "El papel del centro en la problemática metropolitana actual." In *Espacio y vivienda en la Ciudad de México,* ed. Marta Schteingart, 107-119. Mexico City: Departamento del Distrito Federal.

Torres Balbas, Leopoldo. 1987. *Resumen histórico del urbanismo en España.* Madrid: Instituto de Estudios de Administración Local.

Tostado, Conrado. 1998. *The State of Querétaro.* Mexico City: Reproducciones Fotomecánicas.

Tovar G., Consuelo, ed. 1994. *Querétaro: Places and Pathways.* Mexico City: Grupo Editorial Proyección de México.

Tuan, Yi Fu. 1977. *Space and Place*. Minneapolis: University of Minnesota Press.

Valle Arizpe, Artemio de. 1946. *Historia de la Ciudad de México*. Mexico City: Editorial Pedro Robredo.

Vargas, Juan. 1999. "A Link, Not a Barrier at the Border." *San Diego Union Tribune*, January 10.

Venturi, Robert, Denise Scott, and Steven Izenour. 1972. *Learning from Las Vegas*. Cambridge: MIT Press.

Villa, Raul. 2000. *Barrio-Logos : Space and Place in Urban Chicano Literature and Culture*. Austin: University of Texas Press.

Villalpando, R. 1997. Field interview. Mexico City.

Villasante, Tomás. 1989. *Retrato de chabolista con piso*. Madrid: Alfoz/ UIMA.

Violich, Francis. 1944. *Cities of Latin America*. New York: Reinhold.

Ward, Peter. 1993. "The Latin American Inner City: Differences of Degree or of Kind?" *Environment and Planning A* 25:1131–1160.

———. 1990. *Mexico City*. Boston: G. K. Hall.

Webb, Michael. 1990. *The City Square*. London: Thames and Hudson.

Weisberg, Lorie. 1994. "Clusters of Urban Villages Key to New American Housing Dream." *San Diego Union Tribune*, May 1.

Whiteson, Leon. 1994. "Bold New Look, Same Old Hope." *Los Angeles Times*, February 13.

Whyte, William. 1988. *City*. New York: Anchor Books.

———. 1980. *The Social Life of Small Urban Spaces*. Washington, DC: Conservation Foundation.

Wright, Frank Lloyd. 1953. *The Future of Architecture*. New York: Horizon Press.

Zellner, Peter. 2004. "Culture or Bust." Public lecture. INSite Workshop, Centro Cultural de Tijuana, Tijuana, Mexico, May.

Zucker, Paul. 1959. *Town and Square: From the Agora to the Village Green*. New York: Columbia University Press.

Zukin, Sharon. 1991. *Landscapes of Power*. Berkeley: University of California Press.

# Index

and the *ensanche* plan, 48; in Spain, 46–49; and Wars of Independence, 47

Barragan, Luis, 178–179

*barris* (neighborhoods), and redevelopment in Barcelona, 98, 100, 105

*bastide*, 37

Berlin, downtown revitalization in, 232–233

Bohigas, Oriol: and planning strategy in Barcelona, 97–100, 105–107, 113–114; role of, in remodeling of Plaza Real, 108–109

Bonaparte, José, and Plaza Oriente, Madrid, 52–53, 80

Bourbons: in Madrid, 49–55; in Puerta del Sol, 51–52; role of, in Plaza Colón, 70

Brasilia, 24

Broadacre City, 20–22; and aesthetic of flaneur, 21; loss of spontaneous public space in, 21. *See also* Wright, Frank Lloyd

Cárdenas, Cuahtémoc, 161–162, 165

Catalan region, 92, 95; unique culture and urbanism in, 104–105. *See also* Barcelona

CECUT (Centro Cultural de Tijuana), 193–194

Cerdá, Ildefonso, 93–94

*chabolas*, in Madrid, 57, 67

Charles V (king of Spain), 120, 132

Chicano Park, 219–220

church plazas, 170–171

"City of Architects," 91–92

City Walk, 212–213, 218

*Ciudad Lineal* (Linear City), Madrid, 48, 55. *See also* Soria, Arturo

Ciutat Vella (old city), Barcelona, 98

contested public space: and Alameda, Mexico City, 157–162; in downtown Mexico City, 153–157; and hard plazas in Barcelona, 107–110; on Plaza de Oriente, Madrid, 79–83; politics of, 229–231; in Querétaro, 146–148

contextual approach to public space analysis, 224–229

Cortés, Hernán, 115, 120–121, 131

Costa Rica, plazas in, xv

cultural patrimony, and politics of downtown redevelopment in Mexico City, 175–177

culture-ideology of consumerism: in architecture, 22; and globalization, 27–28; and homogenization of urban space, 27–28

cyberspace, ix, 2; critique of, 25–26; and cyberarchitecture, 24–26. *See also* digital revolution, and urban life

Dali, Salvador, 107; and plaza in Madrid, 75–78

Díaz, Porfirio, 183

digital revolution, and urban life, 1–2, 24–26

downtown redevelopment: in Barcelona, 31, 96–104; in Berlin, 232–233; in Frankfurt, 30; in postmodern cities, x, 231; in Latin America, 143; London as, 30; Los Angeles as, 231–232; Madrid as, 89–90; Mexico City as, 141–143, 148–165; 174–177; New York City as, 30–31, 233–235; spectacle spaces in, 30

earthquake, in Mexico City, 153, 158–159

East Los Angeles, and public space, 218–219

edge cities, xi, 3

Eixample, Barcelona, 94, 101, 107

*ensanche* (grid), 55; in Barcelona, 94; in Madrid, 48–49, 61–62

Ensenada, and global tourism space, 197

*evangelista* (evangelist), 136. *See also* Plaza Santo Domingo

forum, 13–14, 116

Fox, Vicente, 149, 155, 162

Franco, Francisco: and buildings on Plaza España, 72; death of, and changes in Barcelona, 92; and housing policy in Spain, 66; impact of, on Spanish cities, 56–57; planning of, in Barcelona, 96; planning of, in Madrid, 61; and Plaza Mayor, Madrid, 84; and Puerta del Sol, 87

Frankfurt, Germany, public space in, 30

García Bravo, Alonso, 121–122

Gaudí, Antoni, 94–95, 107, 112–113

Gehry, Frank, 18

Puerta del Sol, 51–52, 85–89, 227; and cultural identity, 86–87; and Ramón Gómez de La Serna, 86; remodeling of, 87; V. S. Pritchett comment on, 87

pyramids, in Mexico City, 117

Querétaro: aqueduct in, 127; colonial urban design of, 126–129; downtown, 140; and globalization, 29; historic center of, xiii; modernization and public space in, 143–148; suburbs of, xiii

recycling, of urban space, in Barcelona, 110–114

Reichmann International, 160–161

Renaissance: and Madrid public spaces, 42–46; and Plaza Mayor in Spain, 41; and Spanish inquisition, 40; and town squares, 14–15; and urban space in Spain, 38–41

Revolution Avenue, 194–195; as Tijuana functional center, 187

River Zone (Zona del Rio), 192–193

Roman cities, 13–14; legacy of, in Spain, 35

Rosarito, 196–197

Royal Ordinance for Laying Out New Towns. See ordenanzas

Sagrada Familia, 113

Salinas, Carlos, 158–160, 175

San Agustin Plaza, 208

San Antonio, 208–209

Sangremal hill, 129

Santa Fe (New Mexico), 205–207

San Ysidro-Tijuana border crossing, 198–201, 219

sculpture, in public space, 106

sense of place, 6, 7–9

shopping malls, 6, 223; and globalization, 28; in Southern California, 213, 216–218; in South Texas, 208; in Tijuana, 190–192

Social Workers Party of Spain. See PSOE

Soria, Arturo, 48–49

souk (suq), 35

Southern California: culture and public space in, 210, 220–221; Latino

public spaces in, 218–220; Latino street culture in, 219; Los Angeles school of urban research in, ix, 211–212; and Pershing Square remodeling, 214–216; and postmodern urbanism, ix–x, 2–3; public space crisis in, 221; shopping malls in, 213, 216–218; suburban sprawl in, x–xi, 212; traditional squares in, 214

Southwest border region: Anasazi-Pueblo culture in, 202–204; and Arizona, 209–210; and New Mexico, 205–207; public space in, 201–210; and Southern California, 210–220; Spanish colonial towns in, 204–210; and Texas, 207–209

Spain: city and public space in, 33–57, 238–240; expansion of cities in nineteenth century, 48–49; Franco's impact on cities, 56–57; and fusion of urbanism with Mexico, 115–116, 125; in the Middle Ages, 34–38; national housing policies of, 66–68; Renaissance urban space in, 38–42; twentieth-century cities in, 55–57; and unique public space culture, 33–34. See also Barcelona; Madrid

Spanish Civil War, 56, 96

Spanish inquisition, 40

Spanish town planning: impact of, on Southwestern U.S., 204–210; in Mexico, 120–126; and morphology of plazas, 122–126; and Royal Ordinances, 121

"spectacle spaces," 30, 221; and Plaza Colón, 71; and Plaza de España, 73

sprawl, xi–xii

streets: and antiurbanism in U.S. culture, 11; commercial, along U.S.-Mexico border, 194–196; and Latino culture, 219; and public spaces in industrializing societies, 16

street vendors (ambulantes): in Mexico City, 152, 155–157, 230; in Querétaro, 146–147

suburbs: and Barcelona's high rise buildings, 96; celebration of, in U.S., x–xii; and Eixample in Barcelona, 93–94; in Madrid, 62–63, 67, 90; in Mexico City, 141; and poor in Latin America, 143; in Querétaro, xiii, 144; in southern California,

## About the Author

LAWRENCE A. HERZOG (PhD, Syracuse University) is Professor in the Graduate Program in City Planning of the School of Public Administration and Urban Studies at San Diego State University in California. He has written or edited five previous books, including *From Aztec to High Tech* (1999). Herzog has served as an urban/regional planning consultant in Latin America and the United States and has lectured and taught in Spain, England, France, the Netherlands, Mexico, and Peru. More than fifty of his popular essays have appeared in newspapers, magazines, and Web journals, including the *Los Angeles Times, San Francisco Chronicle, Newsday, Times of the Americas, San Jose Mercury News, San Diego Union Tribune, theglobalist.com,* and *voiceofsandiego.org.* His photographs have been exhibited in galleries and shows in Mexico and the United States.